Rhetoric

To
my family
Bill, Willie, Jennifer, and Nicholas
in gratitude for their love and conversation
throughout the years

Rhetoric
An Historical Introduction

Wendy Olmsted

BLACKWELL PUBLISHING
350 Main Street, Malden, MA 02148-5020, USA
9600 Garsington Road, Oxford OX4 2DQ, UK
550 Swanston Street, Carlton, Victoria 3053, Australia

First published 2006 by Blackwell Publishing Ltd

1   2006

Library of Congress Cataloging-in-Publication Data

Olmsted, Wendy, 1943–
  Rhetoric : an historical introduction / Wendy Olmsted.
    p. cm.
Includes bibliographical references and index.
ISBN-13: 978-1-4051-1772-2 (hardcover: alk. paper)
ISBN-10: 1-4051-1772-9 (hardcover: alk. paper)
ISBN-13: 978-1-4051-1773-9 (pbk.: alk. paper)
ISBN-10: 1-4051-1773-7 (pbk.: alk. paper) 1. Rhetoric—History. I. Title.

PN183.O46 2007
808—dc22

                                                                        2005026435

A catalogue record for this title is available from the British Library.

Set in 10/12.5pt DanteMT
by SPI Publisher Services, Pondicherry, India
Printed and bound in Great Britain
by TJ International, Ltd, Padstow, Cornwall

The publisher's policy is to use permanent paper from mills that operate a sustainable forestry policy, and which has been manufactured from pulp processed using acid-free and elementary chlorine-free practices. Furthermore, the publisher ensures that the text paper and cover board used have met acceptable environmental accreditation standards.

For further information on
Blackwell Publishing, visit our website:
www.blackwellpublishing.com

Contents

Acknowledgments

This book is the fruit of many years of teaching and of conversations with colleagues, students, friends, and family. In articulating my project, I have benefited from the advice of Wayne C. Booth, Eugene Garver, and Walter Jost, and from their astute readings of chapters. I am grateful to Janel Mueller, Michael Murrin, Joshua Scodel, and Richard Strier for their perceptive and learned comments on a draft of the Francis Bacon chapter presented to the Renaissance Workshop at the University of Chicago. (Naturally, I remain responsible for my errors.) The students and faculty members of the Renaissance Workshop, Ancient Societies Workshop, and Rhetoric and Poetry Workshop at the University of Chicago have consistently refined and informed my thinking and have been a source of collegiality and scholarly conversation. Dennis Hutchinson graciously provided references and stimulating conversation. Andrew McNeillie, the editor at Blackwell who commissioned this volume, stimulated my ideas and provided wonderful enthusiasm. I benefited from helpful, broad-ranging anonymous readers' reports, and Blackwell Publishing kindly gave me permission to reprint most of Chapter 11, "Exemplifying deliberation: Cicero's *De officiis* and Machiavelli's *Prince*," from *A Companion to Rhetoric and Rhetorical Criticism* (2004), pp. 173–89. Professors John Boyer, Dean of the College, and Dennis Hutchinson, Master of the New Collegiate Division, at the University of Chicago have been unfailing sources of support and encouragement as well as granting a course reduction so that I could finish the book. My husband Bill has been a faithful and discerning reader of drafts. My last and greatest debt is to him for his constant love, patience, and intelligence and to Jennifer and Nicholas for their affection, liveliness, and stimulating conversation.

Abbreviations

Primary Works

Analytica priora	Aristotle, *Analytica priora*, in *The Basic Works of Aristotle*, ed. Richard McKeon (New York: Random House, 1941).
The "Art" of Rhetoric	Aristotle, *The "Art" of Rhetoric*, trans. John Henry Freese (Cambridge, Mass.: Harvard University Press, 1975).
CD	Augustine, *On Christian Doctrine*, trans. and with introduction by D. W. Robertson (Indianapolis: Bobbs-Merrill, Library of Liberal Arts, 1958).
Characteristicks	Anthony Ashley Cooper, 3rd Earl of Shaftesbury, *Characteristicks of Men, Manner, Opinions, Times*, ed. Philip Ayers (Oxford: Clarendon Press, 1999), vol. I.
Confessions	*St Augustine's Confessions*, 2 vols., trans. William Watts (Cambridge, Mass.: Harvard University Press, 1977).
CPW	*Complete Prose Works of John Milton*, 8 vols., general editor Don M. Wolfe (New Haven, Conn.: Yale University Press, 1953–82).
De amicitia	Cicero, *De senectute, De amicitia, De divinatione*, trans. William Armistead Falconer (London: William Heinemann, 1923), pp. 109–211.

A Defence of Poetry	Sir Philip Sidney, *A Defence of Poetry*, in *Miscellaneous Prose of Sir Philip Sidney*, ed. Katherine Duncan-Jones and Jan van Dorsten (Oxford: Clarendon Press, 1973), pp. 73–121.
De inventione	Cicero, *De inventione*, trans. H. M. Hubbell (Cambridge, Mass.: Harvard University Press, 1968).
De officiis	Cicero, *De officiis*, trans. Walter Miller (Cambridge, Mass.: Harvard University Press, 1913, repr. 1997).
De oratore	Cicero, *De oratore*, trans. E. W. Sutton and H. Rackham (Cambridge, Mass.: Harvard University Press, 1959).
Essays	Francis Bacon, *The Essays*, ed. and with introduction by John Pitcher (Harmondsworth: Penguin Books, 1985).
"Flatterer"	Plutarch, "How to distinguish a flatterer from a friend," in *Essays*, trans. Robin Waterfield (Harmondsworth: Penguin Books, 1992), pp. 61–112.
For the Sake of Argument	Eugene Garver, *For the Sake of Argument: Practical Reasoning, Character, and the Ethics of Belief* (Chicago: University of Chicago Press, 2004).
Francis Bacon	*Francis Bacon*, ed. Brian Vickers (Oxford: Oxford University Press, 1996).
Gorgias	Plato, *Gorgias*, trans. Donald J. Zeyl (Indianapolis and Cambridge: Hackett Publishing, 1987).
"Human nature"	Thomas Hobbes, "Human nature," in *The English Works of Thomas Hobbes*, ed. Sir William Molesworth (London: John Bohn, 1840; repr. Germany: Scientia Verlag Aalen, 1966), chapter VIII, para. 8, p. 40.
Lectures on Rhetoric	Hugh Blair, *Lectures on Rhetoric and Belles Lettres* (1819), introduction by Charlotte Downey (Delmar, NY: Scholars' Facsimiles & Reprints, 1993).
Legal Reasoning	Edward H. Levi, *An Introduction to Legal Reasoning* (Chicago: University of Chicago Press, 1949).
Life and Letters	Francis Bacon, *The Life and Letters of Francis Bacon*, 7 vols., ed. James Spedding (London: Longman, Green, Longman, and Roberts, 1861–74).

Mandeville's Travels	*Mandeville's Travels: Texts and Translations*, ed. Malcolm Letts, Works issued by the Hakluyt Society, 2nd series, 101–2 (London: Hakluyt Society, 1953).
Marvelous Possessions	Stephen Greenblatt, *Marvelous Possessions: the Wonder of the New World* (Chicago: University of Chicago Press, 1991).
Nicomachean Ethics	Aristotle, *Nicomachean Ethics*, trans. Martin Ostwald (Upper Saddle River, NJ: Prentice Hall, Library of Liberal Arts, 1999).
Novum organum	Francis Bacon, *Novum organum with Other Parts of the Great Instauration*, trans. and ed. with introduction and notes by Peter Urbach and John Gibson (Chicago: Open Court, 1994).
"Of cannibals"	M. E. de Montaigne, *The Complete Essays of Montaigne*, trans. Donald Frame (Stanford, Calif.: Stanford University Press, 1957), pp. 150–9.
"Of the custom"	M. E. de Montaigne, *The Complete Essays of Montaigne*, trans. Donald Frame (Stanford, Calif.: Stanford University Press, 1957).
On Duties	Cicero, *On Duties*, trans. M. T. Griffin and E. M. Adkins (Cambridge: Cambridge University Press, 1991, repr. 1993).
On Rhetoric	Aristotle, *On Rhetoric: a Theory of Civic Discourse*, trans. George A. Kennedy (Oxford: Oxford University Press, 1991).
Orator	Cicero, *Orator*, in *Brutus; Orator*, trans. G. L. Hendrickson and H. M. Hubbell (Cambridge, Mass.: Harvard University Press, 1971), pp. 306–538.
Peloponnesian War	Thucydides, *The Peloponnesian War*, trans. Rex Warner (Harmondsworth: Penguin Books, 1972).
Persuasion	Jane Austen, *Persuasion*, with introduction and notes by Gillian Beer (Harmondsworth: Penguin Books, 1998, repr. 2003).

PL   John Milton, *Paradise Lost*, in *John Milton: Complete Poems and Major Prose*, ed. Merritt Y. Hughes (Upper Saddle River, NJ: Prentice Hall, 1957), pp. 173–470.

Politics   Aristotle, *Politics*, trans. H. Rackham (Cambridge, Mass.: Harvard University Press, 1990).

The Prince   Niccolò Machiavelli, *The Prince*, 2nd edn., trans. and ed. with introduction and notes by Robert M. Adams (New York: W. W. Norton, 1992).

"Resonance"   Stephen J. Greenblatt, "Resonance and wonder," in *Learning to Curse* (New York: Routledge, 1990), pp. 161–83.

Rhetoric   Aristotle, *Rhetoric*, trans. W. R. Roberts (New York: Modern Library, 1954).

Rhetoric of Fiction   Wayne C. Booth, *The Rhetoric of Fiction* (Chicago: University of Chicago Press, 1961, 2nd edn. 1983).

Select Documents   *Select Documents Illustrating the Four Voyages of Columbus*, 2 vols., trans. and ed. Cecil Jane (London: Hakluyt Society, 1930).

Talking to Strangers   Danielle S. Allen, *Talking to Strangers: Anxieties of Citizenship since Brown v. Board of Education* (Chicago: University of Chicago Press, 2004).

Topica   Cicero, *Topica*, in *De inventione, De optimo genere oratorum, Topica*, trans. H. M. Hubbell (Cambridge, Mass.: Harvard University Press, 1968), pp. 383–459.

Works   Francis Bacon, *The Works of Francis Bacon*, 7 vols., ed. James Spedding, Robert L. Ellis, and Douglas D. Heath (London: 1857–74; facsimile repr. Stuttgart: Friedrich Frommann Verlag, 1963).

Secondary References

Achilles in Vietnam   Jonathan Shay, *Achilles in Vietnam: Combat Trauma and the Undoing of Character* (New York: Atheneum, 1994).

Analogical Imagination   David Tracy, *The Analogical Imagination: Christian Theology and the Culture of Pluralism* (New York: Crossroad, 1981).

Country of My Skull	Antije Krog, *Country of My Skull: Guilt, Sorrow, and the Limits of Forgiveness in the New South Africa* (Parktown, SA, 1998; New York: Times Books, 1999). Page citations from the South African edition.
"Cultivating deliberating"	David J. Smigelskis, "Cultivating deliberating: mindfully resourceful innovation in and through the *Federalist Papers*," in *A Companion to Rhetoric and Rhetorical Criticism*, ed. Walter Jost and Wendy Olmsted (Oxford: Blackwell Publishing, 2004), pp. 190–205.
Emperor of Men's Minds	Wayne A. Rebhorn, *The Emperor of Men's Minds: Literature and the Renaissance Discourse of Rhetoric* (Ithaca, NY: Cornell University Press, 1995).
Ethos and Pathos	Jakob Wisse, *Ethos and Pathos from Aristotle to Cicero* (Amsterdam: Adolf M. Hakkert, 1989).
Excess	Joshua Scodel, *Excess and the Mean in Early Modern English Literature* (Princeton, NJ: Princeton University Press, 2002), pp. 61–76.
"Exemplifying deliberation"	Wendy Olmsted, "Exemplifying deliberation: Cicero's *De officiis* and Machiavelli's *Prince*," in *A Companion to Rhetoric and Rhetorical Criticism*, ed. Walter Jost and Wendy Olmsted (Blackwell Publishing, 2004), pp. 173–89.
"Georgics of the mind"	Stanley E. Fish, "Georgics of the mind: the experience of Bacon's *Essays*," in *Self-Consuming Artifacts: the Experience of Seventeenth-Century Literature* (Berkeley: University of California Press, 1972), pp. 78–155.
"Gift of counsel"	A. R. Ascoli, "Machiavelli's gift of counsel," in *Machiavelli and the Discourse of Literature*, ed. A. R. Ascoli and V. Kahn (Ithaca, NY: Cornell University Press, 1993), pp. 219–57.
"History of the anecdote"	Joel Fineman, "The history of the anecdote: fiction and fiction," in *The New Historicism*, ed. H. Aram Veeser (New York: Routledge, 1989), pp. 49–76.
Human Condition	Hannah Arendt, *The Human Condition* (Chicago: University of Chicago Press, 1958, 2nd edn. 1998).

Humanist as Traveler	Jonathan Haynes, *The Humanist as Traveler: George Sandys's "Relation of a Journey begun an. dom. 1610"* (Rutherford, NJ: Fairleigh Dickinson University Press, 1986).
"Impact"	Clifford Geertz, "The impact of the concept of culture on the concept of man," in *The Interpretation of Cultures: Selected Essays by Clifford Geertz* (New York: Basic Books, 1973), pp. 33–54.
"Incompletely theorized agreements"	Cass R. Sunstein, "Incompletely theorized agreements," *Harvard Law Review* 108 (1975), pp. 1733–72.
"Invention, emotion"	Wendy Olmsted, "Invention, emotion, and conversion in Augustine's *Confessions*," in *Rhetorical Invention and Religious Inquiry: New Perspectives* (New Haven, Conn.: Yale University Press, 2000), pp. 65–86.
The Invisible Man	Ralph Ellison, *The Invisible Man* (New York: Modern Library, 1952, repr. 1994).
"Jane Austen"	Gilbert Ryle, "Jane Austen and the moralists," in *English Literature and British Philosophy*, ed. with introduction by S. P. Rosenbaum (Chicago: University of Chicago Press, 1971), pp. 168–84.
Law, Violence	David Cohen, *Law, Violence and Community in Classical Athens* (Cambridge: Cambridge University Press, 1995).
"Lawyers and rhetoric"	Richard J. Schoeck, "Lawyers and rhetoric in sixteenth-century England," in *Renaissance Eloquence: Studies in the Theory and Practice of Renaissance Rhetoric*, ed. James Murphy (Berkeley: University of California Press, 1983), pp. 274–91.
Legal Discourse	Peter Goodrich, *Legal Discourse: Studies in Linguistics, Rhetoric and Legal Analysis* (London: Macmillan, 1987); see pp. 85–124.
Legal System	Julius Stone, *Legal System and Lawyers' Reasonings* (Stanford, Calif.: Stanford University Press, 1964).
Life of Milton	Barbara K. Lewalski, *The Life of John Milton: a Critical Biography* (Oxford: Blackwell Publishing, 2000).
Machiavelli	Eugene Garver, *Machiavelli and the History of Prudence* (Madison: University of Wisconsin Press, 1987).

Machiavellian Moment	J. G. A. Pocock, *The Machiavellian Moment: Florentine Political Thought and the Atlantic Republican Tradition* (Princeton, NJ: Princeton University Press, 1975).
"Metarhetorics"	James J. Murphy, "Metarhetorics of Plato, Augustine, and McLuhan: a pointing essay," *Philosophy and Rhetoric* 4 (1971), pp. 201–14.
Middle Ages	James J. Murphy, *Rhetoric in the Middle Ages: a History of Rhetorical Theory from Saint Augustine to the Renaissance* (Berkeley: University of California Press, 1974).
A Miracle	Lawrence Weschler, *A Miracle, a Universe: Settling Accounts with Torturers* (New York: Pantheon, 1990).
Muses of One Mind	Wesley Trimpi, *Muses of One Mind: the Literary Analysis of Experience and its Continuity* (Princeton, NJ: Princeton University Press, 1983).
"My life with rhetoric"	Wayne C. Booth, "My life with rhetoric," in *A Companion to Rhetoric and Rhetorical Criticism*, ed. Walter Jost and Wendy Olmsted (Oxford: Blackwell Publishing, 2004), pp. 494–504.
"New Historicism"	Jean E. Howard, "The New Historicism in Renaissance Studies," *English Literary Renaissance* 16 (1986), pp. 13–43.
"A night in the topics"	J. M. Balkin, "A night in the topics: the reason of legal rhetoric and the rhetoric of legal reason," in *Law Stories: Narrative and Rhetoric in the Law*, ed. Peter Brooks and Paul Gewirtz (New Haven, Conn.: Yale University Press, 1996), pp. 211–24, 273–5.
"On analogical reasoning"	Cass R. Sunstein, "On analogical reasoning," *Harvard Law Review* 106 (1993), pp. 741–91.
Overcoming Law	Richard A. Posner, *Overcoming Law* (Cambridge, Mass.: Harvard University Press, 1995).
Partial Constitution	Cass R. Sunstein, *The Partial Constitution* (Cambridge, Mass.: Harvard University Press, 1993).
Personal Patronage	Richard P. Saller, *Personal Patronage under the Early Empire* (Cambridge: Cambridge University Press, 1982).

Rhetoric of Irony	Wayne C. Booth, *A Rhetoric of Irony* (Chicago: University of Chicago Press, 1974).
Rhetoric of Reason	Sarah Spence, *Rhetoric of Reason and Desire: Vergil, Augustine, and the Troubadours* (Ithaca, NY: Cornell University Press, 1988).
Sacred Rhetoric	Debora K. Shuger, *Sacred Rhetoric: the Christian Grand Style in the English Renaissance* (Princeton, NJ: Princeton University Press, 1988).
"Satan as orator"	Nancy Hagglund Wood, "Satan as orator: a rhetorical analysis of the persuasion of Eve in *Paradise Lost*" (PhD dissertation, Rutgers University, New Brunswick, NJ, 1972).
"Science of jurisprudence"	Paul H. Kocher, "Francis Bacon on the science of jurisprudence," *Journal of the History of Ideas* 18 (1957), pp. 3–36.
Senior Statesman	Thomas N. Mitchell, *Cicero: The Senior Statesman* (New Haven, Conn.: Yale University Press, 1991).
Some Words	Stuart M. Tave, *Some Words of Jane Austen* (Chicago: University of Chicago Press, 1973).
Sovereign Amity	Laurie Shannon, *Sovereign Amity: Figures of Friendship in Shakespearean Contexts* (Chicago: University of Chicago Press, 2002).
"The stranger"	Julian Pitt-Rivers, "The stranger, the guest and the hostile host: introduction to the study of the laws of hospitality," in *Contributions to Mediterranean Sociology: Mediterranean Rural Communities and Social Change* (Paris: Mouton, 1968), pp. 13–30.
"Sweetness"	John C. Cavadini, "The sweetness of the word: salvation and rhetoric in Augustine's *De doctrina Christiana*," in *De doctrina Christiana: a Classic of Western Culture*, ed. Duane W. H. Arnold and Pamela Bright (Notre Dame, Ind.: University of Notre Dame Press, 1995), pp. 164–81.
Tanner, *Jane Austen*	Tony Tanner, *Jane Austen* (Cambridge, Mass.: Harvard University Press, 1986).

When Words Lose their Meaning	James Boyd White, *When Words Lose their Meaning: Constitutions and Reconstitutions of Language, Character, and Community* (Chicago: University of Chicago Press, 1984).
Who Speaks for the Negro	Interview with Ralph Ellison by Robert Penn Warren, in R. P. Warren, *Who Speaks for the Negro* (New York: Random House, 1965).
Word of the Law	Dennis R. Klinck, *The Word of the Law* (Ottawa: Carlton University Press, 1992).

Introducing Rhetoric

Rhetoric: an Historical Introduction explores rhetoric as a practical art of deliberation and judgment that can best be taught and learned through historically specific examples of argument and interpretation. Many scholars have "theorized" rhetoric by articulating specific principles that provide direction for inquiry into persuasion and communication. Yet such theories tend to remove themselves from historical contingencies and varied modes of representation. The theories teach ideas about rhetoric without relating texts to the larger intellectual currents of their time. But the art of rhetoric requires reasoning about particular circumstances in light of broad cultural understandings.

Like *A Companion to Rhetoric and Rhetorical Criticism*, this volume demonstrates that the capacities of the good rhetorician – to invent subjects and arguments, to organize discourse, and to make good judgments – cannot be learned from rhetorical theory. These capacities must be actively exercised by beginners and advanced scholars alike.[1] The chapters of this volume introduce readers to classic rhetorical texts that offer themselves simultaneously as concrete works of persuasion and as thoughtful considerations of how rhetoric works. These texts are "simultaneously works *of* rhetoric and works *about* rhetoric."[2] The volume, in which practice grounds and guides theory, articulates rhetoric as an activity of invention and discovery by providing concrete experience in rhetorical inquiry. It interprets texts that form contexts for one another: Plato for Aristotle, Aristotle for Cicero, and so on to the modern era. Contemporary writers such as Edward H. Levi, Wayne C. Booth, Stephen Greenblatt, Danielle S. Allen, and Eugene Garver reinvent terms of Aristotle's *Rhetoric* to tackle practical problems of their times and fields. All of these writers think as rhetoricians and teach others to do so. The volume aims at a wide range of readers, including generalists and specialists alike, and serves as a counterpart to *A Companion to Rhetoric and Rhetorical Criticism*.

I have organized the book into three main parts, each of which illuminates the others. Part I provides the necessary historical background for the study of rhetoric and focuses on terms central to its intellectual development – terms such as "deliberation," "judgment," "topic," "character" (ethos), "argument" (logos), "emotion" (pathos), and "eloquence." Each text formulates these terms in light of the specific practical problems that it engages in its own period. Each uses rhetorical terms that are flexible and suggestive, facilitating inquiry into situations different from those in which they were originally invented.

The choice of terms reflects my own preoccupation with invention (the art of finding subjects and arguments) and with style's integral relation to argument. I investigate a rhetoric that seeks the best possible means of persuasion rather than one that aims to win at any cost. As Aristotle observes, rhetoric works very much like medicine. Doctors practice their art as well as possible even when they cannot achieve a perfect cure. Good rhetorical texts increase our ability to find strong arguments, communicate a trustworthy character, and, as Danielle S. Allen argues, heal the negative political emotions that result from pain at inequitable decisions. Because speakers and writers seek arguments in historically and culturally specific situations, rhetorical texts cannot tell them what to say. Instead they use *topoi*, the Greek name for the places or topics (Latin: *loci*) where materials and arguments can be found. Cicero calls topics the signs or pointers to proofs and compares them to the indications a prospector uses to find gold. But speakers and writers need to do the digging to find the ends and proofs pertinent to their situations. Topics are not universal. They are shared within specific communities. And rhetorical practice varies with the cultural norms and common beliefs that define its limits and possibilities. At the same time, speakers and writers shape the community's character, beliefs, and ideas. This volume is organized to stimulate thought about the interactions of the rhetorical practice with historical contexts.

Part II explores how major literary texts interpret and revise the classical rhetorical works of Part I. The three writers I examine significantly alter previous rhetorical practices. Francis Bacon reinvents maxims and aphorisms to investigate nature. His reinventions influence his treatment of character, argument, and emotion in the *Essays*. Milton extends the plurality of styles available for the purposes of combating vicious deception and healing the errors of the innocent in seventeenth-century Protestant, verbal, religious warfare, and Jane Austen explores a plurality of nineteenth-century English discursive communities. Her novel, *Persuasion*, dramatizes the problems and opportunities of pluralism, telling the story of a woman whose "word had no weight," but who, by the end, achieves the eloquence to "pierce a soul."

Part III argues that the classical rhetorical tradition informs central intellectual movements of our own time. Each of the texts in this section address contemporary issues by transforming terms and strategies introduced in Part I. From the numerous fields affected by rhetoric (including sociology, science, economics, history, religion, literary criticism, and law), Part III chooses to introduce readers to rhetorical analyses of literary texts, politics, and legal arguments. By reading Chapters 3 and 6, readers learn about interconnections between religious inquiry and rhetorical invention. All the chapters in Part III reassess the contribution of important thinkers in each field and speculate on the implications of their disciplines for understanding invention.

By engaging the practice of rhetoric, *Rhetoric: an Historical Introduction* also confronts its challenges. Rhetoric easily slides into deception and emotional manipulation. Speakers and writers need constantly to differentiate their practices from abuses of rhetoric, just as logical truth needs to refute error. In our own time, the press constantly contrasts mere rhetoric with substantive analysis. The belief that rhetoric is associated with deceptive language and false arguments goes as far back as Plato, whose character, Socrates, calls rhetoric the knack of flattering and compares it to cooking sweet pastries that please people and make them ill. In order to please (and to control) others, rhetoricians become chameleons that adapt themselves to the preferences of their audiences. Because demagogues are dangerous, everyone needs to be aware of their strategies and to correct them by using rhetorical argument.

These rhetoricians are rightly suspect, and many of the chapters in this volume distinguish deliberative arguments from fraudulent practices. As a whole, *Rhetoric: an Historical Introduction* provides an articulation of the field of rhetoric and the possibilities of its practice across a broad range of disciplines. It investigates the practice of deliberative rhetoric by offering compelling examples from rhetorical and literary history.[3]

Notes

1   See "Introduction," *A Companion to Rhetoric and Rhetorical Criticism*, ed. Walter Jost and Wendy Olmsted (Oxford: Blackwell Publishing, 2004), pp. xv–xvi.
2   Peter Rabinowitz, Hamilton College, reader for Blackwell Publishing.
3   I have given the nominative case of Greek or Latin words so that readers may consult their own reference works, except where a longer or more extensive context calls for a different case.

Part I

Classical Rhetorical Traditions

Introduction

Part I introduces the ambiguities, challenges, and opportunities of trying to discover the most practical and best actions in the particular murky situations in which we human beings live. Whether we are engaging in "negotiation within ourselves" to settle on a promising course of action for our lives, or listening to political speeches in Congress, or speaking to others in community groups, student organizations, or faculty councils, we are faced with the fact that we deliberate without full knowledge of the things relevant to our decisions, things that are changing even as we speak. Likewise, our choices are affected by our own strengths and weaknesses. And when we deliberate with others, our interactions are influenced by emotions and other interpersonal factors. The impossibility of having expert knowledge about everyday matters, or even about momentous issues such as whether Iraq had weapons of mass destruction, makes deliberative rhetoric imperfect. Plato famously attacked this rhetoric in the *Gorgias* because it was not based on knowledge. He wanted political and ethical decisions to be made by experts. He wanted a rhetoric that did not stir the passions or appeal to everyday human beliefs and opinions.

But no one has found a perfect science or expertise that can disclose the particular, always shifting, partly unknown things that we apprehend from apparently "subjective" points of view in ordinary life and in politics. These are the things relevant to choice and judgment. A sick person can consult a doctor about treatments for his illness and can become informed about the advantages and disadvantages, the probable costs and benefits, of various procedures and medications. In the end, however, he needs to look at his own medical history, his values and hopes for life in order to make a choice. Similarly, a member of Congress voting on the Iraq war had to discover for herself the relevant facts and probabilities to decide whether Iraq was a terrorist threat, whether it had weapons of mass destruction, and whether or not the doctrine of pre-emptive strike was consistent with the political ideals and practices of our democracy. There is no perfectly philosophical, expert, or scientific method for achieving definitive knowledge of such issues. And yet we need to think about them and speak about them. However tempting it may be to believe cynically that politicians are manipulators or that there are no good decisions about medical problems, whenever we equate deliberative rhetoric with manipulation and demogoguery, we deprive ourselves of power, the power to investigate, to test the presentations of facts, to articulate our commitments, and to interact fairly and respectfully with others. Lapsing into skepticism and cynicism only robs us of the capacities we do have for making good decisions. Aristotle's *Rhetoric* aims to develop these capacities by articulating rhetoric as a power of engaging verbally in practical deliberation.

The text posits that all human beings exhort and dissuade; Francis Bacon suggests that we even exhort and dissuade in the "negotiation within ourselves." But we can become better at it by increasing our power of finding facts and arguments, of articulating goals for a particular situation, and of interacting well with others who deliberate. Yes, the sick person will not have perfect knowledge of his condition, nor will he be absolutely sure that his choice will contribute to a good, enjoyable life as he envisions it, but he can improve his ability to find probable facts, seek ends that serve his interests, and interact effectively with others involved in the decision. Aristotle argues that we can increase our ability to discover facts and the ends or "goods" in terms of which to deliberate. We can heal emotional responses such as fear, anger, and envy. But, Plato argues, we need to beware of the tactics of flatterers and abusers who would lead us astray.

The first chapter of Part I explores Plato's famous attack in the *Gorgias* on demagogic speakers who used pleasure to manipulate their audiences. Aristotle's *Rhetoric* responds to Plato's identification of rhetoric with passion by rejecting earlier Greek rhetorical handbooks focused on emotion and by making argument the central issue of rhetoric. Because rhetoric is not a perfect method for informing choice and judgment, he seeks to discern the best possible choice or judgment in a particular situation. His text exemplifies strategies of rhetorical persuasion and develops terms that readers may use to inform their own productions and interpretations of arguments. Speakers need to consider the available facts and arguments (logos), how they manifest a trustworthy character (ethos), and how to produce reasonable emotion in an audience (pathos). My chapter shows how Aristotle's terms illuminate speeches from Thucydides' *The Peloponnesian War*.

The second chapter introduces readers to Cicero's reformulation in *De oratore* of Aristotle's topics of the speaker's character, the speech or argument, and the audience's emotion adapted to the use of advocates pleading in the Roman law courts. Although Aristotle shifts the focus of rhetorical texts from emotion toward argument, Cicero insists that it is appropriate to move emotions in order to persuade judges. Emotion manifests the importance of an issue or person to the speaker. Yet appeals to emotion easily degenerate into manipulation. This chapter engages with the challenge of differentiating appropriate emotion from the abuse of emotion.

The focus on emotion in the second chapter leads to the analysis in the third chapter of Augustine's revision of Cicero in *On Christian Doctrine*, where rhetoric becomes hermeneutics and Augustine uses its terms and arguments to come to know God and to understand the Bible. The interpreter of the Bible seeks an ultimate truth (logos) but runs of the risk of confusing the things that should be used with the things that should be enjoyed for their own sake. References to the *Confessions* will illuminate these risks. Augustine's reader also needs to develop a new, better character (ethos) in order to apprehend a higher truth. Emotion (pathos) plays a role in moving readers toward truth/God. In light of the new ends formulated in Books 1–3 of *On Christian Doctrine*, that text articulates new relationships between the plain or subdued style, the moderate or delightful style, and the grand style explored by Cicero. Augustine turns his attention to how style can help writers heal ignorance, literal-mindedness, inattentiveness, and the inability or unwillingness to act well.

The fourth chapter shows how Machiavelli re-examines the precepts of Cicero's *On Duties* (*De officiis*) to create a handbook for princes seeking power. *On Duties* and *The Prince* exemplify advice to rulers that teach readers (specifically Marcus, Cicero's son, and the Medici family) how to deliberate about actions that seem to be virtuous (but not expedient) or expedient (but not virtuous). *On Duties* challenges his readers to reject what is only apparently honorable and to reject cynical expediency that violates what is honorable. *The Prince* challenges readers' reliance on commonplace moral beliefs (many of them Ciceronian) and teaches them to discriminate between prudent political thought and the search for success by any means. *The Prince* adapts Cicero's topics and maxims to a highly unstable political situation in Italy, very different from the Republican and "tyrannical" contexts that inform *On Duties*.

Chapter 1

The Rhetorician: Demagogue or Statesman? Plato's *Gorgias* and Aristotle's *Rhetoric*

During George W. Bush's first term in office, a spokesman for the United States Department of Health and Human Services responded to criticism of the administration's appointments by saying "this is all just rhetoric that is being thrown around by people who disagree with our appointments" (*Chicago Tribune*, September 7, 2003 in "Nation"). Like many people, the spokesman used the word "rhetoric" to refer to irresponsible language. The accusation is not new. In classical Athens, political leaders attacked oratorical speeches for endangering the city ("Politics of deliberation," pp. 30–1). When the Spartans deliberate about going to war in Thucydides' *The Peloponnesian War*, Sthenelaidas calls for immediate revenge against the Athenians, asserting that "no one" should settle matters "by lawsuits and by words." "Let no one try to tell us that when we are being attacked we should sit down and discuss matters" (p. 86). He scorns rhetoric in favor of immediate action.

Any attempt to explore the power and cogency of deliberative rhetoric needs to address such attacks. Although it can manipulate emotion, when properly used in a democratic setting, it allows citizens to form a community and decide on a wise course of action. Plato's *Gorgias* (c.387–385 BCE) exposes the dangers and deceptiveness of rhetoric, but Aristotle's *Rhetoric* (c.350 BCE) engages with those dangers in order to improve people's abilities to make wise decisions about matters that affect their interests. Aristotle elevates deliberative rhetoric above mere selfishness to make it the basis of political community and practical wisdom ("Politics of deliberation," p. 22).

By contrast, Plato's *Gorgias* criticizes orators for saying what pleases the audience in order to advance their self-interest. Socrates argues that oratory is nothing but a knack for causing pleasure. He undermines Gorgias' definition of rhetoric as persuasion in the law courts and the assembly by claiming that rhetoricians persuade the ignorant, producing belief (*pistis*) and not knowledge in their audiences (*Gorgias* 459a, pp. 17–18). Socrates rejects belief and opinion as modes of knowledge and uncovers the hypocrisy of the demagogue who seduces his audience through flattery, saying that flattery takes "no thought at all of whatever is best" (464d). He compares rhetoric to pastry-baking, a knack that claims to know "what foods are best for the body." If a doctor and a pastry baker had to "compete in front of children" (464d, p. 25), the doctor would lose. Similarly, Socrates argues, if one who knows what is just for the state had to compete with a deceptive flatterer, the flatterer would win.

If Plato had confined his critique to Athenian demagogic oratory, his criticisms would be apt. But he also attacks deliberative rhetoric ("Politics of deliberation," p. 32). He rejects the role of practical wisdom in politics and argues instead that citizens ought to consult experts, scientists, or philosophers, whose knowledge begins from universal principles and provides an explanation of causes. This argument is powerful, but it leaves an enormous gap. By sharply distinguishing speech in a court or assembly from expertise and science, Socrates denies the possibility of a wise deliberation based on common opinion and directed toward particular circumstances. But such reasoning is indispensable. For example, even though experts can inform someone of the odds of a medical cure's being effective or how to build defensive structures to protect a city, patients as well as citizens need to know how to weigh a cure against its side effects or the desirability of military strength against its risks. These are the kinds of issues for which Aristotle's *Rhetoric* provides strategies and ways of thinking.

Because deliberative rhetoric deals with things that can be otherwise than they are, it cannot rely on universal principles for its starting point. Aristotle agrees that rhetoric is not a science, that it has no specific subject matter, and that it produces belief, not knowledge; but he defends its truth and usefulness. Because Aristotle holds, in stark contrast to Plato, that collective deliberation of the many is better than the deliberation of a few experts (*Politics* 3. 6, 1281b–1282a, pp. 225–7), he makes deliberative oratory the basis of political community ("Politics of deliberation"). Rhetoric informs decision-making through a process of discussion and debate.

At the same time, Aristotle was clearly aware of dangers of oratory. He scolds litigants who wrongly "warp the jury by leading them into anger or envy or pity" (*On Rhetoric* 1. 1, 1354a, p. 30).[1] He attacks previous rhetorical handbooks that focus on putting the judge in a certain frame of mind. For friendliness and enmity make the judges unable "to see the truth adequately, but their private pleasure or grief casts a shadow on their judgment" (ibid., p. 31). The Athenian judges could easily be led by self-interest because they were chosen by lot from among the citizens and participated in trials of people they knew. Appeals to the emotions alone were likely to distort their judgments.

While acknowledging that rhetoric easily warps the *emotions* of the audience, Aristotle's *Rhetoric* offers the first account of rhetoric as the power of finding *arguments* to inform decisions. The text shows readers how to invent arguments and find evidence. In doing so, it responds to the problems raised by Plato's *Gorgias*. Whereas the *Gorgias* makes a sharp distinction between science and persuasive rhetoric and between knowledge and mere belief or opinion, Aristotle locates rhetoric as a "counterpart" to dialectical argument. The text addresses ordinary people involved in the common activities of urging and dissuading one another. Instead of pursuing expert knowledge, it seeks to develop more disciplined habits of persuasive argument in everyone (*The "Art" of Rhetoric* 1. 1, 1354a, p. 3). Speakers are encouraged to draw on common Athenian understandings about the law courts and the assembly. They need to know about "ways and means, war and peace, the defense of the country, imports and exports, and legislation," although they do not need to know as much as the expert (1. 4, 1359b, p. 41). Speakers can help their audiences make wise decisions that affect their interests and well-being and in which they have a say.

By locating rhetoric rather broadly as a mode of reasoning, on the one hand, and as having an ethical dimension, on the other, Aristotle overcomes the impasse created by Plato in the *Gorgias*. Because people deliberate about many different kinds of issues, rhetoric can have no defined subject matter. Instead, the function of rhetoric "is not to persuade but to see the available means of persuasion in each case, as is true also in all the other arts; for neither is it the function of medicine to create health but to promote this as much as possible; for it is nevertheless possible to treat well those who cannot recover health" (*On Rhetoric* 1. 1, 1355b, p. 35). Aristotle's comparison of rhetoric with the search for health shows how important he thinks rhetoric is. But, like medicine, rhetoric is not perfect, and it is not always successful (*Talking to Strangers*, pp. 89–91). For this reason Aristotle does not define rhetoric as the art of persuading. Instead, speakers need to concentrate on what *is* within their power, namely, finding the best *possible* arguments. A speaker making an argument for a difficult case, defending, for example, a notorious criminal charged with a crime he seems likely to have committed, strives to find the best possible arguments to defend her client. Her success in this project, not the outcome of the trial, marks her excellence as a rhetorician. Aristotle aims to improve the speaker's ability to investigate facts and arguments, as well as what is just or unjust about particular actions.

Aristotle's word for "ability" (*dunamis*) has a powerful resonance; *dunamis* is the same word that Socrates uses to attack those who seek power (*to dunasthai*) through persuasion (*Gorgias* 466b, but see also 450a). But Aristotle aims to increase people's rhetorical and intellectual agency. This power must not be confused with the rhetorical force that demagogic orators cultivated.

The text's emphasis on rhetorical agency becomes apparent in the distinction between artistic and non-artistic proof. The word "artistic" refers to evidence that is provided by the speakers, while the word "non-artistic" refers to those that pre-exist the speech: "witnesses, testimony of slaves taken under torture, contracts and such like" (*On Rhetoric* 1. 2, 1355b, p. 37). Evidence from witnesses and similar sources is outside the control of speakers, whereas they possess the power to invent by virtue of their choice of persuasive premises. (Of course, speakers also increase their rhetorical agency by using evidence well.)

What kinds of arguments are available to the rhetorician? The text says that the rhetoricians use enthymemes or rhetorical syllogisms and arguments by example (1. 2, 1355a–1355b, pp. 39–40). The word "enthymeme," though it sounds very technical, actually has an interesting root: the Greek *thumos*, which means "life," "heart," "spirit," and "courage." So a good argument not only involves a true inferential process, as in syllogism, but it goes *into* (*en*) the *thumos*. The verb, *enthumeisthai* can mean to "take to heart," "form a plan," "infer," or "conclude." The word "enthymeme" draws on these meanings. Enthymeme does not just lead to a logical conclusion; it also expresses a decision or choice. Indeed, it is in the *Rhetoric* that one finds Aristotle's "study of judgment" (*Talking to Strangers*, p. 141). For example, Alcidamus, a classical orator, argues in his oration the *Messianicus*, "if the war is the cause of present evils, things should be set right by making peace" (*On Rhetoric* 2. 23, 1379a, p. 191). If we add the proposition that "this war *is* the cause of present evils," the conclusion that one should make peace suggests action. Contrarily, a syllogism produces a true statement such as "Socrates is a mortal" that does not by itself lead to a choice.

However, because enthymemes concern only probabilities, they may seem less valid than syllogisms. And because enthymemes are more useful than syllogisms or scientific arguments when addressing a crowd (owing to their brevity), they may seem like watered down versions of detailed rigorous arguments (1. 2, 1357a, p. 41). But Aristotle argues, on the contrary, that because enthymemes concern probabilities, one can argue on both sides of a case. People deliberate when there are at least two possible options from which to choose. Thus one "should be able to prove opposites, as in logical arguments; not that we should do both (for one ought not to persuade people to do what is wrong), but that the real state of the case may not escape us" (*The "Art" of Rhetoric* 1. 1, 1355a, pp. 9 and 11). By seeking the facts and arguments on both sides, speakers have a better chance of discerning "the true state of affairs" (*On Rhetoric* 1. 1, 1355a, p. 34). Facts are not equally available on both sides, "but true and better ones are by nature always more productive of a good syllogism and, in a word, more persuasive." "Rhetoric is useful because the true and the just are by nature stronger than their opposites" (ibid., pp. 34–5).

Aristotle asserts that arguments need to be both true *and* just, and so it makes sense that he places rhetoric as an offshoot of dialectic and ethics or politics

(The "Art" of Rhetoric 1. 2, 1356a, pp. 19, 18). Speakers show that they are credible by reasoning well about practical matters and by showing that they are trust-worthy, honest, and have the audience's interests at heart. Other virtues are required as well. Speakers need to show that they will be fair to the audiences rather than exploiting them. They need to show in the speech that they are courageous (2. 9, 1366b, pp. 91, 93); those whose words seem cowardly cannot be trusted. But even a wise, virtuous speaker will not be heard unless he addresses the concerns of the audience. He needs to recognize the different *kinds* of audiences and their purposes.

The Speaker's Attentiveness to Audience and Social Context

In addition to discovering pertinent facts and arguments, speakers need to demon-strate their cognizance of the audience's purposes by adjusting their speech to the ends presupposed by the communicative situations. The three public contexts for speech in classical Athens were the law court, the assembly, and occasions such as funerals that called for praise and blame. A speaker who addressed the interests of the city in the court, or praised a future action without considering its expediency in the assembly was unlikely to find useful materials for his speech. The *Rhetoric* differentiates audiences according to whether they decide or serve as spectators and according to whether they judge the past, the present, or the future (*On Rhetoric* 1. 3, 1358b, pp. 47–8). Deliberative rhetoric addresses those who are concerned with future consequences, epideictic speakers praise and blame persons as if they were present, and orators in the law courts speak to those who judge past deeds. These audiences have different expectations, and the speaker who disregards their distinct purposes and social contexts will speak beside the point.

Thucydides' *The Peloponnesian War* offers a pertinent historical example. It represents the Corinthians as failing either to persuade or to find available means of persuasion because they disregard their audiences' purposes. They cannot display good will or marshal relevant facts because they are guided by an inappro-priate idea of the Athenians' goals. The Corinthians try to persuade the Athenians to reject Corcyra's appeals for help by arguing that Corcyra's "motives" in avoiding an alliance earlier "were entirely evil, and there was nothing good about them at all" (p. 58). This attack might seem forceful because it charges the opposition with being unjust. But Corcyraean guilt or innocence for a past action is not an overriding issue when deliberating about an alliance for the future. And although the Athenians are initially sympathetic to the Corinthians, they are not persuaded by their arguments. Thucydides does not indicate exactly why they were not. Perhaps the Corinthians fail to convince the Athenians because they do not address their interests. The Corcyraeans, on the other hand, show their attentiveness to Athenian interests: "perhaps the greatest advantage to you is that you can entirely depend on us because your enemies are the same as ours" (p. 57). And the Athenians, unsurprisingly, make an alliance with the Corcyraeans.

However, in distinguishing the three types of rhetoric, Aristotle does not mean to imply that one can never use deliberative arguments in a speech that praises and blames or use epideictic rhetoric in a judicial speech. Instead, he argues that each type of rhetoric has its defining purpose and "includes other factors as incidental" (*On Rhetoric* 1. 3, 1358b, p. 49). For example, Pericles' Funeral Oration at Athens uses the occasion to give advice. He tells his audience there is no relaxing during war, and persuades them to give even more for the cause of Athens than they have already given. Yet he connects this piece of deliberative rhetoric to his larger purpose of praising Athens and her soldiers, telling the audience to "fix your eyes every day on the greatness of Athens as she really is . . . and fall in love with her" (*Peloponnesian War*, p. 149). As this example shows, advice and eulogy can support one another.

In these ways, Aristotle increases speakers' abilities to relate to their audiences. But when it comes to advising them about how to find materials for their speeches, the task becomes more daunting. How can writers of rhetorical texts give advice to readers whose situations they do not know? Aristotle solves this problem by finding *topoi*, translated literally as "places," and Anglicized as "topics," for speakers to use as a resource. Topics help speakers to consider what is most probably advantageous, good, or just in the case at hand. Aristotle organizes the topics (the elements from which enthymemes "may be derived" (*The "Art" of Rhetoric* 2. 22, 1396b, p. 295) under three headings: ethos or character of the speaker; logos, the argument or speech; and pathos, the emotion of the audience. All three come into play when discerning the means of persuasion, for rhetorical speeches recommend ends, celebrate virtues, and evaluate justice; none of these activities can be done independently of the speaker's character and the audience's emotions. As Danielle S. Allen and Eugene Garver argue, rhetorical equity and truth are found in a relationship between speaker and hearer (see Chapter 9 below). And unlike Aristotle's *Nicomachean Ethics*, a science that investigates the most noble ends and actions, the *Rhetoric* seeks the best *possible* ends to be pursued in a specific situation. It enlarges the range of possible ends by using *topoi* such as pleasure, wealth, and friendship to indicate a wide range of goods that might be sought (*The "Art" of Rhetoric* 1. 6, 1362a, pp. 61–9). It focuses on everyday ideas about what human beings desire. Some ends are shared within a particular polity, so orators also need to know the type of political organization under which their audiences live. Aristotle comments: "choices are based on the 'end'." The "end of democracy is freedom, of oligarchy wealth, of aristocracy things related to education and the traditions of law, of tyranny self-preservation" (*On Rhetoric* 1. 8, 1366a, p. 77). An outline of procedures for retaining great wealth would not interest the many and exhortations to increase the freedom of the many will probably not have been heeded by an oligarchic audience.

Aristotle offers headings such as the noble (*kalon*) and the disgraceful (*aischron*) under which to find things to praise and blame, including the virtues of "justice, courage, self-control, magnificence, magnanimity" and "liberality" (*The "Art" of Rhetoric* 1. 9, 1366b, p. 91). Topics also suggest indirect strategies for discovering virtue. Speakers find things to praise by looking at the signs of virtue. One may find what is noble by looking at what is honored. Ethical qualities may not be obvious (ibid., p. 95). Or a speaker might consider the things a person does "while neglecting his own interests," for they are probably noble (1. 9, 1366b–1367a, p. 95). Praise and blame are supposed to *amplify* virtue and vice. They allow persons in a polity to envision the ideals that animate their lives. "Praise is speech that makes clear the greatness of virtue" and the depth of vice (*On Rhetoric* 1. 9, 1367b, p. 84).

A speaker's presentation of her character offers opportunities for discovery and discernment. Speakers use epideictic topics to establish a virtuous ethos for themselves *in the speech* (*The "Art" of Rhetoric* 1. 2, 1356a, p. 17). Although the idea that one can be inventive in presenting one's character seems to open the door to deception, the treatment of maxims in Book 2 suggests that speakers show their characters by making a public choice and commitment to a good. Aristotle shows how speakers discover ways to present their characters. They define themselves by a verbal action. A speaker who demonstrates that she is honest and can think in practical terms will be more credible than one who evidently lacks sense and is dishonest, especially in matters where there is no definitive factual proof that one course of action is better. Indeed, Aristotle affirms, "character is almost...the controlling factor in persuasion" (*On Rhetoric* 1. 2, 1356a, p. 38).

Distinct topics limit and focus the search for matter in judicial rhetoric. Whereas deliberative rhetoric draws on common beliefs about what is advantageous and disadvantageous and epideictic rhetoric focuses on virtue and vice, judicial rhetoric promotes justice and identifies injustice by appealing to the law. "Forensic speech accepts as given the laws of the polis," so the section on judicial rhetoric uses enthymemes to adjust "particular cases to general laws" (*Aristotle's Rhetoric*, p. 96). Aristotle addresses accusation and defense as well as the sources from which their enthymemes should be drawn, investigating "for what, and how many, purposes people do wrong... how these persons are [mentally] disposed," and "what kind of persons they wrong and what these people are like" (*On Rhetoric* 1. 10, 1368b, pp. 87–8). Because Aristotle is interested in causation in order to explain wrongdoing, he finds enthymemes particularly useful in judicial rhetoric.

Some of the most interesting and influential paragraphs on judicial rhetoric focus on equity or fairness. Here, as in the treatments of the ends of deliberative and epideictic rhetoric, we find Aristotle enlarging the repertoire of considerations and arguments speakers may entertain. Equity is important because the law cannot define circumstances precisely, and occasions arise when following the letter of the law would produce injustice. For example, a law may have an excessively broad reference, so that persons who commit misdemeanors are prosecuted as criminals. According to Aristotle, one must not "regard personal failings and mistakes as of equal seriousness with unjust actions. Mistakes are unexpected actions and do not result from wickedness." Instead, Aristotle insists that it is equitable to forgive human weaknesses, "to look not to the law but to the legislator and not to the word but to the intent of the legislator, and not to the actions but to the deliberate purpose" (1. 13, 1374b, p. 106).

Nineteenth- and twentieth-century British and North American legal writers use similar headings to interpret ambiguous statutes. Litigants uncomfortable with the wording of a statute can look to the intent of the legislature to determine the meaning of the statute, or they may look at the purpose of the statute rather than to its precise meaning. Both intent and purpose may be ambiguous but, Edward H. Levi argues, that very ambiguity provides a forum for invention and discussion (*Legal Reasoning*, pp. 28–30), as I will show in Chapter 10.

Aristotle argues that litigants should look "not to the part but to the whole" of the law, "not [looking at] what a person is now but what he has been always or for the most part" (*On Rhetoric* 1. 13, 1372a, p. 106). A single action may need to be viewed in the context of a lifetime of actions. Because equity requires that one consider words in light of legislative intent and the character of the defendant, equity should not be regarded as an escape from a logical process. Instead litigants discover different sources of argument.

It is not enough, however, to know topics that help the speaker find ends like happiness and living well or virtues like courage and justice. Speakers also need to produce emotions in their audiences that are based on wise interpretations. The length of Aristotle's analysis of emotion may seem puzzling, given Book 1's attack on moving the emotions of judges. Has he forgotten that he attacked earlier rhetorical handbooks because they emphasized emotion? Has he caved in to manipulating emotion?

We may also wonder why the treatment of emotion occurs in the same chapter as the analysis of arguments and inferential structures. This grouping of emotion with arguments suggests that speakers must assess ways of moving emotions just as they assess the cogency of arguments. This impression is borne out by Aristotle's analysis of belief or conviction (*pisteis*, s. *pistis*), a term whose various uses generate the structure of the *Rhetoric*. The order of the text follows roughly the process of composing a speech. Book 1, chapter 2 (*On Rhetoric* 1355b–1356a, p. 37) uses the plural *pisteis* with reference to the three sources of persuasive materials (ethos, logos, and pathos), as well as the proofs or conviction (*pisteis*) that they produce (p. 39), and finally the proofs (*pisteis*) that produce belief – enthymeme and argument by example (1. 2, 1356b, p. 40). Aristotle organizes the text in terms of these uses, considering the sources of persuasion in Book 1, and Book 2, chapters 1–12; assessing emotion, enthymeme, and example throughout Book 2; and showing speakers how to produce conviction through style in Book 3. He uses the words *topos* and *topoi* with regard to finding both the materials of speech and the arguments that organize them. But his treatment of emotions also helps speakers understand how to produce a broad range of emotions. He provides cognitive grounds for emotions on the basis of assessments of social interactions. Emotions based on probable interpretations of actions and events should not be confused with passion (*pathê*) that is ungoverned.

Book 2, chapters 1–12 analyze only political emotions, "the affections which cause men to change their opinion in regard to their judgements, and are accompanied by pleasure and pain" (*The "Art" of Rhetoric* 2. 1, 1378a, p. 173). The emotions usually come in pairs like anger and mildness, love and hate, and fear and confidence. One term in each pair names an emotion accompanied by pain (such as anger, fear, indignation, and envy). Speakers use rhetoric to change negative emotions, transforming anger to mildness or fear to confidence. For example, if someone is enraged by an undeserved slight, a speaker may show that the slight was unintended or less significant than it seemed (*Talking to Strangers*, p. 150). Speakers need also to attend to the sensitivity of the slighted person (his disposition). On the other hand, by representing a slight as especially offensive, the speaker may increase another person's anger.

Aristotle's treatment of emotions is rooted in his own culture and provides a "normative repertoire" that speakers use to produce emotion in that context (*Law, Violence*, p. 53). It views people's relationships to each other as subject to rivalry. Men strive for honor and increase their own honor by diminishing the status of others, producing conflict. In this context, slights produce great anger.

But the *Rhetoric*'s treatment of emotions also has broader implications. For example, it defines anger as "affecting a man himself or one of his friends, when such a slight is undeserved." Philip Fisher points out that the reference to whether a slight is deserved relates anger to justice. A person whose worth is unfairly diminished by another feels justifiable anger. And because anger extends to one's family and friends, it is not egocentric. There is a social component to it (*Vehement Passions*, pp. 173–5).

Aristotle's exploration of emotions shows the need for citizens to understand the emotions of others and to interpret people and actions in a variety of ways (*Talking to Strangers*, p. 151). Emotions are persuadable; they can be reasonable sources of energy for practical action. Aristotle also makes friendship central to rhetoric, because a speaker who wishes to demonstrate his credibility needs to know how to make friends with the audience (*Talking to Strangers*, pp. 119–21, 136–40, 152–5; *For the Sake of Argument*, pp. 27–8, 34, 42; see also Chapter 9 below, pp. 114, 115, 128–33, 137).

The essence of this sort of friendship is not sentiment but "wishing for anyone the things which we believe to be good, for his sake but not for our own, and procuring them for him as far as lies in our power" (*The "Art" of Rhetoric* 2. 4, 1381a, p. 193). Friends have the "same ideas of good," so that a speaker who shares an audience's ends becomes a friend. Rhetoricians are also able "to prove that men are enemies or friends, or to make them such if they are not" (2. 4, 1382a, p. 201; *Talking to Strangers*, p. 149) In short, Aristotle treats the problem of understanding the emotions of others as requiring reasonable assessments of people and occasions.

Aristotle's focus on argument permeates the entire *Rhetoric*. As is the case with producing emotion, a speaker needs to use arguments to show that his character is credible. His speech must demonstrate that he can reason. Speakers must demonstrate in the speech that they can reason wisely and effectively about practical matters. Arguments that address the audience's interests demonstrate good will. And maxims show the speaker's beliefs in ethical values. In sum, speakers need to show their "good sense, virtue and goodwill" (*The "Art" of Rhetoric* 2. 1, 1378a, p. 171).

The interpenetration of ethos with argument becomes apparent in the *Rhetoric*'s analysis of how speakers show good will. Orators demonstrate good will and practical wisdom by arguing that an action serves the best interests of the audience (1. 3, 1358b, p. 35). In order to do this, they need to know how an audience perceives its own welfare: a friend wishes "for anyone the things which we believe to be good, for his sake" (2. 4, 1381a, p. 193). We have seen that a speech might address a range of concerns including happiness, success, wealth, and security (1. 5, 1360b, p. 57). But it is not enough to find material for a speech. Speakers need to organize these materials into an argument. For example, King Archidamus draws on ends of safety and welfare in *The Peloponnesian War* when he encourages the Spartans to be deliberate in their decision to wage war instead of acting immediately on their passions. His references to the "lives of men and their fortunes, the fates of cities, and their national honour" (p. 85) manifest his concern for the welfare of his polity. The end of his speech (the people's welfare) becomes the end of the speaker's deliberate choice, manifesting his character. Aristotle asserts that "characters become clear by deliberate choice, and deliberate choice is directed to an 'end'" (*On Rhetoric* 1. 8, 1366a, p. 77). When deliberate choice is manifested by a speech, we cannot disentangle ethos from argument.

Aristotle closely interconnects argument and ethos in his analysis of maxims, encouraging speakers to do the same. Maxims (condensed enthymemes) make a rational argument *and* give a speech character (ethos). For "speeches have character insofar as deliberate choice is clear, and all maxims accomplish this because one speaking a maxim makes a general statement about preferences, so that if the maxims are morally good, they make the speaker seem to have a good character" (*On Rhetoric* 2. 21, 1395b, p. 186). When Socrates uses the injunction, "know yourself," he urges self-knowledge *and* he shows the kind of person he is.

A maxim may also have emotional power illustrating how intertwined argument and emotion can be. Aristotle gives an example of a person who exclaims in anger that whoever says that a person should know himself lies. This angry speaker says derisively, " 'At least, this man, if he had known himself, would never have thought himself worthy of command' " (2. 21, 1395a, p. 185). The emotional effect of this acerbic comment (outrage) cannot be separated from its cognitive content (that if the person knew his weaknesses, he would not think he was worthy to lead). Aristotle argues similarly that ethos should "result from the speech (logos) not from a previous opinion that the speaker is a certain kind of person" (1. 2, 1356a, p. 38). Unlike Ciceronian rhetoric, which depends heavily on the authority of a person within his society, Aristotelian rhetoric emphasizes how the speech creates an impression of the speaker.

The Structures of Argument

Unless a speech assesses arguments judiciously, it can never be persuasive to a rational audience. The *Rhetoric* provides topics for finding these arguments. We have learned the topics or elements like good and bad, fair or foul, just or unjust that serve as matter; now we need to find topics "in another way" (*The "Art" of Rhetoric* 2. 12, 1397a) to organize and assess these elements. Again, topics serve to direct attention to structures of argument *and* to expand the variety of arguments available to a speaker. They indicate how to recognize probative as well as fallacious enthymemes. By looking at the circumstances of a case from the perspective of different strategies of argument, speakers find and test propositions. Modern North American lawyers approach cases in this way. When one person has allegedly injured another, lawyers may consider whether to focus on "fault" and "intent" or on causation (see Chapter 10 below). One of the more effective *topoi* Aristotle mentions is that from division. In itself, division is an abstract structure: "*a* or *b* or *c*," but it helps speakers find propositions. Aristotle offers an example: "there are always three motives for wrong doing; two are excluded from consideration as impossible; as for the third, not even the accusers assert it' " (2. 13, 1398a, p. 305). By dividing the options exhaustively and excluding each one, the orator proves that that the defendant has no motive for doing wrong.

King Archidamus offers a deliberative argument from division in *The Peloponnesian War*. He opposes going to war by arguing that Sparta lacks resources, dividing them into kinds: "What have we to rely upon if we rush into [war] unprepared? Our navy? It is inferior to theirs ... Our wealth? Here we are at an even greater disadvantage: we have no public funds ... [T]he superiority which we have in heavy infantry and in actual numbers, assets which will enable us to invade and devastate their land? ... Athens ... controls plenty of land outside Attica and can import what she wants by sea." He summarizes by asking, "If we can neither defeat [the Athenians] at sea nor take away from them the resources on which their navy depends, we shall do ourselves more harm than good" (p. 83). Insofar as his division is exhaustive, his argument is persuasive.

Aristotle offers twenty-eight *topoi* (topics) for creating enthymemes (*On Rhetoric* 2. 22, 1396b–2. 23, 1400b, pp. 189–204). George A. Kennedy helpfully characterizes topics as "lines, or strategies, of argument useful in treating many different subject matters in all three species of rhetoric" (*On Rhetoric*, p. 190). The kinds are organized under two broad pairs of rubrics – those pertinent to demonstration and those pertinent to refutation, and among the demonstrative topics, some emphasize predication (such as the topic from definition) and others inferential structures (such as the topic from antecedent to consequence). (Looking at predication will help us understand later how Aristotle advises the orator to use style. Greek sentences may also follow inferential structure.) In *The Peloponnesian War*, the speakers from Mytilene, after their revolt had been defeated, argue from antecedent to consequence (*The "Art" of Rhetoric* 2. 23, 1399a, p. 311) in addressing the Spartans:

> But if you give us your whole-hearted support you will gain for yourselves a state which has a large navy (which is the thing you need most); you will be in a much better position for breaking the power of Athens by detaching her allies from her, since the others will be greatly encouraged to come over to you; and you will clear yourselves of the charge that has been made against you of not giving help to those who revolt. (*Peloponnesian War*, p. 201)

The speakers from Mytilene show that Spartan aid will produce three advantageous consequences for the Spartans. *Topoi* give structure and cogency to their speech.

But speakers should not make their arguments too complicated for the audience to follow. If speakers draw on premises from special subject matters, they may find themselves involved in a scientific dispute that is irrelevant to the decision that needs to be made. "To the degree that someone makes better choice of the premises, he will have created knowledge different from dialectic and rhetoric without its being recognized; for if he succeeds in hitting on first principles, the knowledge will no longer be dialectic or rhetoric but the science of which [the speaker] grasps the first principles" (*On Rhetoric* 1. 2, 1358a, p. 46). Then the speech becomes a scientific treatise rather than an effort to inform deliberation. Modern North American lawyers encounter this difficulty when they make use of expert witnesses. In the Supreme Court Case concerning the admission of students to the University of Michigan Law School (*Gratz v. Bollimer*), statisticians served as expert witnesses for the plaintiffs and the defendants. These statisticians needed to avoid lengthy expositions of the principles of statistics understood for their own sake, partly because such expositions would cease to be relevant to the case and partly because, an Aristotelian would argue, general audiences are not able to follow intricate arguments. After all, the decision-making power belongs to a judge not to a statistician, for the judge views the legality of what has been done.

But enthymemes are not the only arguments available to speakers. Argument by example is an equally powerful way to explore and assess issues. Modern legal theorists including Edward H. Levi and Cass R. Sunstein show how argument by example or analogy works in modern English and North American law (see Chapter 10 below). Aristotle stresses the power of example to generate and assess arguments. He compares it to induction. But induction moves from many particulars to a generalization, whereas argument from example needs only one instance. How can inference from a single instance be warranted? In confronting this question, Aristotle makes a puzzling statement that argument by example reasons "neither from part to whole nor from whole to part but from part to part, like to like" (*On Rhetoric* 1. 2, 1357b, p. 44; see also *Analytica priora* 69a, p. 103). Levi illuminates this opaque statement when he writes that in case law, a lawyer or judges moves from one case to another, finding similarities and differences before announcing a similarity or difference as determinative and expressing it through a concept (*Legal Reasoning*, p. 2). For example, when considering whether a person who made an exploding lamp that injures someone should pay damages to that person, a lawyer or judge looks at previous cases to find similarities and differences. Both guns and lamps produce injury, but perhaps a gun manufacturer has a greater responsibility to exercise care than the maker of the lamp because a gun is more likely to be dangerous. Comparison of cases helps litigants find arguments.

Aristotle also treats argument by example as a source of analogies. For example, someone contemplating a strong Persian neighbor might turn to the past to find an argument, namely that "it is necessary to make preparations against the king [of Persia] and not allow Egypt to be subdued; for in the past Darius did not invade [Greece] until he had taken Egypt" (*On Rhetoric* 2. 20, 1393a, p. 179). The analogy between the past and the present suggests what may happen in the present.

Although modern legal rhetoric focuses on examples, deliberative orators use both fable (*logos*) and historical example (*parabolê*) (*On Rhetoric* 2. 19, 1393a). Aristotle argues that while it is easier to invent fables than to find apt examples, historical examples are more useful in deliberative rhetoric "for generally, future events will be like those of the past" (2. 20, 1394a, p. 181). Nevertheless, fables play a role because they invite one to "see the likenesses," as philosophers do, underlining again the cognitive aspect of rhetoric. Aristotle illustrates the use of fable by telling Stesichorus' story of a horse and a stag. This story is a parable, warning against giving Phalaris a bodyguard. It provides a succinct political theory to be used as a paradigm for action. A horse that wishes to avenge himself on a stag asks a man to help him. The man mounts the horse but "instead of getting vengeance the horse found himself a slave to the man." Stesichorus warns the people to "look out, lest while wishing vengeance on your enemies...[you] suffer the same thing as the horse. You already have the bridle [in your mouth], having appointed a general with absolute power; if you give him a bodyguard and allow him to mount, you will immediately be slaves to Phalaris'" (2. 20, 1393b, p. 180). The fable dramatizes the dangers of delegating physical power to others. Its lack of historical truth does not prevent it from disclosing a probable sequence of events.

Classical and humanist political writers made extensive use of fables as models for the structure of a polity. Sir Philip Sidney's *A Defence of Poetry*, for example, refers to the fable of Menenius Agrippa, who, when the "people of Rome had resolutely divided themselves from the senate" tells them a tale about a time "when all the parts of the body made a mutinous conspiracy against the belly" but they understood ultimately that "with punishing the belly they plagued themselves" (p. 93). The artful speaker uses the example to elicit key relations in a political situation.

Aristotle's analysis of enthymeme and example has consequences for style. The *Rhetoric* does not treat style as an end in itself, but as a way to bring an argument home to an audience. Book 3 names perspicuity (*saphê*) as one of the chief merits of style: "For if [*style*] does not make the argument [logos] clear, it does not achieve its function" (*The "Art" of Rhetoric* 3. 2, 1404b, p. 351). Appropriately, given the focus on predication in Book 2, Book 3 emphasizes the choice of nouns and verbs as salient. Nouns and verbs, when properly chosen, make arguments by predication transparent. Someone arguing by definition, for example, would want to "observe due proportion" in choosing a word to express a predicate (3. 2, 1405, p. 355). Consider, for example, those who call actors the "flatterers of Dionysius," whereas actors call themselves "artists." The text adds, "similarly, pirates now call themselves purveyors" (ibid., p. 357). Accusers and defenders of a "pirate" can use the elevating term to lighten the offense or the denigrating term to make the offense heavier. In this way, style contributes to ethical and cognitive meaning rather than serving a merely ornamental function.

Similarly, Aristotle recommends metaphors for their ethical power; metaphors "signify what is fair or foul...*qua* fair or foul" (1405b, p. 359). "For it does make a difference, for instance, whether one says 'rosy-fingered morn,' rather than 'purple-fingered,' or, what is still worse, 'red-fingered'." Aristotle's most humorous comment on style concerns the ethical effect of epithets. It seems that,

> When the winner in a mule-race offered Simonides a small sum, he refused to write an ode, as if he thought it beneath him to write on half-asses; but when he gave him a sufficient amount, he wrote,
>   Hail, daughters of storm-footed steeds.

"And yet," Aristotle concludes, "they were also the daughters of asses" (1405b, p. 361).

The close relationship between argument and style emerges in Aristotle's treatment of metaphor. In a famous analysis, Aristotle praises "smart" or sophisticated style and words that make us learn easily (3. 10, 1410b, p. 395). The words should be neither too strange nor too ordinary for "we do not know the meaning of strange words, and proper terms we know already" (p. 397). But metaphor gives pleasure by making us learn. By arguing that "all style and enthymemes that give us rapid information are smart," Aristotle makes style pertinent to argument.

The *Rhetoric* brings style and emotion, sought by earlier orators for their power to manipulate audiences, into close relation to argument. It offers a way of discovering stylistic strategies that clarify arguments; these in turn inform decisions about contingent matters. The text does not guarantee that a speaker will not make a bad argument seem better; speakers can use rhetoric to do precisely that. But by clarifying the issues at stake when choosing arguments and stylistic devices, Aristotle subjects persuasive speech to discernment and judgment. Those willing to improve their abilities to exhort and dissuade become more able to discover cogent arguments and to criticize the deceptive arguments of others. Instead of serving as a substitute for action or a means of flattering and deceiving audiences, Aristotelian rhetoric provides tools for displaying character, improving practical resourcefulness and judgment, and producing constructive emotion. It exercises the intellect with regard to the ethical and political problems that test human convictions and engage their emotions.

Note

1   I use two editions of Aristotle's *Rhetoric*: George A. Kennedy's *On Rhetoric* and John Henry Freese's translation, *The "Art" of Rhetoric*, for the Loeb Classical Library. The former offers detailed commentary and careful translations and the latter is often more readable and offers the Greek text in addition to the translation.

Chapter 2

Eloquence, Persuasion, and Invention: Cicero's *De oratore*

If Thucydides and Aristotle elevate deliberative rhetoric to make it the basis of political community, Cicero celebrates eloquence because it contributes to the "benefit of mankind." He claims that eloquence led human beings out of a "brutish" life into a civilized existence as citizens (*De oratore* 1. 33, vol. I, p. 25; see *On Duties* 1. 56, p. 61). Eloquence belongs to the republican statesman who shapes the character and arouses the energy of the people (*Senior Statesman*, p. 26).

Cicero's emphasis on persuasion suggests that the chief purpose of oratory is to arouse passion. Antonius, a participant in the dialogue in *De oratore* (55 BCE), doubts that one must have a philosophical knowledge of psychology in order to "kindle the feelings of his hearers, or quench them when kindled." He emphasizes emotion, believing that the business of the orator is to use words to magnify the misery of things believed to be evil while "he enlarges upon and beautifies by his eloquence whatever is commonly deemed delectable" (1. 219, p. 155; 221, p. 157). For this, Antonius insists, he needs "no philosophers' definitions" (1. 222, p. 159). Instead he calls for a person "of sharpness," "ingenious," who "with keen scent will track down the thoughts, feelings, beliefs and hopes of his fellow citizens," language that revives the image of the orator that Plato attacks in the *Gorgias* (1. 223, p. 159). Restating Aristotle's controversy over the relative merits of reason and emotion in persuading audiences, Crassus and Antonius nevertheless agree that "it is in calming or kindling the feelings of the audience that the full power and science of oratory" is "brought into play" (1. 17, p. 15). This emphasis on moving the audience raises the question of how an eloquent speaker can avoid the traps that Plato discovered in demagogic Athenian oratory. Does the Roman orator, a flatterer and a pleaser, manipulate the audience for his own self-interest?

Later writers who draw on Cicero while writing in a princely or monarchist context claim that orators actually control the minds of the people: the ruler's eloquence "transforms the [people] into ideal subjects who continually... need... direction" (*Emperor of Men's Minds*, p. 29). Christian rhetoricians, including Augustine, also looked to passionate rhetoric flowing from the heart to produce an irresistible effect on listeners. Passion enables reason to affect action, "stirring the will to desire what the mind already approves" (*Sacred Rhetoric*, p. 46). *De oratore* debates the relative importance of knowledge and emotion by arguing on both sides of the question and allowing readers to arrive at a decision. Antonius asserts that "nothing in oratory... is more important than to win for the orator the favour of his hearer" and to move their emotions (2. 178, vol. I, p. 325). Rhetoric can "arouse a listless nation, and... curb its unbridled impetuosity." "Who more passionately than the orator can encourage to virtuous conduct, or more zealously than he reclaims from vicious courses?" (2. 35, vol. I, p. 223).

This controversy needs to be understood in relation to the social functions of oratory. Roman orators were more likely to lead the people than to deliberate with them about contested values and conflicting interests, as speakers do in Thucydides' history. For example, *The Peloponnesian War* juxtaposes the Melians' emphasis on justice and courage with the Athenians' concern for self-interest (*Peloponnesian War*, pp. 400–8). But Roman orators drew on a relatively small, agreed-upon "repertory of values" in persuading their audiences. "Courage, discipline, hard work, duty and tradition were continually praised; their opposites, daring, immoderation, vanity, and novelty, were continually derogated." Orators did not innovate or debate values so much as they sought to "properly elaborate and deliver them" ("Text and context," p. 38). The rhetorical strategies of the Hellenic writers, especially those of style, became primary tools of Roman orators wishing to express attitudes toward their topics and to articulate their objectives (ibid., p. 39). An orator could achieve the right elaboration and delivery by means of *decorum*, the appropriateness of style to the matter and purpose at hand. This decorum was not fixed; rather it worked dynamically through the art of the speaker.

Cicero elaborates three styles borrowed from Hellenism: the "grand, which stirs the emotions; the middle, which persuades through pleasure; and the plain or subdued style, which proves points" (*Orator* 69; "Text and context," p. 39). Each style has an appropriate function. B. A. Krostenko comments that an orator would not use the grand style to speak of rainwater because the "objective is to establish, say, a property claim" where "careful argument is more useful than fulmination; fulmination, *in that context*, would give the impression, at the least, of obfuscation, if not lunacy" (*Orator* 99). But when a speaker wants to expand on "the glory of the state and thus rouse hatred against her betrayer... explosive heat is more useful than adroit subtleties" ("Text and context," p. 39). Thus Cicero attends to the appropriate attitude, tone, and emotion toward the matter at hand, for these convey the speaker's sense of the weight and type of issue that is at stake.

However, Cicero's focus on style should not imply that he was uninterested in argument. Antonius articulates only one side of the issue (probably representing the rhetorician Hortensius), while Crassus, representing Cicero, insists that eloquence must be united with wisdom. The dialogue links the two by making subject matter the source of eloquence, copiousness, and fervor. Crassus insists, "a full supply (*copia*) of facts (*rerum*) begets a full supply (*copiam*) of words *(verborum)*" (*De oratore* 3. 125, vol. II, pp. 99, 98). Without a grasp of the subject, the speaker can produce only a feeble speech. "Unless there is such knowledge, well-grasped and comprehended by the speaker, there must be something empty and almost childish in the utterance" (1. 20, vol. I, p. 17). Just as Crassus links style, emotion, and subject matter, Antonius himself creates a role for argument when he draws on Aristotle's headings of logos, ethos, and pathos and turns them to the distinct situation of Roman politics (2. 162–216, vol. I, p. 165).

This revision of Aristotle's tripartite schema shows Cicero's rhetorical inventiveness. Because rhetorical terms are general and ambiguous, they can be redefined to fit new circumstances. Cicero finds new meanings and uses for ethos, logos, and pathos. *De inventione*, a rhetoric he wrote as a young man, articulates the way that common topics "as arguments . . . can be transferred to many cases" (2. 48, p. 209). It praises topics used in one case that can be applied to another.

Topics lead speakers to matter and arguments for their speeches. Shifting to the point of view of the orator, Antonius in *De oratore* uses a metaphor of hunting for gold to show how topics (*topoi* or *loci*) lead orators to facts and arguments even when Antonius himself cannot tell them what the facts and arguments actually will be in the specific case. He views the orator as like a prospector: "For if I wished to reveal to somebody gold that was hidden here and there in the earth, it should be enough for me to point out to him some marks and indications of its positions, with which knowledge, he could do his own digging, and find what he wanted . . . so I know these indications of proofs, which reveal to me their whereabouts when I am looking for them; all the rest is dug out by dint of careful consideration" (*De oratore* 2. 174, vol. I, p. 323). Orators must do their own digging, but topics point the way. By topics Antonius has in mind strategies of argument such as argument from the greater and the lesser, which could yield the particular proposition "If good repute is above riches, and money is so keenly desired, how far more keenly should fame be desired?" (2. 172, vol. I, p. 321). One only has to link this proposition to a particular premise to make it practical.

De oratore uses Aristotle's categories of ethos, logos, and pathos to help speakers find arguments, create good will, and move their audiences. But it redefines the categories to emphasize the importance of sympathy, public reputation, and passionate speech. These redefinitions also depart from *De inventione*'s treatment of topics. By analyzing *De inventione*'s approach, we will be better prepared to consider the method of *De oratore*. *De inventione*, like Aristotle's *Rhetoric*, shows speakers how to find material and a point of view from which to argue. As we have seen, Aristotle's headings of speaker, speech, and audience (ethos, logos, and pathos) point to places speakers can look for matter. The process of considering these multiple points of view discovers propositions and materials that need not be in conflict. *De inventione*, however, does not recognize a rhetorical issue in the law courts without a conflict of pleas. It addresses rhetoric as a mode of controversy. It also organizes the inventive process very tightly. It lists a series of questions, each of which provides a place for decision, and the sum of which help the orator find the issue (*constitutio*) that he wishes to address in his speech. The conflict between verbal expressions generates the first issue: "The 'issue' is the first conflict of pleas which arises from the defence or answer to our accusation, in this way: 'You did it', 'I did not do it', or 'I was justified in doing it' " (1. 10, p. 21). If the plaintiff and the prosecutor disagree about the deed (*factum*) (i.e. whether he did it), they have found an issue about which to speak. If the plaintiff and the prosecutor agree about the facts, they make a definition, and if their definitions disagree, they focus their arguments on this dispute (whether, for example, a killing is murder or manslaughter) (*nominis controversia*) (1. 11, pp. 23, 22). Otherwise, they consider the nature of the act to find whether they disagree about that (*generis controversia*). Cicero calls that dispute qualitative because "there is a question . . . about how important it is or of what kind" it is (1. 12, p. 25). But if the participants agree an all these matters, the orator may still have a controversy about procedure.

Compared to Aristotle's extremely open, multisided approach, *De inventione* focuses on areas of choice quite narrowly. But *De oratore* treats invention more expansively. Antonius introduces the questions in an account of his own process of arguing a case in court. Having emphasized the necessity of gaining mastery over documents, evidence, contracts, and so forth, he raises questions of fact ("what has been done, or what is being done, or going to be done" (2. 100, 104, vol. I, pp. 273, 275). When the terms in which a fact is defined or an "act should be described" are in dispute, the advocate raises a "question . . . of definition" (2. 107, vol. I, p. 277). For example, when Antonius argued that Norbanus was not guilty of treason and the opposition argued that he was, they were engaging in a dispute about definition. The focus on definition emphasizes the extent to which legal deliberation may turn on the use of words; later it played an important role in biblical hermeneutics.

Once the fact and the definition of the act has been agreed upon, *De inventione* stipulates that a dispute about a qualitative issue may arise; this question becomes pertinent when the "letter" of the law and the "spirit are at variance." (2. 110, p. 279). By moving from the question of fact, to definition, and to quality, Cicero progressively zeroes in on the place where a conflict of pleas can be found in a particular case and, therefore, where an opportunity for rhetorical argument can be found.

Disputes about the moral quality of an action have important and far-reaching implications because they give the orator an opportunity to address the broadest ethical and interpretive questions. Wesley Trimpi demonstrates the importance of the qualitative issue for understanding how fiction works by examining the philosophical questions out of which the rhetorical questions arises. Philosophical questions focus on "whether something exists or happened," "what the thing is (*quid sit*)," and "what its character is (*quale sit*)." The first question is answered by inference and conjecture (*coniectura*), the second question is answered by definition (*definitione*), and the third "by distinctions between right and wrong (*iuris et iniuriae distinctione*)" (*Muses of One Mind*, p. 252; *Topica* 82–6). Questions of right and wrong provide the broadest scope for exploring possible interpretations of an action. They provide a perspective that allows one to interpret the "confusing detail of a particular case" (*Muses of One Mind*, p. 254). Quintilian also believes that the qualitative issue provides the most scope for oratory (ibid., p. 257). He argues that, depending upon how speakers define the motive for a murder, the question will yield different points for the judge's consideration. Opponents could dispute whether Orestes ought to have obeyed the oracle or whether he should have avenged his father's murder. Trimpi infers from this variety that fiction has the capacity "to receive unlimited qualification through the manipulation of circumstances" (ibid.).

De oratore approaches the problem of how to articulate a full account of the ethical and emotional implications of an action differently from *De inventione*. After Antonius introduces the questions of fact and of definition, instead of raising the qualitative issue, he draws on Aristotle's tripartite distinction (ethos, logos, and pathos), focusing on "the proof of our allegations, the winning of our hearers' favour, and the rousing of their feelings to whatever impulse our case may require" (2. 115, vol. I, p. 281). These three considerations allow orators to consider ethical questions previously raised by the qualitative issue in ways more closely bound up with inventing matter for a speech.

Whereas school rhetoric proceeded through the parts of the speech to find topics for invention, Antonius' account relies on the three factors for finding the materials for a speech. As a result, ethical, emotional, and probative emphases permeate the whole speech, rather than being limited to the introduction or peroration. Like Aristotle, Cicero makes character as important as argument but he values emotion more than Aristotle does. However, there are important differences between the two accounts that dramatize how Cicero adapted the earlier scheme to meet the distinct needs of Roman oratory.

Like Aristotle, Cicero focuses on the character of the speaker in order to make the speech more ethical. But Aristotle's account stresses the good will, virtue, and practical sense of speakers as what manifests their trustworthiness. As Jakob Wisse puts it, Aristotle focuses on those aspects of ethos that make a speech "reliable by suggesting that a speaker with those qualities will tell the truth." Cicero, on the other hand, expands ethos to include all the qualities that will "win the sympathy of the hearers" (*Ethos and Pathos*, p. 7). Aristotle argues that the orator's ethos should be displayed in the speech, but Cicero relies on the character that a speaker or a client has achieved in public office. Antonius insists,

> A potent factor in success, then, is for the characters, principles, conduct and course of life, both of those who are to plead cases and of their clients, to be approved and conversely that of their opponents condemned; and for the feelings of the tribunal to be won over, as far as possible to goodwill towards the advocate and the advocate's client as well. Now feelings are won over by a man's merit, achievements or reputable life, qualifications easier to embellish, if only they are real, than to fabricate where non-existent. (*De oratore* 2. 182, vol. I, p. 327)

Whereas Aristotle's speaker needs to display prudence in his speech to show that he is reliable and trustworthy, Cicero stresses the speaker's display of good will (*benevolentia*) and his ability to win sympathy (*conciliare*), an attitude particularly important in the law courts.

Although it is tempting to view Cicero's term for sympathy as equivalent to Aristotle's ethos, doing so fails to capture Cicero's distinct idea. Cicero's idea of ethos is broader than Aristotle's because it refers to the existing reputation of the speaker and the client. The reference in the quotation to "man's merit, achievements or reputable life" suggests a notion of character that is socially defined and unchanging (See *De officiis* 1. 107–14, pp. 109–17; *Trials of Character*, p. 5). Character in this sense can be passed from one generation to another; Romans respected the customs of the ancestors (*mos maiorum*) and revered authority. The orator's style embellishes his achievements as well as his client's worth and reputation, and he enhances his own ethos by the expression on his face, and kindliness in the use of his words (*Ethos and Pathos*, p. 21). *De oratore* emphasizes the need for the orator to give "the tokens of good-nature, kindness, calmness, loyalty and a disposition that is pleasing" (2. 182, vol. I, p. 329). Antonius advises using a mild tone of voice and gentleness to display character. He argues that "to paint their characters in words as being upright, stainless, conscientious" often has a "wonderful effect" and is "often to be worth more than the merits of the case" (2. 184, vol. I, p. 329). Style conveys qualities that reconcile the judges and make them friendly to one's position. Since "the repertory of values" available to the orator in the late Roman Republic were small and less open to debate than those in classical Athens, orators relied on style to show the force of their adherence to those values in the case at hand.

Cicero's treatment of pathos also has a practical emphasis. Pathos, like ethos, becomes as important or more important than judgment and deliberation. We can understand Antonius' emphasis on emotion easily because he plays the role in the dialogue of the defender of emotion who claims that "nothing in oratory... is more important than to win for the orator the favour of his hearer, and to have the latter so affected as to be swayed by something resembling a mental impulse or emotion, rather than by judgement or deliberation" (2. 178, vol. I, p. 325). But Crassus, who argues for the crucial role of learning in oratory, makes a similar point when he argues that "there is to my mind no more excellent thing than the power, by means of oratory, to get a hold on assemblies of men, win their good will, direct their inclinations wherever the speaker wishes, or divert them from whatever he wishes" (1. 30, vol. I, p. 23). Crassus identifies this art with the existence of a "free nation" in which talent emerges. He envisions a gifted orator arising from the company of humankind who can lead by his words. Though not radically democratic like Aristotle's society, the Republic fosters freedom, which allows excellence to emerge. The Roman Republic became exemplary for many later writers, including John Milton.

Cicero's treatment of the emotions seems similar to the position Aristotle attacks in Book 1 of the *Rhetoric*, when he criticizes earlier rhetorical handbooks for concentrating on the emotions. Aristotle warns that "it is wrong to warp the judge's feelings, to arouse him to anger, jealousy, or compassion, which would be like making the rule crooked which one intended to use" (The "Art" of Rhetoric 1. 1, 1354b, p. 5, translation modified). Antonius, on the other hand, tells Catulus that nothing is more important than swaying the audience with an impulse or emotion, rather than by judgment or deliberation. "For men decide far more problems by hate, or love, or lust, or rage, or sorrow, or joy, or hope, or fear, or illusion, or some other inward emotion, than by reality, or authority, or any legal standard, or judicial precedent, or statute" (*De oratore* 2. 178, vol. I, p. 325). Because Antonius' position resembles the one Aristotle attacks, we might infer that Cicero's rhetoric is less cognitively based than Aristotle's. And, in fact, Cicero's rhetoric does insist on the centrality of vehemence in a way Aristotle's does not. However, Cicero and Crassus repeatedly emphasize the need to unite wisdom and eloquence. Without eloquence, learning is impotent to affect public action. Antonius regards the power to "arouse a listless nation, and to curb its unbridled impetuosity" as part of the orator's authority. The greatest orator passionately encourages virtuous action and "zealously" turns the people away from vicious ways (2. 35, vol. I, p. 223). Passion becomes an antidote, and even a medicine against the vicious. In the "battles of the law-courts," the judge may be "ill-disposed" or "angry" or "friendly to the other side," and these perturbations need to be "reined back" or "spurred on" or "swung round" if the effect of his perturbations is to be overcome (2. 72, vol. I, pp. 251, 253). Antonius goes so far as to compare the orator to a "careful physician who, before he attempts to administer a remedy to his patient, must investigate not only the malady of the man he wishes to cure, but also his habits when in health, and his physical condition" (2. 185, vol. I, p. 331). This comparison suggests that passions can put the judge into a diseased state that the orator must cure. This cure requires not only vehement rhetoric, but the orator's sensitivity and discernment, his willingness to "explore the feelings of the tribunal," to "scent out with all possible keenness their thoughts, judgements, anticipations and wishes, and the direction in which they seem likely to be led away most easily by eloquence" (2. 186, vol. I, p. 331).

In spite of Antonius' confidence, one cannot help thinking that orators may misuse the ability to lead others in the way they want them to go. But he makes two arguments that qualify this understanding. He asserts that in order to make an audience feel "indignation, hatred or ill-will, to be terrified of anything, or reduced to tears of compassion," the orator must have all these emotions "branded" upon his visible appearance (2. 189, vol. I, p. 333). But in order to appear moved, in order to move others, one must oneself be really stirred by the "very feelings" one seeks to prompt in others (2. 189, vol. I, p. 335).

Renaissance reiterations of this idea interpret the orator's feeling emotion himself as a sign of authenticity. Antonius, however, does not go quite so far. Rather, he compares the orator to an actor and a poet (2. 193, vol. I, p. 337). The comparison to the actor emphasizes role-playing and makes his experience of emotion a performance. Yet the comparison does not undercut Antonius' insistence on feeling emotion himself, because the actor really is caught up emotionally in his speech. Similarly, the orators' feelings are stirred up by the very nature of the orations by which they intend to stir the emotions of their audiences. By tying emotion to the oration, Cicero gives feeling a cognitive dimension.

Antonius links emotion to composition and invention by making the point that no one can be "a good poet who is not on fire with passion, and inspired by something very like frenzy" (2. 194, vol. I, p. 339). The moment of being seized by a subject coincides with strong emotion. Moreover, Antonius links the orator's strong emotions to her attitudes to the actions about which she speaks. If the speaker does not care about the case she is making, how can she expect the audience to be moved? For, "it is not easy to succeed in making an arbitrator angry with the right party, if you yourself seem to treat the affair with indifference" (2. 190, vol. I, p. 335). Strong emotion expressed by means of style indicates the speaker's attitudes toward a topic; emotion and style elaborate and deliver the basic values of the Roman Republic as they are pertinent to the situation being addressed. Not to feel compassion for an unjustly accused victim or hatred for his accuser, Antonius argues, would make a speaker who tries to arouse these emotions ridiculous or disgusting. Emotion is not detached from the values and circumstances that inform the speaker's eloquence.

Antonius also links emotion and the grand style to the tripartite Aristotelian scheme for finding materials for a speech. The three sources of material from a speech, namely, the "the winning of our men's favour...their enlightenment, and . . . their excitement call for three different styles, the gentle, the acute, and the energetic (2. 128–9, vol. I, p. 291). The orator must teach, win over or delight, and move (2. 128, vol. I, p. 291; 2. 310, vol. I, p. 435; 3. 104, vol. II, pp. 83–4). These three provide the principles of his rhetoric. The three are separable: an orator can use a gentle style to show kindliness and benevolence to the audience without appealing strongly to their emotions by means of the vehement style, or can teach using a plain style unelaborated with passionate figures. The grand or vehement style seeks richness, diversity, and copiousness that move the audience cumulatively. Moving the passions takes time. "You could not awaken compassion, jealousy or wrath at the very instant of your onset, in the way that a proof is seized upon as soon as propounded" (*De oratore* 2. 214, vol. I, p. 355). Introducing proofs into a vehement speech could interrupt its cumulative effects.

In spite of the fact that the styles often need to be kept separate, Antonius acknowledges that the mild and emotional styles influence one another. He claims that no style is "better blended than that wherein the harshness of strife is tempered by the personal urbanity of the advocate, while his easy-going mildness is fortified by some admixture of serious strife" (2. 212, vol. I, p. 355). The speaker's mildness bespeaks equanimity and benevolence while the grand style creates ardor in the audience. Cicero uses an intense, fiery, melodramatic style when he attacks Catiline, but his tone toward the Senate is milder ("Text and context," p. 47). The styles are flexible and dynamic, appealing to core republican values but articulating and elaborating them in styles appropriate to the speaker's objective (ethos), the audience's state of mind and potential for emotion (pathos), as well as the situation under consideration (articulated in a logos).

Chapter 3

Rhetoric and the Search for God: Augustine's *On Christian Doctrine* and *Confessions*

Rhetorical Invention, Hermeneutics, and Style in *On Christian Doctrine*

Augustine creates a dramatic turn in the history of rhetoric by adapting rhetorical invention to the goal of interpreting the Bible. He intervenes in the way that rhetoricians consider the ends of rhetoric. Whereas Cicero and Quintilian praise the grand style for moving humankind away from savagery and toward civilization, Augustine illuminates the *dilemma* that confronts those who try to persuade others to good. How can preachers reach people who know what they should do, but do not do it (*CD* 4. 28, p. 137)? This became a dominant problem for Augustinian and Reformation thinking. In response, Augustine articulates a new rhetoric and a new psychology that draw on the Ciceronian relationship between knowing and moving. He practices the rhetorical inventiveness so important to my argument by using Ciceronian terms in light of new circumstances and new ends.

Augustine unifies the intellectual and affective aspects of rhetoric that appear more differentiated in Cicero with the consequence that rhetoric comes to address the whole person. Cicero had already gone some distance in this direction. Cicero's Crassus insists in *De oratore* that a speaker's grasp of the subject generates an abundance of words (3. 125, vol. II, pp. 99, 98; see Chapter 2, p. 27), linking style to knowledge. Adding to this, Antonius argues that the passion of the speaker is generated by his own speech. Unifying Cicero's language of separate faculties, Augustine characterizes the grand style as "forceful with emotions of the spirit," and "carried along by its own impetus." He links passionate style to a deeply convinced character (ethos). Eloquence comes into being through "the force of the things discussed" (the logos) and the "ardor of the heart" (pathos) (*CD* 4. 42, p. 150). Thus emotion cannot be separated from knowledge of a subject and neither of these can be separated from the person speaking. The ardor that results from wholeheartedness seizes the audience and turns them toward good actions.

The goal of rhetoric, then, is not only assent but also the engagement of the whole person in truth and action. Augustine has never been surpassed as a model for this kind of persuasion. According to *On Christian Doctrine*, "grand eloquence" moves the "minds of listeners, not that they may know what is to be done, but that they may do what they already know should be done" (4. 27, p. 137). The text retains a distinction between knowing and being moved to do in order to show that eloquence "does not circumvent rationality but enables it, stirring the will to desire what the mind already approves" (*Sacred Rhetoric*, p. 46). On the whole, the text uses terms drawn from the three sources of argument (ethos, logos, pathos) separately, but the end of Book 4 brings them together to appeal to the whole psyche. "Volition, subjectively experienced, is emotion," and is directed toward truth (*Sacred Rhetoric*, p. 46; "Two faces," pp. 10–11). ·

But *On Christian Doctrine* also raises problems for the student and scholar of rhetoric. Augustine rejects the sophistic understanding that rhetoric is purely a matter of eloquence *and* the idea that persuasion should depend on truth alone, a position that James. J. Murphy identifies as the "Platonic rhetorical heresy" ("Invention, emotion," p. 65; *Middle Ages*, p. 60). But readers tend to emphasize one side or the other, partly because Augustine wrote Book 4 about thirty years after Books 1–3. As a result, most scholars have disregarded the importance of Books 1–3 for Augustine's understanding of rhetoric. They have thought of Book 4, which argues for the need for eloquence in Christian preaching, as "the first manual of Christian rhetoric" (*Middle Ages*, p. 58). It would be a misunderstanding, however, to assume that Augustine advocates purely stylistic strategies for persuading audiences. When we consider rhetoric as secondary to knowledge, as focusing on presentation rather than inquiry and "as handmaid to master" then the role of rhetoric becomes limited to propagating known religious truths ("Rhetoric and religion," p. 62). This approach diminishes rhetoric. However, if we understand Book 4 (written in 427) as completing the arguments of Books 1–3 (written *c.*397– 400), then the work becomes one whole argument with two parts ("Charity," pp. 256, 259, 261). Augustine relates these parts by arguing that "there are two things necessary to the treatment of the Scriptures: a way of discovering those things which are to be understood (rhetorical invention) and a way of teaching what we have learned (presentation and style)" (*CD* 4. 1, p. 117). The first subject is covered in Books 1–3, the second in Book 4. The two processes need to be used together. We should not consider style to be independent from invention. The preacher who has studied the Scripture and knows what he has discerned still has to inquire into his audience, whether they need to be taught, to be made attentive, or to be moved to action. Both kinds of inquiry require arts that the *On Christian Doctrine* teaches.

However, Augustine emphasizes the difficulty of teaching these arts. He, like previous rhetoricians considered in this volume, needs to point the way to others who wish to interpret the Bible rather than passing on his own interpretations. Antonius in Cicero's *De oratore* addresses this problem when he compares the orator to a prospector who must do his own digging to find gold (2. 174, vol. V, p. 323; see Chapter 2, p. 27). Accordingly, Augustine discriminates between two kinds of teaching. He contrasts the teacher who reads to a student with one who teaches the student to read. One teaches information and the other a method. Likewise, one teacher of a text "explains to listeners what he understands" whereas another offers precepts that students may use themselves to interpret obscure passages (*CD*, "Prologue," 9, p. 7). Augustine defends his use of precepts to teach students "so that they may profit not only from reading the work of expositors but also in their own explanations of the sacred writings to others" (*CD* 1, p. 3).

The text provides indicators to mark the interpreter's path. Readers must have vision to connect distinctions and the precepts to their own inquiries. Distinctions between things and signs and between enjoyment and use demarcate the area of the students' rhetorical and interpretive inquiry. A " 'thing' (*res*) is that which is not used to signify something else, like wood, stone, cattle, and so on" whereas "signs" are either things used as "signs of other things" or "signs whose whole use is in signifying, like words" (*CD* 1. 2, p. 8). By exploring things before words, the text expresses its commitment to finding the matter of a speech and to discerning truth before approaching a written text or giving a speech.

Things can be distinguished in turn by whether they are to be "enjoyed or to be used." Augustine follows the *topos* of division recommended by Aristotle and Cicero to set up exclusive categories that organize his argument. The distinction between things to be enjoyed and things to be used provides a basic but ambiguous definition of the good toward which the interpreter and the speaker aim. If, in Aristotle, the deliberative orator aims his inquiry and his speech toward what is advantageous or disadvantageous for his audience, the Augustinian interpreter of the Bible aims toward the things to be enjoyed or to be used. For, "to enjoy something is to cling to it with love for its own sake. To use something, however, is to employ it in obtaining that which you love provided that it is worthy of love" (*CD* 1. 4, p. 9). The text sets up a process of means/ends reasoning that makes the Trinity the sole thing to be enjoyed for its own sake and all other things, including human beings, useful means in reaching this enjoyment. God is "Wisdom" itself, and the mind of creatures "should be cleansed so that it is able to see that light and to cling to it once it is seen" (1. 10, p. 13). Possessing a wisdom that is the goal of inquiry, God becomes the rhetorical logos, while the mind that aims to reach wisdom "by good endeavour and good habits" needs a certain ethos to inquire successfully (ibid.). In this way, the text puts rhetorical invention in the service of Neoplatonic ascent to wisdom and goodness. But because human beings prefer to enjoy the world and its creatures, God made the "Word" flesh to heal their wounds and provide a way toward an ethos or character capable of loving God. Unlike either the Neoplatonic wisdom or the Aristotelian logos, God is active in giving grace to heal the inquirer ("Charity," pp. 263–4).

Inquiry presupposes not only the logos to be sought and an ethos that enables seekers, but also a pathos that incites the search. This pathos is love or caritas. Augustine articulates pathos through the maxims "Love God" and "Love thy neighbor"; readers use these precepts to guide their interpretations of Scripture and their actions (*CD* 1. 24, p. 20; 1. 27, p. 22).

The practical and rhetorical character of the advice comes through when Augustine affirms that no one who thinks he understands Scripture but does not use it to "guide the double love of God and of our neighbor" understands it "at all." True interpretation leads to charitable emotion and action. On the other hand, anyone who finds a lesson that "builds charity," even if she cannot show that the author intended that lesson, is not deceived. A person's charity expresses itself in "doing well" and "obeying the rules of good customs"; again, actions express understanding. The better people become, the more clearly they understand Scripture and love God and neighbor, and the more clearly they understand and love, the better they are; thus the text generates a hermeneutic and rhetorical circle of ever-deepening inquiry and action.

Having established the "things" to be sought in Christian rhetorical inquiry, *On Christian Doctrine* examines the natural and conventional signs through which things are understood. Book 2 focuses on conventional signs that "living creatures . . . show to one another for the purpose of conveying . . . the motion of their spirits or something which they have sensed or understood." The text constructs its sign system with reference to intention, for signs convey by "bringing forth and transferring to another man the action of the mind in the person who makes the sign" (*CD* 2. 3, pp. 34–5). The sending and receiving of signs relates to the will: "when we nod, we give a sign only to the sight of the person whom we wish by that sign to make a participant in our will" (2. 4, p. 35). This volitional aspect of language becomes crucially important in the activity of interpreting Scripture and converting souls.

Although Book 2 concentrates on conventional, literal signs, it also calls attention to the importance of the "obscurities and ambiguities" that can deceive readers. Despite the danger attributed to obscurity, as David Tracy has shown, *On Christian Doctrine* gave new energy to the "Western theological figurative readings of the scriptures" and to " 'obscurity' as an intellectual" and ethical "value" ("Charity," p. 260). More explicitly and thoroughly than the earlier rhetorical works analyzed in the present volume, Augustine's work defends figurative, ambiguous languages. Whereas Aristotle's *Rhetoric* claims that "easy learning is naturally pleasant to all" and that "metaphor . . . above all produces this effect" (*The "Art" of Rhetoric* 3. 10, 1410b), Augustine argues that God made the Scripture ambiguous in places because "things which are easily discovered seem frequently to become worthless" (*CD* 2. 7, p. 37). He praises similitude because "things are perceived more readily" through them and "what is sought with difficulty is discovered with more pleasure," bringing together considerations of logos and ethos, wisdom, and (later) eloquence (2. 8, p. 38).

The importance of figurative reading is brought home by his *Confessions* (c.400), the story of his conversion that closes with a figurative reading of Genesis. The *Confessions* tells how such figurative reading freed Augustine from the literal meanings produced by his contempt for the Scriptures. Even after he had been awakened to the love of truth by reading Cicero's *Hortensius*, he rejected the Scriptures because his "swelling pride soared above the temper of their style, nor was my sharp wit able to pierce into their sense" (*Confessions* 3. 5, p. 113). But his discovery of figurative reading gave him delight in truth, not just in eloquence.

Figurative language cures pride, teaches humility, and enables the intelligence to penetrate obscurities. The style of the Christian preacher Ambrose leads Augustine to truth; when he opened his heart to Ambrose's eloquence, the truth of his proof concerning the interpretation entered with it. Ambrose's figurative interpretations of Scripture give Augustine new life, for he hears "one or two hard places of the Old Testament resolved . . . which when I understood literally, I was slain" (*Confessions* 5. 14, pp. 257, 259).

On Christian Doctrine, whose first three books were written at approximately the same time as the *Confessions*, insists on the need for understanding the clear passages in Scripture before tackling the obscure ones. But concerns with ethos, with delight, and with truth permeate the treatment of both obscurity and clarity. Through obscurity God conquers "pride by work," and allows Augustine to recognize more "pleasantly" the saints "as shorn sheep having put aside the burdens of the world like so much fleece" (*CD* 2. 7, pp. 37, 38). But in order to interpret obscure passages, one must consult clear ones, for "hardly anything may be found in these obscure places which is not found plainly said elsewhere" (2. 8, p. 38).

The understanding of clear passages, though they do not present the same problems as obscure ones, requires a disciplined character. Accordingly, the text provides steps to combat pride and to induce the fear of God that leads toward a "recognition of His will." The healing pathos of fear leads through the ethos of meekness and piety to the love of God for his own sake and love of neighbor for God's sake; consolation then leads to fortitude and the love of eternal things and ultimately to wisdom (logos) (*CD* 2. 9, pp. 38–9). The student seeks to know the books of Scripture and to study the clear precepts for living. Inquiry has a practical aspect pointing to a way of life.

Once students have developed the proper character and knowledge of Scripture, they learn to distinguish literal from figurative signs: the latter are things designated by literal signs that "are used to signify something else" (*CD* 2. 15, p. 43). In order to resolve questions raised by "unknown literal signs" (2. 16–62, pp. 43–76), they acquire the knowledge of languages, of various translations, of whatever things that may aid in interpreting similitudes, and of human institutions and non-superstitious practices. Like Aristotle and Cicero, Augustine insists on the centrality of knowledge in shaping rhetorical decisions. Once students have been instructed and made gentle so that they can dispute without controversy, they may attend to inquiring into and resolving scriptural ambiguity.

Interpreting figurative language is crucial to biblical interpretation and spiritual growth; otherwise students undergo a "miserable servitude of the spirit in this habit of taking signs for things" (*CD* 3. 9, p. 84). Augustine himself suffered from this servitude, according to his *Confessions*, because he could not imagine God as anything other than a material substance, an idea that led to many contradictions. When he practiced the Manichean religion, he took signs for things. He believed with the Manicheans that the sun and moon were divine rather than works of the divine. *On Christian Doctrine* insists, contrarily, "he is a slave to a sign who uses or worships a significant thing without knowing what it signifies" (3. 13, p. 86). A slave might take the command to eat "of the Body and Blood of our Lord literally" instead of venerating it "in spiritual freedom" (3. 9, p. 87). But figurative reading insists on the need for the interpretation of signs and things. One should never take one's interpretations for truth or love them because they are one's own (1. 41, p. 31).

The text provides a method students may use to ascertain the meaning of signs. Like Cicero, Augustine defines the point of conflict between statements as a place for making a rhetorical choice and conducting inquiry. *De inventione* outlines a method of identifying the points of disagreement in a legal plea (see Chapter 2, p. 28). When one side argues that "he did it," and the other side replies, "he did not," a point of disagreement emerges to which the sides may address their arguments ("Invention, emotion," p. 80; *Rhetoric of Reason*, p. 100). *On Christian Doctrine* provides an analogous method. When the student encounters a conflict between the literal signs of the Bible and the precepts to love God and neighbor, conflict becomes a place for inventing a figurative reading (3. 14, p. 88).

Figurative reading allows for flexible interpretations and a genuine multiplicity of readings. Augustine does not argue for rigid equivalences of point to point. For example he interprets "'take hold of arms and shield: and rise up to help me' [Ps. 34: 2 (35: 2)]" as obscure until one links it to "a passage which reads 'O Lord, thou has crowned us, with a shield of thy good will' [Ps. 5: 13 (5: 12)]." The second passage allows him to interpret the shield and other means of defense as signifying the good will of God. Yet not every biblical passage that refers to a shield ought to be interpreted in this way (CD 3. 37, p. 101). Furthermore, if readers find two or more meanings in Scripture and both are congruous with charity, then both are acceptable even if the author did not intend them. Divine truth, not authorial intention, serves as the criterion for judging an interpretation. Augustine encourages a plurality of readings adapted to the multiple concerns that engage readers in seeking a virtuous life.

Having taught readers a method of rhetorical invention, the text turns to the question of style. Many have taken Book 4 to be a manual of Christian rhetoric that can be read independently from Books 1–3. And, as I have noted, it was written much later. However, the treatment of style presupposes the close interconnection of style with the matter and with the articulation of ethos, logos, and pathos in Books 1–3. Like Aristotle and Cicero, Augustine links style to truth, whether it be a truth that teaches, that moves, or that delights. Books 1–3 focus on the discovery of "things . . . to be understood," and Book 4 on "teaching what we have learned," but teaching should not be understood as a mere distribution of previously discovered conclusions (CD 1. 1, p. 7). Rhetoric is not a handmaid to theology but fully integrated into it because God himself "poured forth" words "both wisely and eloquently" (4. 21, p. 132). The "Prologue" insists that those who learn need "vision" to connect what the speaker or writer says and the idea to which he gestures (CD 3, p. 4). Book 4 teaches preachers to facilitate this connection by means of their style. Since the connection being sought is intellectual and affective, preachers use different styles to overcome the obstacles to their listeners' responses. Augustine argues that "just as there is one kind of eloquence for youth and another kind for age" and yet another for those in great "authority" (following Cicero) so there is eloquence "clearly inspired by God." He discovers a new Christian eloquence that benefits the understanding of readers "by the discovery of what lies hidden" and "by exercise" that makes us learn (4. 9, p. 123).

Augustine follows Cicero in arguing that wisdom without eloquence benefits no one but eloquence without wisdom can be very harmful (De inventione 1, p. 3; CD 4. 7, p. 121). Reason and emotion must work together, for one who speaks wisely first looks "into the heart of the Scriptures with the eye of their own hearts" (CD 4. 7, p. 122). The metaphor, "the eye of the heart," suggests that the heart represents the whole person as an affective, wise center. Style informs wisdom when the obscurity of Scripture works eloquently to exercise the understanding and help it discover "what lies hidden" (4. 9, p. 123). Matter cannot be detached from manner.

Augustine makes palpable the eloquence of the Bible, which he had despised in his early years. The sweetness of scriptural tropes disentangles readers from worldly enjoyments and delights them with "sweetness that would make us blessed" (CD 1. 4, p. 10; "Sweetness," p. 166). Delightful style is not cultivated for its own sake, but so that listeners may "feast delightedly on [the] truth" (CD 4. 26, p. 136). The grand or moving style unblocks our "affections" attached to a thorny way and moves hearts to full conviction and action (*CD* 1. 16, p. 16; "Sweetness," p. 166). Finally, those who are held back by misunderstandings, as Augustine himself was during the long philosophical quest for truth described in the *Confessions*, can be taught by a subdued style that makes difficult ideas clear. Each style contributes distinctively to the conversion of listeners to truth known, loved, and enjoyed.

Augustine recommends the three Ciceronian styles he was taught as a student of rhetoric. But, in a spirit of invention, he adapts Cicero's approach to its new Christian context in ways that have enormous consequences for the history of rhetoric. Cicero, as my Chapter 2 argues, recommends that speakers use stylistic techniques appropriate to their topic and their objectives ("Text and context," p. 39). *Decorum*, the appropriateness of style to the matter and purpose at hand, produces the right elaboration and delivery. But Cicero does not interpret decorum rigidly; instead the speaker shapes it dynamically by his speech. Each of the three styles, the "grand, which stirs the emotions; the middle, which persuades through pleasure; and the plain, which proves points," has an appropriate function (*Orator* 69; "Text and context," p. 39). The grand style is appropriate to large issues such as the glory of the state, whereas the plain style works for more legalistic matters when precision and clarity are appropriate.

Augustine reiterates but adapts the styles. First he quotes Cicero who claims "he therefore will be eloquent who can speak of small things in a subdued manner, and of moderate things in a temperate manner, and of great things in a grand manner" (*CD* 4. 34, p. 142; *Orator* 29. 101). But because Christian values are pertinent to what seems small, speakers may use the grand style to address "small" issues (*Sacred Rhetoric*, p. 44). Whereas Cicero would use the subdued style about such legal matters as finances, a Christian orator might consider money a great matter if it related to the welfare of someone's soul. In such circumstances, Augustine recommends the use of the grand style (*CD* 4. 35, p. 143).

Augustine shifts the focus of style from the topic (logos) to the audience's relation to the truth (pathos). He argues that speakers should make style appropriate to the problems of audiences and recommends the subdued style when listeners are confused, the moderate style when they are inattentive, and the grand style when they need to do something but do not wish to do it. He also uses the "grand manner if he is moving an adverse mind to conversion" (*CD* 4. 38, p. 146). The purpose of the grand style is to bend hardness of heart (4. 54, p. 161). If an orator has done everything possible to "be heard intelligently, willingly, and obediently," he is eloquent whether or not the audience gives its full assent. Good style need not involve ornament or other specific devices; rather ornament arises from the ardor of the heart. Like Aristotle, Augustine discriminates between the good use of the art and its successful use.

The examples of ornament cited by Augustine in his defense of the eloquence of Scripture show how closely interconnected devices of sentence structure are to structures of thought. Although he does not believe that Paul learned how to write the climax or the periodic sentence from Greek rhetoric, he shows how Paul uses eloquence. Paul's enthymeme, "we glory also in tribulations, knowing that tribulation worketh patience; and patience trial; and trial hope, and hope confoundeth not" (Rom. 5: 3–4), is organized around the figure "called *klimax* in Greek and *gradatio* in Latin," where words and meanings are ranged in a pattern. "For we see that here patience arises from tribulation, trial from patience, and hope from trial" (*CD* 4. 11, p. 125). The structure of the sentence mirrors and emphasizes the causal pattern of the thought. Likewise, Augustine praises the prophet Amos, citing the passage 6: 1–6, for resisting the delight that would have accrued by making each of six phrases depend upon a repeated pronoun in favor of joining two phrases to each pronoun to yield three sentences. The first pertains to captivity, the second to lust, and the third to gluttony; the sequence of thought makes them beautiful (*CD* 4. 18, pp. 130–1).

The eloquent passages from Scripture dramatize the difficulties orators face in teaching their audiences and show how Hebrew writers and Paul use the styles to meet these difficulties. The subdued style explains what lies hidden or cannot be understood by the ignorant, for example, the doctrine of the Trinity. Decorum depends on the adequacy of a statement to the truth and focuses on explaining truth to the ignorant. A teacher who seeks clarity does not hesitate to use vulgar speech when Latin is too ambiguous or obscure, "not caring for what sounds elegant but for what well indicates and suggests what he wishes to show" (*CD* 4. 24, p. 133).

Although truth is more important than delight in the subdued style, Augustine does not make the effects of the three styles mutually exclusive, arguing, for example, that "matter itself is pleasing when it is revealed simply because it is true," as in the exposure of falsehood (*CD* 4. 28, p. 137). But because the delight in truth may not make all audiences attentive, teachers use the moderate style to produce delight when they wish an audience to "adhere more tenaciously to that which is being said" (4. 55, p. 161). Augustine relates this style to the central distinction in Book 1 between things to be enjoyed and things to be used. When audiences are unable to "cling" to the divine, a delightful style helps them "adhere." The Sermon on the Mount uses this style for the beatitudes.

Although the truth does not lack emotional power for "when . . . things are learned, the [listeners] may be . . . moved by a knowledge of them," the grand style moves "an adverse mind to conversion" (*CD* 4. 28, p. 137; 4. 38, p. 146). The mind may be adverse because unwilling or hard, but Augustine's choice of examples implies that external challenges can daunt even the most faithful. He notes how Paul uses the grand style to exhort the Romans under the pressure of persecution: "For thy sake we are put to death all the day long. We are accounted as sheep for the slaughter. But in all these things we overcome, because of him that hath loved us. For I am sure that neither death, nor life, nor angels, nor principalities, nor powers, nor things present, nor things to come, nor might, nor height, nor depth, nor any other creature shall be able to separate us from the love of God, which is in Christ Jesus our Lord (Rom. 8: 36–9)" (4. 43, p. 151). The words, though ornamented, are "determined by the ardor of the heart rather than by careful choice" (4. 42, p. 150). Their force comes from matter passionately expressed to overcome the uncertainties and fears of the audience.

Ultimately Augustine views the three styles, along with ethos, logos, and pathos, as interconnected. Orators should mix the three in order to hold the audience's attention. Whenever a difficult question emerges, no matter what the dominant style of a speech, the orator needs acumen, the appropriate quality of the plain or subdued style. Similarly, praise or blame calls for the moderate style, even in the midst of teaching or moving the emotions. Augustine uses the metaphor of the ebb and flow of the sea to indicate the tact with which an orator moves from a fervent speech to explain something in the subdued style and then returns to the things that must be expressed in the grand style (*CD* 4. 51, p. 159). Style requires a subtle sense of the demands of the material and the capacities of the audience. The three styles cannot be always be separated from one another in practice.

Confessions: Rhetoric and Conversion

If *On Christian Doctrine* provides a rhetorical method for inventive interpretation and teaching, the *Confessions* (c.397–400) provides a rhetoric of conversion. Like classical rhetorical texts, the *Confessions* seeks practical knowledge of things to seek and things to avoid. This practical activity is informed by the art of rhetoric as invention. It finds arguments, molds characters, and moves hearts. Far from being a mere handmaid to theology, inventive rhetoric requires substantive thinking and does not limit itself to style. When we bring the broad range of classical sources of persuasion (ethos, logos, and pathos) into play in interpreting the text, we discover how inadequate rhetorical approaches confine their users to partial, and therefore inadequate beliefs ("Invention, emotion," p. 67; "Rhetoric and religion," p. 63), whereas inquiry makes possible a growing understanding that leads to better questions. Augustine represents his own infancy and childhood as "dogmatic," driven to short-term and poorly understood desires. He uses rhetoric understood in broadly Aristotelian and Ciceronian terms as discovery of what is advantageous, virtuous, and beneficial to characterize the infant's rhetoric as lacking inventive power. He looks back on his own infancy and watches other children, concluding that the infant cannot deliberate about which desires injure her and which lead to happiness. By relating desire to language, the child eventually grows, seeks, and becomes transformed. She can change her understanding of ends and desires, becoming more practically wise. By encountering new arguments that changed his character, led him to wisdom, and inflamed his heart, Augustine was converted from eloquence to philosophy and then to Christianity.

The text formulates his mistaken and his mature beliefs in rhetorical terms. It criticizes his early training in rhetoric for emphasizing style and emotion to the exclusion of truth. It bemoans an education that taught him to read Terence and to declaim Virgil in order to internalize their styles and emotional appeals; imitating and acting out their language, Augustine used imagination for "self-stimulation" rather than "leading desire beyond itself." The text also attacks the theater for aestheticizing emotions like pity and mercy that should lead to action. In writing about the theater, Augustine "represents emotion as isolated from persuasion and action and turned into an object to be dwelt on, delighted in, and reproduced" to stimulate the audience ("Invention, emotion," p. 69).

Augustine's immature rhetoric contains the chief elements of the classical method (ethos, logos, pathos and delighting, teaching, and moving), but they are detached from one another and used manipulatively for preordained goals rather than leading to inquiry. Such rhetoric seeks to please and move the audience without fully teaching them, in order to bend minds to the will of the speaker. The text represents the youthful Augustine as unable to put together the elements of a full rhetoric or to use them to search for wisdom and happiness.

Augustine traces five rhetorical conversions that change his life. First, Cicero's *Hortensius*, a text that has been lost, breaks into his self-absorption in language and passions. This book, using the *full* power of rhetoric and discovery, changes his affections (pathos), his idea of truth (logos), and his character (ethos), indeed his whole way of life. "Now this book altered my affection, turned my prayers to thyself, O Lord, and gave me new purposes and desires" (*Confessions* 3. 4, p. 113). It was the book that "stirred up, and enkindled, and inflamed me," p. 113). But Cicero's style, his words, did not by itself transform Augustine and lead him to new purposes. Instead, "I made not use of that book... to sharpen my tongue... nor had it persuaded me to affect the fine language in it, but *what it said* persuaded me" (3. 4, translation altered, my emphasis). Moving beyond style to truth, Augustine fell in love with wisdom (*sapientia*). The idea of wisdom pointed like a *topos* beyond itself to further discovery, rather than appearing as something fully known.

But Augustine's enthusiasm for truth leads not to more knowledge but to the word "truth" espoused by the Manichean religion. The text represents his attraction to the sect as based on the images of the sun and moon, and he associates the Manicheans with pleasure in images and words. The leader of the sect, Faustus, uses delightful, moving language (*Confessions* 5. 3, p. 211; 5. 6, pp. 223–4). But Augustine's mature rhetoric redefines decorum, delight, and affect by linking them to truth. However, Augustine does not arrive at a mature rhetoric easily. The naïveté of Manichean belief as Augustine describes it manifests itself in taking the word "truth" for wisdom and collapsing the difference between images and the physical universe they represent (*Confessions* 3. 6, pp. 116–17). Manicheans and the young Augustine are too literal in their use of images and language. Only Ambrose's spiritual, figurative reading of the Bible begins to free Augustine from this literalism. The *Confessions* account of Augustine's meeting with Ambrose illuminates his emphasis on figurative reading and ambiguous meaning in *On Christian Doctrine*.

In order to understand this third conversion, we need to recognize that even though Augustine rejects sophistic oratory (which emphasizes eloquence and style at the expense of matter and argument), the *Confessions* and *On Christian Doctrine* do not envision truth as separate from a speaker and audience. Truth is embedded in a wise person. When he meets Ambrose, Augustine is drawn to him "not . . . as a teacher of the truth," but as a man who is benevolent toward him. When he listens to Ambrose, his rhetorical habits lead him to focus on Ambrose's eloquence. But while Augustine listens to the style, the substance, the truth he had "neglected" steals in "upon his mind" (*Confessions* 5. 14, p. 257). At first, he had "weighed every word of his very attentively, but of the matter" he was "careless and scornful" (5. 13, p. 257). Now he discovers a new union of matter *and* words (*res* and *verba*). Moreover, Ambrose *proves* his claims, something that the Manicheans do not do. Augustine moves from rhetoric as style to probative rhetoric (5. 14, p. 259). Rhetorically probable arguments serve to free Augustine from his naïve Manichean beliefs. He falls into a fearful skepticism that hinders his thought for a while, but eventually, attending to Ambrose's refutations of literal reading, he learns that he can evaluate and criticize improbable beliefs. He also learns the need for figurative interpretation that acknowledges "a gap between sign and signified" ("Invention, emotion," p. 74). The *Confessions* reading of Genesis emphasizes that one word can be understood in a multiplicity of ways. Because people read the Scripture in light of their own lives, their insights differ. "These discoveries make up the activity of *inventio* through which people seek a wise and blessed life" ("Invention, emotion," p. 74; "Charity," p. 254 on *CD*).

Augustine's Manicheanism is inadequate from a rhetorical point of view because it does not provide arguments, critical doubt, or awareness of ambiguity and the power of tropes. From a religious point of view it is inadequate because it does not acknowledge the role of belief or "risk faith in an expression of the meaning of life 'as related to, indeed as both participating in *and distanced from*, what is sensed as the whole of reality' " (*Analogical Imagination*, pp. 20, 73; "Invention, emotion," p. 74). Eventually, when he can accept the probative power of probable arguments, Augustine begins to believe in the authority of the Bible. The obscurities of Scripture do not stop him from investigating how interpretation leads to a wiser and happier life.

Ambrose prepares Augustine for his conversion to Neoplatonism by making the distinction between the literal and the figurative. As I mentioned earlier, Augustine's religious belief had been blocked by his conviction that God is an infinite material substance at war with evil, another more enmattered substance. But Neoplatonism, i.e., the commentaries of Porphyry and Plotinus on Plato, combined with his reading of the Gospel of Saint John, encouraged him to turn inward, to move from things known, to his own mind in knowing, and finally to the light of truth as making knowledge possible. Gradually he came to believe that God was more like truth and mind than like matter. But at the same time that he discovered the unchangeable light (logos), he recognized his own inability to see it (ethos). He believed that some agency, namely God's charity (pathos), was needed to change him and bring him toward truth. Grace, in combination with the reading of Scripture, transforms the human ethos.

Augustine's conversion to Christianity is prefaced by a period of reading and meditating. Although Neoplatonism made him more certain of God, he was not able to stand fast in his belief and to change his life by surrendering his mistress and the idea of marriage to the celibate life. His indecision leads to an insightful treatment of the will and of deliberation. In Book 8, chapters 8 and 9, he puzzles about how his mind can command him to give up sexuality and marriage *and* can refuse to obey. What is the mystery of the fallen will that is divided against itself? Eventually he asserts that he has many wills, seeking many different conflicting goods without being able to choose any. "Deliberative conflict emerges into discovery only through the combination of reading, listening, meditating, and being moved rhetorically" ("Invention, emotion," p. 78).

The examples of others who read and converted provide him with a rhetorical model for conversion. A friend of a friend, Ponticianus, changes when he reads the life of Saint Anthony; he "began to read, wonder at it, and to be inflamed with it" (*Confessions* 8. 6, p. 435). Augustine uses the word *accendi*, related to Cicero's word for kindle or inflame, *incendi* (*De oratore* 2. 190). *On Christian Doctrine* also comments that the good listener warms to (*accendit*) the Scripture when it is pronounced ardently (4. 21, p. 132). He praises the grand style because it can inflame and seize and convert a person to action.

Ponticianus compares his own life with the conversion narrative (logos), and is moved to change. The contrast between his life and Anthony's leads him to discover new possibilities for a happy life. Similarly in the garden, Augustine, having experienced conflict, finally gives up, grieves, and calls for God's help. He hears the words "take up and read"; interpreting them as meant for him, he takes up the Bible and reads "not in rioting and drunkenness, not in chambering and wantonness . . . but put ye on the Lord Jesus Christ." His doubt vanishes (*Confessions* 8. 12, p. 465; "Invention, emotion," p. 79). Alypius reads a different passage and treats it as a command. "Hearing and reading . . . are part of a deliberative activity" in which Augustine and Alypius determine what is authoritative for them. Rhetoric works in Books 6–8 through this interaction between readers and texts.

"Rhetorical ethos is supplanted" by charity "as a principle of communicability that links a speaker or author and a reader" ("Invention, emotion," p. 80; "Metarhetorics," p. 208).

From the beginning the rhetorical search for God required a relationship between a human and a divine person expressed in the medium of prayer. Through prayer, Augustine seeks God, but the stimulus for his search comes from God: "Man is desirous to praise thee; thou so provokest him, that he even delighteth to praise thee" (*Confessions* 1. 1, p. 3). "Provoketh" (or "kindle") and "delight" echo the rhetorical terms associated with moving and pleasing, but now an eloquent God is their source. Because Augustine's narrative produces emotional and intellectual effects, it needs to be interpreted in terms of the full breadth of rhetorical terms, including ethos, logos, *and* pathos, along with the styles that delight, teach, and move.

Augustine's rhetoric can best be understood in light of rhetorical texts that stress invention, not eloquence and style alone. Intellectual and literary historians have shown how Augustine brings emotion and argument together: "the orator moves by giving reasons" ("Invention, emotion," p. 82; "Philosophical foundations," pp. 47–64). A rhetorical understanding of the need for tropological reading complements Augustine's insistence on God as distanced from human understanding. In the *Confessions* deliberation examines grounds of belief as "part of a well-founded, well-thought through religious commitment, while [it] eschews skepticism as inadequate by itself." Finally, "insofar as conversion implies a change of life and just not a shift in ideas, it involves human beings in deliberative activities" ("Invention, emotion," p. 82). In deliberating, readers compare their own lives with the text and are changed by the rhetorical arguments they discover in the process. These arguments accord with a divine will that neither the text alone nor the reader can fully express, but that emerges in the energy of their interaction. "The text has no absolute, accessible, intended author or meaning apart from the activity of reading and deliberating through which it lives" ("Invention, emotion," p. 83).

Chapter 4

Practical Reason or Interested Calculation? Cicero's *On Duties* and Machiavelli's *The Prince*

Whereas Augustine transforms Cicero's treatments of emotions and style, Machiavelli explores how to adapt, correct, and reject customary *topoi* in considering new particular circumstances (see "Exemplifying deliberation"). *The Prince*'s revision of Ciceronian topics offers a sophisticated reworking of deliberative rhetoric in light of the problem of how to found a new state. *On Duties* (44 BCE) and *The Prince* (1513) cultivate the reader's practical aptitude for using topics and maxims to judge possible action in the once durable Roman Republic, on the one hand, and to found a new state in the unstable conditions of Renaissance Italy, on the other.

On Duties and *The Prince* are admirable models of deliberation because they engage specific practical issues *and* larger intellectual currents of their times. Unlike many twenty-first-century discussions of rhetoric that remain abstract and theoretical, these texts use rhetorical topics to teach their readers how to deliberate about particular ethical and political dilemmas.

To understand these texts as deliberative, we need to observe the ways in which they address contingent issues. Responding to Plato's charge (*Gorgias* 449) that rhetoric lacks a subject matter, Aristotle was the first to discriminate the field of rhetoric as that of the contingent and elevate it to a form of "practical wisdom." D. P. Gaonkar has shown that contingency in Aristotle's sense has two main features. First, "the contingent is posited . . . as the opposite of the necessary (or necessarily true) and in conjunction with the 'probable' " ("Contingency," p. 7). The probable refers not to mathematical or statistical criteria but "things that normally . . . happen" (See *The "Art" of Rhetoric* 1. 2, 1357a, p. 27). Second, Aristotle locates contingency in practical possibilities that lie within our power of action. "For it is about our actions we deliberate and inquire, and all our actions have a contingent character" (*Nicomachean Ethics* 3. 3, 1112b, quoted in "Contingency," p. 153). If there were not at least two possible actions in which to engage, we would not deliberate.

Rhetorical arguments are drawn from probabilities and from what people believe. Cicero shows his awareness of this aspect of rhetoric when he distinguishes between the study of perfect duties and of common duties. The former are right in themselves, but the latter comprise "duty for the performance of which an *adequate reason*" may be given (*De officiis* 1. 8, 11, emphasis added).

He focuses on the contingent when he divides deliberation into three questions: "whether the contemplated act is honorable or shameful"; whether the action . . . is or is not conducive to comfort and happiness," and what to do when "that which seems to be expedient seems to conflict with that which is virtuous or honorable." The last question offers the greatest challenge because the norms of the honorable and the expedient seem to pull in two directions: "the result is that the mind is distracted in its inquiry and brings to it the irresolution that is born of deliberation" (*De officiis* 1. 8).[1]

Cicero considers the relations of the honorable to the beneficial or expedient by taking up particular issues of action. The efficacy of his terms depends upon their remaining in tension, providing two point of view from which to evaluate possible actions. Having argued that keeping faith is basic to justice, for example, he argues that duties alter with circumstances. "Occasions often arise, when those duties which seem most becoming to the just man and to the 'good man' . . . undergo a change and take on a contrary aspect" (1. 1). What is just in one situation may turn out to be unjust in another if it harms someone or if it is disadvantageous to the person who made the promise. For example, if someone has promised to appear as an advocate in court, but his son falls seriously ill, he does not violate his duty by staying away from court. One can reach this conclusion by deliberating about the action under two principles of justice, namely that one should not harm another and that common interests should be served. In this way, one clarifies priorities.

Against Marcia L. Colish's argument that Cicero "reformulate[s]" the honorable itself "as a mode" of the expedient, however, I propose that the meanings of the two terms shift as Cicero considers examples ("Cicero's *De officiis*," pp. 87–8). But the shifts do not obscure the distinctiveness of the terms. Instead the honorable and the expedient form a range within which the prudent leader can inquire. The *topoi* allow Cicero to discriminate manipulation and cunning from practical wisdom. Having commented "things are in a bad way when that which should be obtained through virtue is attempted by means of money," Cicero nevertheless acknowledges, "since . . . there are times when such assistance is necessary, I shall talk about how it should be used" (*On Duties* 2. 22). Understood by itself this statement seems to advocate sheer opportunism, but later it turns out that the virtue of liberality requires deliberate judgment in order to hit its mark.

Problems of expediency and virtue define the field of deliberative rhetoric. One finds analogous problems and tensions in Aristotle's *Rhetoric*. As we saw in Chapter 1, Aristotle argues that deliberative rhetoric has the expedient and the inexpedient as its end, and as *topoi* of deliberation, he lists health, friends, and excellence in action as life conditions and activities that constitute happiness. Aristotle's *sumpheron* and Cicero's *utilitas* can be translated as "the expedient" in the *OED*'s second sense, "namely, what is conducive to advantage generally," or "what is fit, proper, suitable to the circumstances," but not in the third sense as " 'useful' or 'politic' as opposed to 'just' or 'right'." Cicero limits his concept of the useful to what is advantageous for mankind, eschewing a debate about whether the "supreme good" can be measured by one's "own interests" (*On Duties* 1. 5). He urges readers to deliberate about actions where a duty is unclear, because doing something absolutely good (like seeking truth) might cause one to neglect duties toward others and doing one's duties toward others may degenerate into self-serving action.

Cicero uses his *topoi* to teach his son Marcus and other readers to deliberate about actions where a duty is not clear initially. The words "the honorable" (*honestas*) and the beneficial or expedient (*utilitas*) are topics in a broadly Aristotelian and Ciceronian sense. Aristotle lists such topics as the good or bad, fair or foul, just or unjust, from which rhetorical arguments may be drawn (*The "Art" of Rhetoric* 2. 18, 1396b, p. 295) and alludes to common features such as the possible and impossible, the more and less, that define the field of deliberation (1. 3, 1359a, p. 37). The more or the less also serve as strategies of argument. *On Duties* considers not only whether an action is morally right or wrong, but also "when a choice of two morally right courses is offered, which one is morally better; and likewise, when a choice of two expedients is offered, which one is more expedient" (*De officiis* 1. 10). Deliberative judgments are not always clear-cut; they are capable of comparison and degree.

At times *On Duties* appeals to the honorable or virtuous as a philosophical principle rather than as a topic to be used jointly with the expedient. The analysis manifests little tolerance of inconstancy or trickery and rejects deception unequivocally, a position Machiavelli reverses. These principles lead some readers to consider Cicero's treatment of politics as a philosophical ethics, which they contrast to Machiavelli's apparently unadulterated pragmatism ("Cicero's *De officiis*," pp. 82, 84).

But Cicero, far from allowing philosophy to determine his judgments independently of practical concerns, argues that deliberative reason permits people to adjudicate between the demands of the honorable and the expedient. Having established the precepts of justice, such as that one person ought not to harm another "unless provoked by wrong" (1. 20), he analyses the weaknesses that cause men to violate justice. For example, those who have great spirit desire wealth "with a view to power" (1. 25); they seek expedient means for benefiting themselves and the Republic. Their desires are honorable. But spirited men easily forget the limits set by justice. They become caught up in competition at the expense of fellowship. Rather than simply attacking these wrongdoers, Cicero seeks a balance and a check to excess: "I do not mean to find fault with the accumulation of property, provided it hurts nobody, but unjust acquisition of it is always to be avoided" (1. 25). He corrects the ungoverned, shortsighted pursuit of the expedient without abandoning the idea of expediency altogether, because one cannot judge whether an action is virtuous without taking into account its actual effects.

Similarly, because the desire for glory and power gives rise to abuses, reason needs to adjudicate between purportedly liberal actions that succeed and those that fail to live up to their name (1. 42–9). In order for liberality to be a virtue, it must not harm others, it must not impoverish the giver, it must be exercised with an eye to the benefits that one has received, and it must be proportional to the worth of the recipient. A liberality that harms the receiver or impoverishes the giver violates justice and undermines itself. For these reasons, the choice of honorable and virtuous actions requires attention to practicality. Although it may sound as if Cicero advocates cynical expediency in adjusting gifts to the worth, standing, or character of a recipient and to the gifts already accepted from a person, he urges regard for human society and not a fixed calculus to measure reciprocal giving (1. 50; *Personal Patronage*, pp. 16–17).

In offering Marcus a deliberative exercise in reasoning practically, Cicero appeals to expediency to defend the value of the honorable. However, his appeal does not imply that virtue can be reduced to expediency. The relation between the two terms is illuminated by Aristotle's argument in the *Rhetoric* 1. 6 that deliberative rhetoric always addresses what is expedient (*sumpheron*), useful, or profitable. The *Rhetoric* addresses the topics of good action, wealth, friends, and happiness, the activities that promote these ends. Likewise, Cicero uses *topoi* of "the honorable" and "the beneficial" to discover particular actions that facilitate desirable ends. He teaches his readers to exercise wise control over circumstances by cultivating virtue rather than reacting to events. Whatever is virtuous is also truly expedient; shrewdness and craft are not enough. Book 2 aims to persuade Marcus of this: "Only by moral character and righteousness" may leaders attain their ends (*De officiis* 2. 10). When Cicero considers the recent destruction of armies and the hatred of the people, and, on the other hand, "successes" and "civil and military... victories," he concludes that "though all these contain an element of chance, still they cannot be brought about, whether for good or for ill, without the influence and the cooperation of our fellow[s]" (2. 20). Accordingly, Book 2 focuses on the problem of how to engage the cooperation of others. The answer lies in the "peculiar function of virtue to win the hearts" of people and to "attach them to one's own service" (2. 17). How is this accomplished?

In *On Duties*, as in Aristotle's *Rhetoric*, trust links people to the leader. Some scholars follow Machiavelli by implying that Cicero is idealistic (not realistic) in this respect, but the text argues that in practice that "the power of good will is ... great, and that of fear ... feeble" (*On Duties* 2. 29). *On Duties* prudently provides evidence that love is stronger than fear by citing the violent deaths of tyrants such as Caesar, Alexander of Pherae, and Phalaris. Good will, on the other hand, is obtained by beneficent acts, and rulers' good sense and justice lead others to have faith in them (2. 32–3). *On Duties* draws on Aristotle's *Rhetoric*, which argues that effective speakers need to show good will, practical wisdom, and virtue if they want their audiences to believe them. Without a belief in the good will of a speaker, an audience cannot trust the advice it receives. If speakers do not demonstrate their prudence, audiences will not believe them capable of giving good advice; and if they do not demonstrate their virtues, the audience will not believe that they can be trusted to treat them well. *On Duties* argues in more affective terms that beneficence produces love in others, focusing on action more than on eloquent speeches. The text asserts that a reputation for goodness attracts the love of the people.

Machiavelli, of course, introduces a fissure between appearing to have good will, prudence, and virtue and actually having them; but the difference between his project and the Aristotelian and Ciceronian projects diminishes when we recognize that Machiavelli attacks conventional virtue, substituting his own mode of agency (*virtù*) in its place. He never goes so far as to argue that the prince may obtain power through the sheer pretense of ability and prudence. Cicero states the point more strongly in asserting that nothing wins lasting glory more than striving "to be what you wish to be thought to be ... For if anyone thinks that he can win lasting glory by pretence, by empty show, by hypocritical talk and looks, he is very much mistaken" (2. 43). *On Duties* argues that people will have confidence in us if they think we have practical wisdom and justice, and admire us if they think we are magnanimous. Each virtue has its proper emotional and ethical effect; a leader's lack of prudence, for example, must eventually come to light when he or she gives advice.

The strong links that Cicero forges between virtue and advantage make his argument pragmatic *and* ethical. He advocates the cultivation of the people's good will, admiration, and confidence as more efficacious for achieving influence than fear or money because they are linked directly to the ruler's own capabilities and virtues (2. 21–6). Later arguments make clear that helping others defend themselves in court and to achieve advancement produces greater advantages than do gifts of money because "the more people they assist, the more helpers they will have in works of kindness" (*De officiis* 2. 53). Liberality with respect to money is less useful, because "the more people one has helped with gifts of money, the fewer one can help" (2. 52–3). Beneficence and gratitude, on the other hand, are virtues (not mere means to advantage) because they cultivate the givers' and receivers' capacities for leadership.

Having articulated his topics of the honorable and the expedient, Cicero uses argument by example in Book 3 to raise hard cases for his deliberative approach. He considers cases where the apparently virtuous course conflicts with the seemingly expedient. These cases offer the greatest scope for deliberation because they produce doubt and require thought. The process of deliberation proves challenging because it is "unlawful...to weigh true morality against conflicting expediency" (*De officiis* 3. 17): "for it is most immoral to think more highly of the apparently expedient than of the morally right, or even to set these over against each other and to hesitate to choose between them" (3. 18). Only doubts about the character of an action ought to give rise to deliberation.

At times the ethics articulated in the text appears to preclude prudence. Some rules seem to be fixed guidelines that decide cases in advance: "nature's laws... forbid us to increase our means, wealth, and resources by despoiling others" and each person ought "to make the interest of each individual and of the whole body politic identical" (3. 26, see 3. 22,). However, Cicero takes his term for rule, *formula* ("rule of procedure"), from Roman law where it guides the determination of relevant facts (*On Duties*, p. 107 n. 3). In doing so, he states his preference for an approach that uses the precepts "whatever is virtuous is expedient" and "nothing is expedient that is not virtuous" to illuminate difficult cases. He chooses the Stoic approach over the Peripatetic system that Marcus has been taught because it strengthens his own emphasis on expediency. Peripatetics believe that the virtuous ought always be preferred to the expedient, whereas Cicero links the two to produce the sphere of the practical. Cicero's use of Panaetius' principles and his appeals to philosophy can be understood as rhetorically adjusted to Marcus' background and education.

Nevertheless, because of the generality of Cicero's rules and maxims, it is tempting to interpret him as promulgating idealistic (i.e., unrealistic) philosophical principles and to contrast his maxims with Machiavelli's counter-maxims. Cicero speaks vehemently against the error of men who are not strictly upright. They seize upon an action that seems to be expedient and dissociate it from the question of moral right: "To this error the assassin's dagger, the poisoned cup, the forged wills owe their origin" (*De officiis* 3. 36).

Machiavelli states, on the contrary, "any man who tries to be good all the time is bound to come to ruin among the great number who are not good" (*The Prince*, p. 42). "A prince who wants to keep his authority must learn how not to be good, and use that knowledge, or refrain from using it, as necessity requires." Machiavelli apparently privileges the expedient (i.e., the necessary) over the virtuous. His rhetoric cuts against custom and religion, including the humanist interpretations of *On Duties*, dramatizing the almost shocking single-mindedness he advocates for the prince. Yet, when we understand how the two texts use commonplaces to deliberate about difficult cases and to enhance the ruler's agency in these circumstances, they can be seen to share a prudential method.

Machiavelli's text belongs to the humanistic genre of advice to princes; like *On Duties* it is addressed in particular to a potential ruler (Lorenzo de' Medici, Duke of Urbino), though it recommends a course of action in addition to educating him in prudence ("Gift of counsel," pp. 219–57). It is " 'performative' in the sense of attempting to effect significant change through the rhetorically persuasive deployment of language, by convincing the Medici" to employ Machiavelli as an adviser and to use *The Prince* as a plan for restoring "stability and a certain autonomy to Italy under the guidance of a new, secular prince" (ibid., p. 220). *The Prince* "refuses to cloak his advice in the pieties of Scholastic or Christian humanist idealism," but uses a deliberative method, while it redefines the ethos appropriate to the ruler ("*Virtù*," p. 195). Rather than focusing on Italian humanist readings of *On Duties*, however, I will consider *The Prince*'s rewritings of Cicero's commonplaces as prudential innovations that spur deliberation in readers.

Both texts use commonplaces to explore cases in order to penetrate the "specious appearance" of expediency or good (*De officiis* 3. 40–1). Cicero's commonplace that the good of one is the same as the good of all leads him initially to prohibit a good man's robbing the tyrant Phalaris of his clothes to benefit himself; but this does not prevent him later from condoning robbing or even killing Phalaris because "we have no ties of fellowship with a tyrant" (3. 32). Likewise, he judges that Brutus' deposing of his colleague Collatinus may seem unjust, but in truth, Cicero argues, he was following the policy of the leaders of Rome of removing Superbus' relations in the interests of the country (3. 40). In a quite similar way, Machiavelli seeks truth beneath appearances. According to John Najemy, "Machiavelli is uncompromising in his insistence that imagination and truth can indeed be differentiated, and that *he* will speak on the basis of truth alone" (*Between Friends*, p. 43).[2] Machiavelli asserts that his discourse will occur by "leaving behind, therefore, things imagined about princes, and speaking of those that are true." In political rule, "something resembling virtue, if you follow it, may be your ruin, while something else resembling vice will lead, if you follow it, to your security and well-being" (*The Prince*, p. 43). And in just this way Cicero argues with regard to Brutus. The difference lies less in their method than in the ways they deploy topics to define the area of efficacious action. Cicero cares about the advantage of the ruler as related to what is expedient for the polity, whereas Machiavelli considers what is expedient for a new prince's efforts to acquire and maintain power in unstable circumstances.

However, I am less interested in similarities and differences between the positions or conclusions of the two texts than in how each deploys related sets of opposed topics to examine particular cases from two sides. Extending Cicero's characterization of topics "as arguments which can be transferred to many cases" beyond his context of the law courts (*De inventione* 2. 47–8), I propose that *The Prince* takes up, adapts, and sometimes reverses, central topics that shape the arguments of *On Duties*. The topics serve as sources of rhetorical invention, tools that readers may similarly adapt in prudently assessing new circumstances.

Readers must be thoughtful because, for many issues, judgment cannot be fully determined by the text; rather, as Machiavelli asserts with regard to good will, "the prince can earn the good will of his subjects in many ways, but as they vary according to circumstances, I can give no fixed rules and will say nothing of them. One conclusion only can be drawn: the prince must have the people well disposed toward him; otherwise in times of adversity there is no hope" (*The Prince*, p. 29). Because circumstances vary, princes must use their own prudence; they may learn prudence by reading and imitating, but imitation requires invention in order to be adequate to circumstances ("*Virtù*," pp. 196–9). Machivelli's practice with respect to Ciceronian *topoi* exemplifies a prudent, flexible use of a text. At the same time, Machiavelli also provides clear limits for his reader: good will is essential to the prince in adversity.

My necessarily condensed analysis of *The Prince* derives from the notion that the text itself works as a "typology of innovators and their relations with *fortuna*" (*Machiavellian Moment*, p. 158). To go a step further, it follows Eugene Garver's claim that "the prince becomes an innovator by following Machiavelli's innovative argument," adducing this innovation by way of Cicero's topics (*Machiavelli*, p. 28). Machiavelli adapts and reverses these topics to discover possibilities of the prince's political agency outside the constitutional sphere where civic virtue operates to control *fortuna* (*Machiavellian Moment*, p. 157).

Machiavelli discovers (in the rhetorical sense of *inventio*) the opportunity for *virtù* by running through an exhaustive set of antitheses until he finds a situation where the prince has acquired territories by the exercise of *virtù* over *fortuna* (*The Prince*, p. 158). The acquisition of hereditary monarchies does not require *virtù* because they are not much subject to *fortuna*; free republics do not provide opportunities for princely *virtù* because people will not surrender their freedom. Only in new principalities does rule depend on the prince's ability (*virtù*) to acquire and stabilize power. Thus Machiavelli's handbook adapts itself to the distinct problems and opportunities of the new prince, namely how to increase his *virtù* so that it controls *fortuna* rather than merely reacting to it. In order to address this problem, *The Prince* uses the *topoi* and maxims through which *On Duties* endeavors to increase the agency of the republican ruler, but redefines them to articulate a *virtù* that encounters fortune directly rather than commanding the cooperation of others in order to reach success (though Machiavelli confronts this latter challenge in the second part of his argument).

On Duties meets the problem of fortune and success, understood as "civil honors, military commands, and victories," by advising the ruler to enlist the resources and support of others (2. 20). The task of Book 2, then, is to advise how to gain control over men's cooperative responses through the prudent use of advice, help in promoting careers, liberality, and respect for private and public property. All of these actions require what is honorable (*honestas*), for the honorable promotes independence from and control over circumstances. Machiavelli, on the other hand, establishes a direct relation between *virtù* and *fortuna* in the case of the new prince: "a new prince taking charge of a competely new kingdom will have more or less trouble in holding onto it, as he himself is more or less capable [*virtuoso*]" (*The Prince*, p. 16). Though new princedoms are the most difficult to achieve, "the less one trusts to chance, the better one's hope of holding on." Using the common topic of more and less, Machiavelli establishes a sphere for action for the new prince. As J. G. A. Pocock formulates it so well, "The more the individual relies upon his *virtù* the less he need rely upon his *fortuna*, and – since *fortuna* is by definition unreliable – the safer he is" (*Machiavellian Moment*, p. 167). Greater dangers offer more opportunities to talented princes for learning how to overcome obstacles (*The Prince*, p. 58). By working with the rhetorical proportions of more and less, the aspiring prince maximizes his control over circumstances.

In articulating *virtù*, *The Prince* also uses the relation between commonplaces and examples to make readers think; otherwise they would slavishly imitate examples and would not improve their ability to use maxims to deliberate about circumstances ("*Virtù,*" pp. 196–9). But "*virtù* is not a general rule of behavior that can be applied to a specific situation but is rather, like prudence, a faculty of deliberation about particulars" ("*Virtù,*" p. 206). Without arguing that Machiavelli directly derived this strategy from *On Duties*, I will note that Cicero, like Machiavelli, brings his precepts in line with hard cases to force his reader to give up their customary beliefs. For example, having stated the maxim that *The Prince* reverses, namely that "no cruelty can be expedient; for cruelty is most abhorrent to human nature," Cicero criticizes the destruction of Corinth and the wrong that Athenians did in "decreeing that the Aeginetans, whose strength lay in their navy, should have their thumbs cut off" (*De officiis* 3. 46). Though mutilating the Aeginetans may have seemed expedient because their navy was a menace, Cicero believes the cruelty abhorrent. In Book 1, however, Cicero modulates his criticism of the destruction of Corinth, writing that he would prefer they had been spared because they were not savage in warfare, but that he believes "they [Cicero's respected elders] had some special reason for what they did – its convenient situation, probably – and feared that its very location might some day furnish a temptation to renew the war" (1. 35). Apparently, concern about safety provides some warrant for cruel treatment. Cicero's citation of the stoning of Cyrsilus as a splendid example of an occasion when the apparent expediency of the polity has been set aside for the sake of the honorable also raises questions. The Athenians stoned Cyrsilus because they intended to abandon their city, take to their ships, and fight for their freedom against the nearly overwhelming power of the Persian invasion, but Cyrsilus "proposed that they should stay at home and open the gates of their city to Xerxes" (3. 48). The people stoned him because his proposition was reprehensible even though it seemed expedient. (In time the plan of evacuating the city led to the Greek victory at Salamis so the plan actually turned out to be more expedient than Cyrsilus' proposal.)

When Cicero refers, then, to integrity or virtue, he does not mean what we (or Renaissance Christian humanists) might have found virtuous. Virtue, as he says, is expedient. Even Regulus' refusal to break his oath to the Carthaginians and his choice to return to death by torture at their hands, though they bespeak character (*honestas*), also display relentless courage. The possible consequences of such courage emerge from Cicero's next example in which the Senate refused to ransom 8,000 Romans held by Hannibal: "The senate voted not to redeem them, in order that our soldiers might have the lesson planted in their hearts that they must either conquer or die. When Hannibal heard this news...he lost heart completely" (*De officiis* 3. 114). Thus character displays its own kind of efficient power.

Like Cicero, Machiavelli offers examples whose consideration generates new insights that qualify the original commonplace. As Eugene Garver puts it, "Machiavelli's challenge is to explicate *virtù* in such a way that it becomes an ethics of principles without degenerating into an ethics of results" – a challenge that also faced Cicero (*Machiavelli*, p. 32). *The Prince* teaches that *virtù* is neither a matter of luck nor of success by offering the example of Cesare Borgia. Initially, Machiavelli uses Cesare Borgia to show how one who acquires rule by fortune loses it "in the same way" (*The Prince*, p. 19). However, the story of Borgia's rise to power eventually shows that one who receives a principality through good fortune may consolidate his power, founding it on a new basis in *virtù*. Borgia kills the families of the "noblemen he had ruined," "enlists all the gentry of Rome...to keep the pope in check," and makes the College of Cardinals subservient to him (p. 22). By the end of the analysis, Machiavelli offers him "as a model for all those who rise to power by means of the fortune and arms of others," even though Borgia – because of Alexander's death – does not succeed (p. 23). Lest the reader jump to the conclusion that *virtù* consists of cruelty, *The Prince* then introduces the puzzling example of Agathocles, whose crimes seem equivalent to those of Borgia but who does not receive glory, for Machiavelli can "scarcely attribute to either fortune or virtue [*virtù*] a conquest which he owed to neither" ("*Virtù*," pp. 202–8; *The Prince*, p. 25). Though he attributes Agathocles' early rise through the ranks of the army to both *virtù* and cruelty, he refuses the name *virtù* to his murdering of the senators and the wealthy people later, for it is not a *virtù* to "betray his friends, to be devoid of truth, pity, or religion." Thus, though Machiavelli begins by praising Borgia's *virtù*, shocking his readers with his narrative of Borgia's dramatic expedient of displaying the body of Orco in two pieces to persuade the people that he himself rejected cruelty, he sets limits on cruelty in section 8, recommending that cruelty should be used well, i.e., only when necessary, to reach power. His examples of Agathocles leads to the insight that *virtù*, not excessive cruelty, maintains power once it has been acquired (*Machiavelli*, pp. 32–3).

Whereas Cicero states principles in defense of virtue and then modifies them in light of expediency, Machiavelli defends expediency apart from virtue, reversing Cicero's emphasis in order to shock his reader. First he renounces conventional virtue, but then he brings back something like virtue in his analysis of how to maintain a state once it has been acquired. Having taken up the Roman and Ciceronian precept that "the foundations on which all states rest... are good laws and good arms," Machiavelli immediately reverses the Ciceronian emphasis on the priority of laws over arms by asserting that "since there cannot be good laws where there are not good arms, and where there are good arms there are bound to be good laws, I shall set aside the topic of laws and talk about arms" (*The Prince*, p. 34): "A prince... should have no other object, no other thought, no other subject of study, than war" (p. 40). Having shown that possessing one's own arms (rather than relying on mercenaries or the arms of others) is crucial to *virtù* (or ability), and having apparently rejected the Ciceronian emphasis on counsel and law, Machia-velli advises aspiring princes to hunt and read history in order to exercise their minds in prudence (the virtue of practical wisdom). Likewise, having defined himself against humanism by asserting that "the prince who wants to keep his authority must learn how not to be good... as necessity requires," thus making expediency prior to virtue, he acknowledges that the prince ought to have as many good qualities as possible, especially if he can be shrewd enough to avoid vices that will lose him the state. Yet, when he recommends that princes limit giving (here following a Ciceronian *topos* that confines liberality to what is within one's means and is advantageous to giver and receiver), Machiavelli comments that the prince "will be acting liberally toward all those people from whom he takes nothing," thus redefining virtue (p. 44). A mercy that allows civil disturbances proves less merciful than the cruelty to a few that produces peace. In his recommendations with regard to virtue versus vice, liberality versus stinginess, cruelty versus clem-ency, love versus fear, keeping one's word versus not keeping one's word, and integrity versus craftiness, Machiavelli skillfully takes up topics that Cicero used to teach Marcus about Republican rule in Rome; he alters them to fit a situation where there is no political stability because "new states are always in danger" (p. 45). In his deployment of maxims and examples, Machiavelli executes activities of deliberation, of appropriating language, so that the Medicis may learn.

Like Cicero he uses oppositional topics to form a ground for deliberation on two sides of the question. These *topoi* prove not to be mutually exclusive, any more than integrity and expediency are for Cicero. Raising the question of whether "it is better to be loved than feared," Machiavelli argues that both are good, that if one must choose, "to be feared is much safer than to be loved," reversing Cicero's argument that fear never lasts and that it leads to the tyrant's death (*The Prince*, p. 46). Yet Cicero himself acknowledges that those who exercise command by force may need to be severe (*De officiis* 2. 24). Indeed, for him insanity lies in using fear in a free city though he argues that even despots tend to be killed when they produce fear in their people. Love, however, is particularly good for securing "influence and hold[ing] it fast" in a republic (2. 23). Moreover, as Cicero's analysis advances, love shades into good will or esteem and is supplemented by admiration, the opposite of the contempt people feel for those who have no virtue, that is, "no ability, no spirit, no energy" (2. 36). Machiavelli likewise recommends that the prince avoid the contempt he would attract by appearing "changeable, trifling, effeminate, cowardly, or indecisive." Instead he should "make sure that his actions bespeak greatness, courage, seriousness of purpose, and strength," all of which are virtues. Granted, he emphasizes the *appearance* of these virtues, but he also goes on to say that "a man with such a reputation is hard to consider against, hard to assail, as long as everyone knows he is a man of character and respected by his own people" (*The Prince*, p. 50). Thus, again, he shifts from his original emphasis on using fear and manipulating appearance to finding a role for greatness and respect. Additionally, once a prince's power has been established, the good will of the people becomes the best protection against conspiracy (*The Prince*, p. 51). Indeed, it seems that the *virtù* of Marcus Aurelius makes him "an object of reverence to all," he was "never hated or despised," and he retained his power, unlike Pertinax and Alexander, who were also lovers of justice. However, in the very next paragraph, Machiavelli argues that "hatred may be earned by doing good just as much as by doing evil," a seemingly contradictory statement until his examples show that, by doing apparently good deeds that are supposed to earn the support of the people, the army, or the nobility, and by adapting oneself to their humors, the ruler shows weakness rather than strength. Once again, "good" here means "apparently good." So Alexander, who seemed good, was so swayed by his mother that people had contempt for him and the army killed him.

Severus, on the other hand, was "cruel and rapacious," and was harsh to the people, but he displayed such *virtù* that, "by keeping the soldiers friendly to him, and oppressing the people, he was able to reign in prosperity all his life long: his talents (*virtù*) made him so remarkable, in the eyes of the people as well as the soldiery, that the former remained awestruck and appeased, the latter astonished and abashed" (*The Prince*, p. 54). Severus succeeds because of his ethos, i.e., his ability to overawe his people by his *virtù* and to amaze his soldiers. The relationship between character, virtue, and admiration is similar to that displayed in *On Duties*, but the specific content has been changed to fit despotic rule. The examples of Caracalla, Commodus, and Maximin also show the danger of incurring the people's hatred. Like Cicero, Machiavelli recommends that princes not offend their subjects by taking their property and killing them *en masse*. In the end, though, neither Marcus nor Severus serves as a model to be followed; rather, the "new prince, coming to power in a new state . . . should take from Severus those elements of his conduct that are necessary to found his state, and from Marcus those that are useful and creditable in preserving a state already stabilized and secure" (p. 57), using the deliberative skills that Machiavelli seeks to teach.

Though we can find Ciceronian *topoi* and emphases in many of the terms that Machiavelli uses, they disagree about the importance of integrity and craftiness, especially lying. Initially, Machiavelli seems to adopt Cicero's distinction between the human and the beastly. Cicero argues that "there are two ways of settling a dispute: the first by discussion; second, by physical force; and since the former is characteristic of a man, the latter of a brute, we must resort to force only in case we may not avail ourselves of discussion" (*De officiis* 1. 34). Cicero makes what seems a firm distinction, only to accept force when it is necessary. Machiavelli similarly asserts "there are two ways of fighting, one with laws and the other with force. The first is properly a human method; the second belongs to beasts. But as the first method does not always suffice, you sometimes have to turn to the second" (*The Prince*, p. 47). However, Cicero stresses codes of warfare in his subsequent analysis whereas Machiavelli passes on to praise deceit. Here they part company: Cicero rejects the fox (which represents cunning) whereas Machiavelli writes that "you must be a great liar and hypocrite" (p. 48). Machiavelli's support of lying develops into a full-blown defense of the need to manipulate appearances; but Cicero, though he acknowledges that orators win favor by advocating both truth and apparent truth in court, rejects trickery as cowardly. His rejection can be illuminated by Julian Pitt-Rivers's comment that those who lie and play the charlatan remain permanent strangers within a social group ("The stranger," p. 16). The trickster falls outside of the bonds of society, becoming like the tyrant in Book 3 who can be robbed or killed with impunity. For "we have no ties of fellowship with a tyrant . . . and it is not opposed to nature to rob, if one can, a man whom it is morally right to kill" (*De officiis* 3. 32). For Cicero, to speak truth is to maintain one's freedom, courage, independence, and social bonds with others. In *On Friendship*, he strongly rejects flattery and dishonesty in favor of open, sharp speech when a friend does not act virtuously (pp. 88–99). But for Machiavelli, aspiring princes always live outside society; their ambition is to found a state and, in doing so, they treat their opponents as enemies.

In addition, Machiavelli, in spite of his care in the chapter on advice to help princes protect their independence, makes them subservient to fortune in sections XX and XXV. For the new prince "has to have a mind ready to shift as the winds of fortune and the varying circumstances of life may dictate," not departing from good if possible, but willing to shift to evil should necessity require it. Likewise in section XXV, "a prince will be fortunate who adjusts his behavior to the temper of the times, and on the other hand will be unfortunate when his behavior is not well attuned to the times" (*The Prince*, p. 68). The moments when *virtù* can make *fortuna* into opportunity are rare; only when extreme instability and danger can be taken advantage of by an exceptional leader will opportunity arise for the new state.

Thus, neither *De officiis* nor *The Prince* can best be read as political theories separate from the specific indeterminacies of their respective practical situations. Cicero and Machiavelli teach deliberation by constructing, adapting, and reinterpreting terms, commonplaces, and examples in light of the distinct problems and opportunities they face in teaching Marcus and the Medici. Their "theories," insofar as one can attribute theories to them, emerge only in the practices of the texts, and in the practices toward which the text aims. These practices are deliberative because they engage the multiple, sometimes recalcitrant, contingencies of human action in circumstances that are only partly amenable to change.

Notes

1   I use two editions of Cicero's *De officiis*. The Loeb Classical Library *De officiis* contains the Latin text along with an English translation. The Cambridge edition of *On Duties* is readable and informative.

2   I am indebted to Julius Kirschner of the University of Chicago for this reference, and to Eugene Garver, Walter Jost, and William Olmsted for reading a draft of this chapter. However, I accept responsibility for my errors.

Part II

Classical Rhetoric and Literary Interpretation

Introduction

Part II examines three literary works seminal for our understanding of how rhetorical writers reinvent classical *topoi* to redefine the relationships between rhetoric, inquiry, and persuasion. Bacon draws on Aristotle, Cicero, and Machiavelli to transform a seventeenth-century English rhetoric that had become limited to issues of style. Attacking the French rhetorician Peter Ramus, who relegated rhetoric to style and whose logic made rigid binary distinctions in order to organized received knowledge, Bacon called for "the will not only to cling to and make use of knowledge already discovered, but to penetrate further; to conquer, not an opponent in argument, but nature herself in action" ("Preface," *Novum organum*, p. 40). He developed a new mode of invention appropriate to science and reanimated persuasive rhetoric as a powerful political and ethical force, capable of healing diseased imaginations and fervid passions. His innovative writing helped to initiate while also transforming the genre of the essay (begun by Montaigne), into a discourse replete with arguments that teach practical wisdom. Influenced by his scientific method, which used negative (in addition to positive) examples as the basis for maxims and aphorisms, Bacon's *Essays* challenge received knowledge, using positive *and* negative examples to generate new propositions and to teach readers more thoughtful ways of praising, arguing, and moving the emotions.

Milton's early pamphlets and *Paradise Lost* refashion the vehement style praised by Cicero and Augustine to the purposes of seventeenth-century political and religious polemics. The pamphlets make Ciceronian and Augustinian categories of style more capacious in order to confront the conflict and the diversity of beliefs generated by the English Reformation as well as to address a wide range of personality types. The pamphlets use invective as a weapon against those perceived to disguise truth under bland generalizations, unmasking the hypocrisy of their arguments and moral stances. *Paradise Lost* represents Satan as a vicious deceiver and Abdiel (the unfallen angel) as the champion of strong speech that brings hidden assumptions into the open and exposes hypocrisy. Far from using agreed-upon commonplaces to persuade readers, the pamphlets intensify opposition and use conflict to test truth, while using mild speech to explore truth with reasonable people. They represent two ways of addressing the challenges of pluralism.

Jane Austen's *Persuasion* confronts the irreducible plurality of sociocultural and rhetorical frameworks in early nineteenth-century England. The novel challenges the idea that commonplaces express the shared values and beliefs of a polity. Instead of a single, English commonwealth, the novel distinguishes at least three discursive commonwealths. Only within a commonwealth can a person's words be heard, understood, and heeded. But in the beginning, the heroine, Anne Elliot's words are not heard and so not heeded. The novel tells the story of her discovery and refashioning of new rhetorical powers and new commonwealths, of her movement from being "nobody," because unheard, to piercing a heart. It comments tellingly on the implications of sociocultural diversity for rhetorical cogency and power.

Chapter 5

Tradition and Invention: Bacon's Aphorisms and the *Essays*

Like Machiavelli, Bacon challenges inherited maxims and mores.[1] Machiavelli seeks terms for deliberation that do not depend on custom or religion and that are adequate to the problems of politically unstable sixteenth-century Italy. I have shown how he reworks Ciceronian maxims from *De officiis* in shocking ways, arguing most famously that "a prince who wants to keep his authority must learn how not to be good" (*The Prince*, p. 42), undercutting the belief derived from classical ethics and rhetoric that the great leader and orator must be a good man. Defying the precept that human beings should never do what is inhuman, Machiavelli asserts, "a prince must know how to make good use of both the beast and man" (pp. 47–8). Yet, as I have also shown, a close reading of *The Prince* in light of Ciceronian deliberation discloses that the text teaches a flexible activity of discovery and judgment. Machiavelli does not exploit shock for its own sake. *The Prince* adapts classical rhetorical strategies to radically different circumstances in Italy. Similarly, Bacon reshapes rhetorical *topoi* to explore distinct historical problems and opportunities.

I have argued that Machiavelli teaches his reader to be thoughtful about circumstances that the Medici might encounter but that the text itself cannot predict. Customary ethical categories cannot handle the new problems presented in acquiring a new princedom. But, far from abandoning ethical concerns entirely, Machiavelli redefines the prince's ethos in light of what is possible and desirable in a dangerous situation. His recommendations sometimes build on those of Cicero's *De officiis* and sometimes revise and reverse them in order to guide action in the rare and challenging task of founding a new state.

Bacon shares many of Machiavelli's preoccupations; but does not aim exclusively to increase the rhetorical and political agency of a leader; instead, Bacon also attends to human agency over nature. He calls for "the will not only to cling to and make use of knowledge already discovered, but to penetrate further; to conquer, not an opponent in argument, but nature herself in action" ("Preface," *Novum organum* I, p. 40). He departs significantly from previous rhetorical practices to make *topoi*, induction, examples, and aphorisms into tools of scientific inquiry. I argue that Bacon extends his reinvented rhetorical art into his deliberative essays ("Bacon's *Essays*," pp. 272–92; "Georgics of the mind," pp. 78–155).

Bacon attacks the method of Peter Ramus (1515–72), a French humanist who redefined the art of rhetoric and whose method for organizing knowledge dominated English thought during the late sixteenth and early seventeenth centuries. Ramus divided subjects into exclusive categories. He sharply distinguished rhetoric from logic, making invention part of logic and limiting rhetoric to issues of style and composition. The distinction reduced rhetoric to presentation and ornament.

Bacon faults the Ramists for creating hard binary distinctions; "these men press matters by the laws of their method, and when a thing does not aptly fall into those dichotomies, either pass it by or force it out of its natural shape" (*Works* IV, p. 448; *Francis Bacon*, p. 140). He criticizes thinkers who merely organize what is known without promoting discovery: "the sciences we now have are nothing more than nice arrangements of things already discovered" (*Novum organum* I, Aphorism 8, p. 45). Rejecting Ramism as a method for science or rhetorical invention, he reinvents rhetoric.

First, instead of making a fixed dichotomy between logic and rhetoric, he links them and praises Aristotle for doing the same: "Aristotle doth wisely place rhetoric as between logic on the one side, and moral or civil knowledge on the other, as participating of both" (*Works* III, p. 411). He attacks his contemporaries' excessive interest in style, deploring those who "hunt more after words than matter; and more after the choiceness of the phrase ... than ... worth of subject, soundness or argument, life of invention, or depth of judgment" (III, p. 283). He also unites argument and reason with imagination, character, and emotion to make rhetoric capable of moving people to action.

Bacon's treatment of rhetoric moves away from Ramism toward an art capable of informing political deliberation and persuading others. It draws on resources of reasoned argument (logos) and emotion (pathos) and character (ethos) to make arguments that are probably true, manifest the trustworthiness of the speaker, and move listeners toward rational action. Whereas many other sixteenth- and seventeenth-century English writers on rhetoric (with notable exceptions such as Thomas Wilson) emphasize style and figure at the expense of argument, Bacon stresses the centrality of argument and reason (*Works* III, p. 283).

But he does not formulate a systematic rhetoric. Believing that rhetoric had already been well developed, Bacon focuses on elements that have been neglected (*Works* III, p. 409). For that reason, we must piece together Bacon's recommendations about how to invent arguments and look for his concepts of ethos, logos, and pathos, in works such as *The Advancement of Learning*, *De augmentis*, and the *Essays*. But neither the rhetoric of the *Essays* nor Bacon's ideas about ethos, logos, and pathos can be understood without studying his reinvention of maxims and aphorisms for the sake of a new science.

Bacon uses maxims in new ways to ground law and science in reason. Maxims had been fundamental to legal reasoning for a long time. For example, Edmund Plowden, a prominent English jurist (1518–85) states, "A maxime is the foundation of Law, and the conclusion of reason" (quoted in "Science of jurisprudence," p. 9). But Bacon discovers a new basis for maxims. Criticizing those who fly precipitously from a few particulars to broad generalizations, he argues that one should move slowly from a large number of particulars to reach a *middle order* generalization, which he calls a legal maxim or scientific axiom. He stresses the need to include negative as well as positive instances along with the maxim. For example, in discussing the maxim "a man's deeds and his words shall be taken strongliest against himself," Bacon comments, "this rule; as all others which are very general, is but a sound in the air... except it be duly conceived in point of difference, where it taketh place, and where not" (*Works* VII, p. 23). In other words, the maxim only helps when one looks carefully at circumstances. Sometimes a man's words and deeds should not be interpreted most stringently when they refer to himself and sometimes they should be.

Analogously, Bacon's science does not just accept generalizations, but recommends true induction, which moves "by proper rejections and exclusions" to "come to a conclusion on the affirmative instances" (*Novum organum* I, Aphorism 105, p. 111; see also *Works* III, p. 387; and "Science of jurisprudence," p. 7.). By looking at positive and negative instances, one tests and refines the generalization. Bacon's discovery shares the emphasis on relating maxims to particulars with traditional rhetoric; but it differs in the scope of the empirical studies and in the extent to which true induction seeks certainty in the long run. Bacon had hoped to make law more just and reasonable by working through the laws of England and Scotland, relating them to maxims and then correcting the maxims in light of further laws. He believed his approach would deepen the foundation of law. He follows a similar procedure in science.

Bacon's Reinvention of the Aphorism in his Science

Bacon wrote most extensively about innovations in the uses of aphorisms in his new science. Without this background knowledge, one can easily misunderstand the reasoning of his *Essays*, which may seem doubtful, inconclusive, or even subversive because they challenge common beliefs ("Georgics of the mind," pp. 78–155). Bacon, like Machiavelli, has often been taken as a skeptic and narrowly pragmatic thinker. But by studying his rhetoric in the context of his science, we discern the roles of skepticism and prudence in an inquiry that comes to terms with recalcitrant aspects of the empirical world.

Bacon distinguishes two kinds of invention, "the one of arts and sciences; and the other, of speech and arguments." He finds the former "deficient" and seeks to restart the "operation of the mind" involved in it, setting it on a new path (*Works* III, p. 384; *Novum organum* I, p. 38). The difference between the two kinds of invention appears most clearly in the treatment of arrangement and composition. Bacon distinguishes "magisterial" style from what he calls "initiative." The magisterial style delivers knowledge "in such form as may be best believed, and not as may be most conveniently examined…He who receives knowledge desires present satisfaction, without waiting for due inquiry." But if one wants to stimulate inquiry and the growth of knowledge, knowledge should be delivered "in the same method wherein it was originally invented" in a style that initiates thought (*Works* IV, p. 449). Because Bacon wishes the initiative style to generate inquiry in the sciences, he favors the use of aphorisms. He thinks of aphorisms as striking statements that are incomplete and disconnected, calling upon the reader to investigate further.

Good aphorisms are "made but of the pith and heart of sciences" precisely because they do not round off thought. Because the aphorism contains no illustrations, examples, or descriptions of practice, one is left with "nothing to fill the aphorisms but some good quantity of observation" (*Works* III, p. 405). Whereas Ramists divide a subject into parts and then list all of them so that they appeared comprehensive, Bacon's aphorisms are incomplete and break up such impressions ("Editor's Introduction," *Novum organum*, p. xii). Bacon writes his *New Science* as a series of aphorisms, arguing in Aphorism 8,

> Even the works already invented owe their existence to casual experience more than to the sciences; for the sciences we now have are nothing more than nice arrangements of things already discovered, not methods of discovery or pointers to new works. (*Novum organum* I, p. 45)

The sciences should point to discoveries that unfold new truth and new works, as I will show in a moment.

The use of the word "pointers" in Aphorism 8 recalls Cicero's emphasis on topics as signs that point to facts and arguments in particular situations without naming what they will be (*De oratore* 2. 174, p. 322). Bacon's method of bringing a general (gathered from past acquaintance with particulars) into relation with a new particular also recalls Aristotle's use of the enthymeme to find facts and arguments in particular situations. Ironically, however, Bacon adapts the broadly Aristotelian method of invention to attack the science of Aristotle, who, he argues, "utterly enslaved his natural philosophy to his logic, rendering it more or less useless and contentious" (*Novum organum* I, Aphorism 54, p. 62).

The *Novum organum* (1620) focuses on illusions, which produce misleading arguments. One central class of fictions that must be eliminated arises from Aristotle's use of "names of things that do not exist," such as " 'fortune', 'prime mover', and 'planetary orbs' " (I, Aphorism 60, pp. 64–5; *Excess*, p. 61). The word "idols" designates the illusions that block human beings from perceiving nature; invention corrects these illusions. Most pertinent to my later argument are the idols of the marketplace that creep into the human mind because of the connection of words and names. "For while men believe their reason governs words, in fact, words turn back and reflect their power upon the understanding, and so render philosophy and science sophistical and inactive" (*Novum organum* I, Aphorism 59, p. 64). Words mislead and cause controversy over definitions. But defining the words is not sufficient; instead inquirers need "to go back to particular instances and to their due order" (ibid.). Bacon's methods of inquiry aim to penetrate these particular instances.

Bacon calls for a "true induction" that arises gradually from particulars. Aphorism 13 criticizes the syllogism because it is "quite unequal to the subtlety of nature . . . While it commands assent, it fails to take hold of things." Instead of trying to apply syllogisms to nature, Aphorism 14 advocates working in the other direction and moving from things, to notions, to words:

> The syllogism consists of propositions, propositions of words, and words are tokens of notions. Therefore – and this is the heart of the matter – if the notions themselves are muddled and carelessly derived from things, the whole superstructure is shaky. The one hope, therefore, lies in true *induction*. (I, p. 46)

The text uses the example of heat to show how true induction works. First, it presents "*to the understanding* all of the known *instances* which agree in the same nature, though in the most dissimilar materials" (II, Aphorism 11, p. 144), including the sun's rays, hot vapors, bodies rubbed hard, and horse dung. Then it presents "instances that lack the given nature," i.e., the negative instances showing the absence of heat, such as the sun's rays in the air between the moon and the earth and the "body of a glow-worm." Finally a third table lists instances that possess the nature being investigated to a greater or lesser degree, such as fertilizer, putrefaction, and animals in motion. Then it considers all the tables to discern "a nature of such a kind that it is always present or absent with the given nature" (II, Aphorism 15, p. 168), and it excludes impossible "natures." (Because of the sun's rays, for example, heat cannot be an *element*.) True induction makes all the exclusions and then arrives at a preliminary affirmative, for example, that "*Heat is an expansive motion, checked, and exerting itself through the parts of smaller bodies*" (II, Aphorism 20, p. 179). Guided by this preliminary affirmation, Bacon studies further instances.

This cautious approach reflects Bacon's distrust of the human mind because it is "rash and premature" (I, Aphorism 26, p. 50). The text rejects what it calls "anticipations" of nature. Because our minds color or anticipate what we see, we miss what is there. For this reason, Bacon insists on the need for *interpretations* of nature. Interpretations gather widely scattered things that "seem harsh and discordant" and do not give rise easily to quick intuitive guesses. He recommends experiments that get at hidden natural processes that occur in many different and unexpected places.

Bacon's method, then, provides safeguards against the mind's own defects. In this respect he can, again, be compared to earlier thinkers. Cicero and Machiavelli also provide a rhetorical method for checking common belief against particular instance so as to avoid the duplicity of appearances. Neither writer accepts the most ordinary understanding of terms. Like Machiavelli, Bacon seeks an elusive truth beneath appearances, but Bacon is the first to make the correction of appearances and illusions the primary goal of his inventive method. His scientific method, like Machiavelli's rhetoric but more systematically, brings maxims to bear on difficult cases to force readers to give up or alter customary beliefs.

His scientific method has other features in common with rhetorical invention. Like Aristotle, Bacon emphasizes strategies of argument that use questions of degree and of comparison. Comparing the heavy and the light in *De augmentiis*, he recommends the consideration of degree, that is, "what bodies weigh more, and what less" (*Works* IV, p. 424). Analogously, when it comes to questions of good and evil, he looks for arguments that show that one evil is worse than another or one good is better than its alternative (*Life and Letters* III, p. 308). Arguments of degree are useful also in deliberating with another person and in "considering and resolving anything with ourselves" (*Works* IV, p. 423). Bacon even applies his flexible mode of thinking to the inner life.

Despite similarities between scientific and rhetorical invention, I wish to note important *differences* that affect how we understand the arts and how we read the essays. Although both types of invention seek knowledge of particulars, the scientist aims for knowledge new to mankind whereas orators seek knowledge new to themselves. Deliberative rhetoric works with common agreement and often leads to an assent that closes inquiry. Because, in his view, rhetorical invention does not discover new knowledge, Bacon may seem to devalue it in comparison with scientific inquiry ("Bacon and rhetoric," p. 226). But even though eloquence can hinder "the severe inquisition of truth, and the deep progress into philosophy... because it is too early satisfactory to the mind of man," and "quencheth the desire of further search," it has its own important power (*Works* III, p. 284). The very quality that hinders inquiry facilitates an ethical use of rhetoric. The art of eloquence *cultivates* exactly the imaginative vivid sayings that Bacon rejects for science. Imagination rounds off expression and makes a strong impression in order to guide action.

Eloquence leads people to love the good of the commonwealth, and, in this sense, rhetoric has a positive ethical function.

Rhetoric, like logic and ethics, provides a necessary corrective when the mind deceives itself. Bacon, more than any of the other rhetoricians in this volume, emphasizes the inadequacy of the human mind for knowing the world, especially in the sciences. He writes, "the intellect alone, unregulated and unaided, is . . . unfitted to overcome the obscurity of things" (*Novum organum* I, Aphorism 21, p. 48). As we have seen, the mind is beset by "idols." The first kind, "the *idols of the tribe*," arises out of human nature and from the fact, as Bacon sees it, "that all our perceptions, both of our sense and of our minds, are reflections of man, not of the universe" (I, Aphorism 41, p. 54). Individual personality also produces illusions ("the *idols of the cave*"), language leads to error ("the *idols of the market-place*"), and philosophy engenders deceiving dogmas ("the *idols of the theatre*") (I, Aphorisms 42–4, pp. 54–5). Idols can be corrected by true induction, which forces the mind to look at unexpected facts and to correct its generalizations by setting them against negative instances. The mind needs analogous correction in its ethical and political activity.

The mind needs ethical guidance because, left to itself, Bacon argues, it would become the slave of passions. Bacon joins many sixteenth- and seventeenth-century writers when he points to "the nature and condition of men; who are full of savage and unreclaimed desires, of profit, of lust, of revenge, which as long as they give ear to precepts, to laws, to religion, sweetly touched with eloquence and persuasion of books, of sermons, of harangues, so long is society and peace maintained" (*Works* III, p. 302; VI, pp. 720–2). But eloquence can coerce those who live by passion alone by setting "affection against affection," and using "*fear* and *hope*" to bridle unruly passions, preventing the unruly from destroying the commonwealth (III, pp. 437–8). Imagination is equally dangerous because it presents things as the human being wants them to be and turns him away from difficulties where "sober things . . . restrict his hope" (*Novum organum* I, Aphorism 49, p. 59).

While the ideas of coercing the passions and purifying imagination are common in Renaissance rhetoricians, Calvin, Melanchthon, and others, Bacon innovates by drawing on faculty psychology to argue that rhetoric can make imagination less dangerous. Whereas poetry (and imagination) "submits the shews of things to the desires of the mind," rhetoric helps reason that "doth buckle and bow the mind to the nature of things" (*Works* III, pp. 343–4). Bacon distinguishes the arts of logic, morality, and rhetoric on the basis of this psychology, giving to each the power to remedy some inadequacy. "For the end of logic is to teach a form of argument to secure reason, and not to entrap it; the end of morality is to procure the affections to obey reason, and not to invade it; the end of rhetoric is to fill imagination to second reason, and not to oppress it" (III, pp. 409–10). Rhetoric changes imagination from an oppressor of reason into a follower of reason.

Bacon creates a political model for this action. Instead of allowing imagination to create dangerous monsters and false objects of desire that overwhelm reason, rhetoric wins "the imagination from affection's [passion's] part, and contract[s] a confederacy between the reason and imagination against the affections" (III, pp. 410–11, my brackets). Imagination by itself focuses on what is present and vivid, but reason *"beholdeth the future and sum of time"* (III, p. 411). Since rhetoric uses imagination to make the future seem present, people will, through their foresight, be moved to action. The filling and winning of imagination by rhetoric are much more effective, Bacon claims, than "sharp disputations and conclusions, which have no sympathy with the will of man" (III, p. 410).

Rhetoric, like ethics, must be able to give "descriptions of the several characters and tempers of men's natures and dispositions" (III, p. 434) and study how to bring the mind to virtue (III, pp. 441–2). Bacon acknowledges that these subjects "are touched a little by Aristotle as in passage in his rhetoric," but scolds him slightly for not incorporating the study of emotion into the study of ethics (III, pp. 436–7). But Bacon himself does not elaborate on arguments from ethos and pathos in the *Advancement of Learning*. However, as Ronald S. Crane shows, Bacon's *Essays* supply much of what is lacking in the earlier works ("Bacon's *Essays*," pp. 274–5). "Of discourse," "Of praise," "Of honour and reputation," and "Of goodness and goodness of nature" articulate many of the *topoi* speakers may use as sources of argument, not only for making speeches but for their own inward negotiations with themselves.

The New Science and the *Essays*: Ethos, Logos, and Pathos

Unlike other works (such as "Apophthegms," "Promus of formularies and elegancies," and "Maxims of the law" (see *Works* VII)) that list sayings and maxims which writers might use, the 1625 essays provide commonplaces in the context of an inquiry. But these essays build on earlier lists of commonplaces for and against a position. Bacon extends Cicero's argument on two sides of the question from forensic to deliberative and epideictic rhetoric ("Introduction," *Essays*) For example, the translation of "De augmentis" in the collection of commonplaces under "Praise, reputation" (*Works* IV, p. 476) lists the antitheses:

For: Praise is the reflexion of virtue.

Against: Fame is a worse judge than messenger.

John Pitcher puts it well when he writes that "once we appreciate that much of Bacon's writing is compounded from the acknowledged contradictions between such *sententiae*, then the *Essays*, in particular, can be understood as a rhetorical art form rather than . . . a set of fireside homilies" ("Introduction," *Essays*, p. 24). In addition, the list of commonplaces displays analogies with the emphasis in the *New*

Science on the need for positive *and* negative instances. Maxims and examples for and against certain positions guide discovery in the 1625 essays of how and in what circumstances one might display ethos or move emotion. The essays sometimes affirm and, at other times, redefine central terms and commonplaces; they bring up difficult cases and use negative instances to challenge readers' assumptions. But these "complicating qualifications," as Stanley E. Fish calls them, do not lead to radical skepticism and subversion as Fish argues they do ("Georgics of the mind," p. 138; *Resistant Structures*, pp. 27–41).

Fish rightly emphasizes the role of proper rejections, exclusions, and negatives in arriving at a scientific axiom ("Georgics of the mind," p. 86), but although he argues correctly that the axiom arrived at according to these procedures is provisional, he misrepresents Bacon's argument when he claims that the essays produce a refining "experience" that says nothing about its subject. Yet Fish asserts his position very strongly: "the essay... says nothing at all about the nominal subject love," nor do the other essays say anything about their subjects (p. 91). Richard Strier shows that "Fish's readings systematically... *eliminate the particular content*" from the essays and "equally systematically assert a generalized (negative) content for them" (*Resistant Structures*, p. 28). The same can be said for Fish's treatment of the science. But, I have argued, Bacon's science uses "rejections and exclusions" to "analyze *nature*," i.e., they focus on the subject of heat. He lists negative instances, for example that "the sun's rays do not give out heat in the middle region of the air" (*Novum organum* II, Aphorism 12, p. 148), and after exclusions, he concludes from the "affirmative instances" and defines the nature of heat as an "expansive motion... through the smaller parts of bodies" (II, Aphorism 21, p. 179). Nothing could be more focused toward a particular than the aphorisms focused on the tables of instances. And even though the definition of heat is provisional, it is much closer to the truth than something like "heat is a body."

Likewise the *Essays* sometimes affirm maxims and sometimes criticize or revise them in order to direct inquiry into particulars. By refuting false beliefs, Bacon produces a more adequate method for investigating and understanding the subjects of his essays, subjects such as proper praise, praise of oneself or one's office, honor, anger, envy, and friendship. He is unequivocal, for example, in arguing that envy is bad. The *Essays* also teach ways to use pathos and ethos well. The linking of positive and negative instances provokes readers to think in terms of particulars and to deliberate about whether an argument holds weight when it comes to articulating ethos in practice. Bacon takes up the Ciceronian and Machiavellian emphasis on how actions should "alter with circumstances" ("Cicero's *De officiis*," p. 85; "Exemplifying deliberation," p. 175). The *Essays* not only admit exceptions; they help readers to look for hard cases.

The essays pertinent to ethos examine the circumstances in which one can display character. "Of discourse," "Of praise," and "Of honour and reputation" address the matter most directly. The first two focus on speakers' explicit use of language to commend themselves. Whereas Aristotle's *Rhetoric* argues that the means of showing that one is practically wise and good are the same as those used in characterizing the virtues of others (2. 1, 1378a), Bacon confronts the disadvantages of speaking of oneself at all. He argues that "speech of a man's self ought to be seldom and well chosen. I knew one was wont to say in scorn, *He must needs be a wise man, he speaks so much of himself.*" His sarcasm implies that a speaker who wishes to appear wise by talking much of himself is very foolish. Bacon's positive recommendation about how to display character is formulated as a narrow instance: "And there is but one case wherein a man may commend himself with good grace, and that is in commending virtue in another, especially if it be such a virtue whereunto himself pretendeth" ("Of discourse," *Essays*, p. 161).

"Of praise" exhibits an even more cautious and critical spirit to arrive at an understanding of dangerous and ethical uses of praise. Explicitly rhetorical in addressing itself to *epideixis* (praise and blame), it begins with a fundamental equivalence – "praise is the reflection of virtue" – a succinct articulation of the ideal relationship between rhetorical ethos and virtuous character. But the essay immediately qualifies this hopeful idealization, cautioning that praise "is as the glass or body which giveth the reflection." In debunking the ability of fame to reflect the truly worthy, "Of praise" initially makes the reader aware of the pitfalls of praise. Indeed, Bacon, writes, "There be so many false points of praise, that a man may justly hold it a suspect." After linking praise to flattery and finding self-flattery a basic constituent of human beings, the essay cautions that if a speaker "be a cunning flatterer, he will follow the arch-flatterer, which is a man's self" ("Of praise," *Essays*, p. 215). What follows then delineates ways that cunning and impudent flatterers gull their victims. Thus, instead of recommending ways to show oneself of good character or to praise the characters of others, Bacon takes his readers through a rigorous course on the dangers and false points of praise. He reverses a commonplace, stimulating readers to think when he asserts, "certainly fame is like a river that beareth up things light and swollen and drowns things weighty and solid," attacking the humanist belief that the reputations of the best of antiquity survive into the present.

However, Bacon's uses of maxims and aphorisms, though provoking and challenging, *do not* subvert the ideas of praise or of ethos. He *celebrates* teaching by praising, as when one addresses "good wishes and respects" to "kings and great persons," and "by telling men what they are, they represent to them what they should be" (p. 215). He gives praise a highly moral emphasis. Though speakers can praise "maliciously" to the "hurt" of others by making their peers envious and jealous, "moderate praise, used with opportunity... doth... good." Having reminded the reader once more of the danger of "magnifying" a man because it may provoke "contradiction, and procure envy and scorn," Bacon argues on the negative side that it cannot be "decent" "to praise a man's self," but he concludes positively "to praise a man's office or profession, he may do it with good grace and with a kind of magnanimity." An example brings home his point: "St. Paul, when he boasts of himself, he doth oft interlace, *I speak like a fool*; but speaking of his calling, he saith, "I will magnify my ministry (Romans 11: 13)" ("Of praise," *Essays*, p. 216). Bacon's argument, far from consuming itself, clears away the deceptions and pitfalls of praise in order to recommend a more ethical and efficacious mode of *epideixis*.

"Of honour and reputation," my third example, links the creation of ethos to the pursuit of reputation. Unlike Aristotle, who focuses on the character a speaker presents *in the speech*, Bacon agrees with Cicero that the speaker's previous reputation in society influences an audience's judgment of his character. The essay begins with a straightforward statement: "The winning of honour is but the revealing of a man's virtue and worth without disadvantage" ("Of honour and reputation," *Essays*, p. 219). Like "Of praise," this essay distills the ideal relation between honor and virtue in a maxim. But it soon corrects any assumptions the reader might have that the link between honor and virtue is easy to achieve. A series of dangers and exceptions flood to the fore. Those who woo and affect honor and reputation . . . are "commonly much talked of but inwardly but little admired." Also it seems that virtue is not enough; persons must "temper" their "actions" so as to "content every faction or combination of people" to make the "music" of reputation "fuller." Outstripping competitors also increases one's honor. "Honour that is gained and broken upon another hath the quickest reflection, like diamonds cut with facets" (p. 219). Display (not just virtue) evidently matters. The list goes on, seeming to overwhelm the belief in the maxim that "honour is but the revealing of a man's virtue," roughly following the apparently subversive approach that Fish outlines ("Georgics of the mind," pp. 92–3, 107–8). Yet, when warning against "envy, which is the canker of honour," Bacon discovers a more informed way to link virtue to honor, and that is to extinguish envy "by declaring a man's self in his ends rather to seek merit than fame, and by attributing a man's successes rather to divine Providence and felicity, than to his own virtue or policy" ("Of honour and reputation," p. 219). Negative instances give rise to a new maxim more focused than the maxim that sets the direction of the essay at the beginning. From complications and qualifications, a formulation better able to guide action emerges in response to the problem of envy.

When it comes to the subject of pathos, Bacon's essays refine common beliefs, linking issues implicated in the moving of emotion to problems of action and practice. Bacon defends moving the emotions on the grounds that "if the affections in themselves were pliant and obedient to reason . . . there should be no great use of persuasions and insinuations to the will" (*Works* III, p. 410). But the passions are mutinous, and so human beings need rhetoric. The task of moving the emotions may seem straightforward, but "Of anger," while drawing on Aristotle (*Rhetoric* 2. 2, 1378b), pits maxims against each other. Whereas Aristotle treats anger as having cognitive grounds in persons' interpretations of insults and slights, Bacon features a very different emphasis on anger as "a kind of baseness." Nevertheless, he refuses to reject anger utterly: "To seek to extinguish anger utterly is but a bravery of the Stoics." Given the impossibility and undesirability of totally eradicating anger, he modifies his advice, urging readers to *"Be angry, but sin not. Let not the sun go down upon your anger."* He advises limiting and confining anger rather than rejecting it *in toto* ("Of anger," *Essays*, p. 226).

Having laid the groundwork for a thoughtful investigation of anger, he becomes more Aristotelian in searching the causes that produce anger and in arguing that the ways in which injury is apprehended and interpreted affect anger. If a speaker emphasizes that the injury he has received implies contempt for him, that "contempt . . . putteth an edge upon anger, as much or more than the hurt itself." Therefore, those who are "ingenious in picking out circumstances of contempt," do "kindle their anger much." Insulting a man's reputation or honor does also "multiply, and sharpen anger." These observations guide the inward negotiations of his readers and can be used in speeches. Bacon is also Aristotelian in considering how to raise anger or appease "anger in another" (p. 227).

"Of envy" illuminates the persuasive use of pathos by suggesting how to recognize what sorts of people are likely to be envious and what sorts of people are likely to be envied. These suggestions contribute to a larger argument about the baseness of envy. The essay is straightforward in its use of maxims. Early in the argument it states directly, "a man who has no virtue in himself ever envieth virtue in others" ("Of envy," *Essays*, p. 83). Instead of challenging his organizing maxim, Bacon draws on Aristotle and directs his readers to look at the persons who envy and those whom they envy in order to develop social indicators by which to recognize the envious (*The "Art" of Rhetoric* 2. 10, 1387b–1388a, pp. 239–43). He adapts these *topoi* to the monarchical and aristocratic society for which he wrote, focusing on issues of birth, rank, and upward mobility to identify those likely to feel envy. For example, "men of noble birth are noted to be envious towards new men when they rise," and "kinsfolk and fellows in office . . . are more apt to envy their equals when they are raised. For it doth upbraid unto them their own fortunes" ("Of envy," p. 84). Those whose status cannot be compared to others, on the other hand, are "less subject to envy." "Where there is no comparison," there is "no envy; and therefore kings are not envied but by kings." Likewise, inherited status minimizes envy for "persons of noble blood are less envied in their rising, for it seemeth but right done to their birth" (p. 85).

In spite of the emphasis on public advancement, hereditary status, and social mobility, Bacon also points to less fixed characteristics and virtues as playing a role. He cautions against attempting excellence in too many areas: "They that desire to excel in too many matters, out of levity and vainglory, are ever envious" ("Of envy," p. 84). He argues by implication that lack of virtue predisposes people to envy: "those are most subject to envy, which carry the greatness of their fortunes in an insolent and proud manner, being never well but while they are showing how great they are" (p. 86). His cautions imply that people who wish not to appear envious ought to avoid levity, vainglory, insolence, and pride. The insistence in "Of praise" and in "Of honour and reputation" that a person's actual reputation over time affects the ethos displayed in any speech extends also to the manifestation of pathos.

"Of friendship" surpasses the previous essays in its critical deployment of maxims and adages, its revision and reversal of those adages and its redefinition of *topoi* crucial to its argument, the *topoi* of beast and god, solitude and company, friendship and counsel, counselor and physician to name a few. Rather than entertaining a pithy, widely believed commonplace at the beginning, the essay qualifies the maxim: "It had been hard for him that spake it to have put more truth and untruth together in a few words, than in that speech, *Whosoever is delighted in solitude is either a wild beast or a god*" ("Of friendship," *Essays*, p. 138). Aristotle uses this maxim to define the nature and ethical character of human beings as inextricably tied to their role in the polity (*Politics* 1. 1). The maxim establishes from the outset that ethics and politics are parts of a single science. Bacon challenges the truth and the foundational character of the maxim before reiterating it, leaving the reader to sort through what is "truth" and what is "untruth" in the maxim. Affirming that hatred of society characterizes the beast, he first asserts directly that it is "most untrue" that hatred of society "should have any character at all of the divine nature," an apparently blanket statement that he then partially undercuts by referring to five false and feigned attempts to "sequester" the self "for a higher conversation." Only the "ancient hermits and holy fathers of the church" seem to have truly drawn away from society in order to have a higher conversation ("Of friendship," p. 138).

Bacon's meditation on the problem of solitude intervenes in a sixteenth- and seventeenth-century debate about the ideals of civility and conversation. Many psychologies and books on counsel advise readers to avoid solitude in favor of educating themselves and bringing stability to their emotions by means of conversation with others in company. Writers are extremely wary of solitude until the seventeenth century, although they find some use in it for religious contemplation.

"Of friendship" decisively denies the linguistic and epistemological basis of this discourse, which had been based on the opposition between solitude and company. The essay asserts "little do men perceive what solitude is, and how far it extendeth. For a crowd is not company, and faces are but a gallery of pictures, and talk but a tinkling cymbal, where there is no love" ("Of friendship," p. 138). By warning that "a crowd is not company," this saying sharply complicates sixteenth-century texts (such as Stefano Guazzo's *The civile conversation*) that celebrate company as the antidote to solitude. Association with others may not correct the weaknesses instilled by solitude. Only friendship informed by a love without which talk is "but a tinkling cymbal" (an allusion to 1 Corinthians 13: 1) can heal solitude.

Yet even this denial does not stand unqualified. Bacon does not utterly reject the discourse on solitude. Rather, as in his new science, he rubs his idea against other maxims and examples in order to refine it, using one of Erasmus' adages to reshape his meaning. He acquiesces to but also adapts Erasmus' adage that "a great city is a great solitude" (*magna civitas, magna solitudo*), because, he explains (and in explaining realigns) the adage toward friendship: in a large town, "friends are scattered." But he goes further than Erasmus and his own earlier saying to "affirm most truly that it is a mere and miserable solitude to want true friends, without which the world is but a wilderness" ("Of friendship," p. 138). "Wilderness" had been a term identified with an extreme, debilitating solitude that is dangerous to the health.

Bacon goes beyond the claim that friendship is medicinal to make friendship a biological necessity. Whereas earlier writings celebrated friendship because it sprang from virtue and corrected temporary swervings from virtue, in "Of friendship," as Laurie Shannon argues, "The self is no longer simply liable to occasional error; a medico-scientific vision of the constant organic processes of the body serves as the basis of a metaphor for moral health" (*Sovereign Amity*, p. 195). Friendship allows for "the ease and discharge of the fullness and swellings of the heart" as Bacon puts it, analogizing friendship to a prescription that "openeth the heart" ("Of friendship," p. 139). This argument redefines Ciceronian and Plutarchan *topoi* of friendship and counsel.

Cicero's dominant influence on the Renaissance ideal of friendship had made truth-telling and free, sharp speech the distinguishing markers of friendship. Cicero argues that only the virtuous, independent friend is capable of offering the strong counsel needed when his counterpart deviates from virtue (*De amicitia* 24–5, pp. 198–203). But Bacon draws on an alternative Plutarchan model that modifies the stringency of the Ciceronian ideal by introducing the idea of friend as a physician and, for Bacon, a minister to whom one "may impart griefs, joys, fears, hopes, suspicions, counsels, and whatsoever lieth upon the heart to oppress it" ("How to tell a flatterer," *Essays*, p. 139). Bacon applies a medicinal model to a heart that, far from erring only occasionally, requires constant processing. The opening of one's emotions to the friend clears the heart much as sarsaparilla and iron open the "stoppings and suffocations of the mind."

"Of friendship" also revises the maxims of friendship and counsel according to which friends are equal. In a long meditation on the desirability and the difficulties of friendship between kings and their subjects, it uses examples that cut across the grain of the main thesis, namely that "great kings and monarchs" set a high value on friendship and that the "wisest and most politic," seeking friendship, raise and join to themselves "some of their servants" (p. 139). The tensions and hazards of this practice emerge in the examples of L. Sulla and Pompey, Julius Caesar and Decimus Brutus, Augustus and Agrippa, Tiberius Caesar and Sejanus, and others, all of whom suffered at the hands of their friends. The examples "proveth most plainly that they found their own felicity (though as great as ever happened to mortal men) but as an half piece, except they mought have a friend to make it entire" (pp. 140–1). Although these men wanted the friendship and each one needed it lest "*closeness did impair and a little perish his understanding*," they enjoyed friendships at their peril. Bacon's partly negative examples point to dangers that he investigates here and in "Of counsel."

Two other central arguments heavily qualify customary beliefs about friendship, the first belief being that a person receives "faithful counsel" from a friend and the second "*that a friend is another himself*," a maxim advanced by Aristotle in the *Nicomachean Ethics* 9. 4, 1166a and by Cicero in *De amicitia* 21. 80 ("Of friendship," *Essays*, pp. 142, 144). Bacon modifies the first by arguing that even before a friend gives counsel, the "wits and understanding do clarify and break up, in the communicating and discoursing with another." Using the metaphors of tossing and marshaling thoughts, Bacon pictures the sorting and ordering of ideas that people achieve in the effort to communicate to their friends. He features the expressive over the admonitory offices of friendship, stressing disclosure above all else. And in revising the Aristotelian and Ciceronian maxim, Bacon transforms it into a statement about delegated agency, for far from being "another himself," the friend is "far more than himself" because he continues his counterpart's work, becoming a deputy who furthers his purposes before death and after ("Of friendship," p. 144). The friend can do many things that a person cannot; he expands the "implementable 'Offices of Life'" (*Resistant Structures*, p. 36; *Sovereign Amity*, pp. 198–9).

"On friendship," then, does more than establish a relationship between beliefs of the audience that are formulated in maxims and a course of action that the writer recommends. Instead Bacon takes his reader through an inquiry into the validity of customary beliefs, challenging basic assumptions about the nature, purpose, and social definition of friendship. He explodes the belief that company can be an adequate remedy for solitude, offering much more stringent criteria for healing solitude than those recommended by humanists. Only an intimate friendship that performs offices both medical and charitable can achieve "the ease and discharge of the fullness and swellings of the heart" and allow persons to order their thoughts. Bacon's challenges of maxims and his redefinitions of the customary inflections of words such as "solitude," "company," "friendship," and "counsel" rework previous models of friendship to achieve new understanding. He confronts problems of social relationship in a hierarchical society that values the educative and affective powers of friendships which must be and yet cannot be based in equality.

Bacon's treatments of ethos and pathos also confront received opinion of rhetoricians about the desirability of displaying character through speech and of praising oneself or others. Yet, after vigorously examining the pitfalls of praise, the essays, I have argued, discover decent ways to praise, namely by celebrating "a man's office or profession" ("Of praise," *Essays*, p. 214). Bacon argues that a man fulfills ethical ideals only by dedicating himself to the good of the commonwealth, and his treatment of ethos and praise bears out this emphasis. Far from consuming its own maxims and aphorisms as Fish argues, his writings use examples to test, to refine, and to support them. But, as he himself argues, his use of examples is not "servile." For, "it hath much greater life for practice when the discourse attendeth upon the example, than when the example attendeth upon the discourse," a maxim that he follows in the essays analyzed here. His examples do not always follow from his maxims or the expected shape of his argument. He believed that such illustrative examples are servile, for "the examples alleged for the discourse's sake are cited succinctly and without particularity, and carry a servile aspect toward the discourse which they are brought in to make good." Like Machiavelli, he corrects maxim and example against each other. For "the form of writing which of all others is fittest for this variable argument of negotiation and occasions is that which Machiavel chose wisely and aptly for government; namely, *discourse upon histories or examples*. For knowledge drawn freshly and in our view out of particulars, knoweth the way best to particulars again" (*Works* III, p. 453). The examples of great men who risked and sometimes gave their lives in order to find caring partners provide opportunities for readers to think their way through the specific values and dangers of friendship as encountered in their own particular circumstances.

Note

1   I am indebted to the Renaissance Workshop at the University of Chicago, especially to Michael Murrin, Joshua Scodel, and Richard Strier for their knowledgeable, astute, and helpful comments. Janel Mueller graciously read this chapter, offering incisive and telling responses to my arguments. I, of course, take responsibility for my errors.

Chapter 6

Deception, Strong Speech, and Mild Discourse in Milton's Early Prose and *Paradise Lost*

John Milton wrote during a turning point in the use of rhetoric when persuasive argument explicitly confronted radical social, political, and religious differences. The Reformation generated a plurality of irreconcilable belief systems and political models that came into conflict before and during the English Civil War. The concept of toleration had barely formed. Conflict between Protestants and Roman Catholics was extremely intense, while Presbyterians and Independents sometimes fought one another and sometimes joined together. Speakers and writers could not appeal to pluralism and the respect for differences without also attending to bitter conflicts. Nor could they assume a common ground between speakers and audiences.

Milton's early prose defends constitutional government and Protestant belief, deploying scathing rhetoric against the National Church and arguing for limited toleration for the many Protestant sects whose beliefs even the Presbyterians rejected. He developed a variety of genres and styles of persuasion to meet the complex challenges produced by a deeply divided public world, reshaping Cicero's ideas of decorum. He thought hard about when and why he should use confrontational public speech to uncover the dangerous euphemisms of his opponents and when a different style was required. He rethought the issue of how to rouse and soothe political emotions by adapting Ciceronian republican rhetoric to religious controversy. His early pamphlets draw on the Bible as a model of decorum, introducing a broad variety of styles to deal with the varying shortcomings of audiences. He shifts from the humanist genre of advice to princes to a republican genre of advice to Parliament, to the people, and to his opponents (*Life of Milton*, p. 190).

Milton's early prose redefines the roles of ethos, pathos, and argument in public speech. He draws on Cicero to articulate the ethos of a republican speaker addressing an assembly ("Civic hero," pp. 71–101), and on Aristotle to defend angry and indignant speech against opponents whom he believes have denigrated his person and his deepest beliefs. By forging classical rhetoric and biblical example into a unity, he creates new possibilities for persuasive speech (*Life of Milton*, pp. 20, 28, 138, 346). He makes angry speech inventive.

The true orator in Milton's prose and *Paradise Lost* (1667) has a heroic ethos, ready to test truth in open battle. This orator uses a vehement style to cut through deception and disclose error, folly, and perfidy. His emotional and moral character infuse arguments with conviction; he stands fast and alone for the sake of truth. Milton casts his own ethos and that of Abdiel, the truth-telling angel of *Paradise Lost*, in epic terms. He marks as a coward the warrior who refuses to appear openly in battle; Edmund Spenser's knights in *The Faerie Queene* tear off the helmets of their opponents to display their true identities, and Milton's verbal weapons seek to accomplish the moral equivalent. Milton calls for free, open, agonistic speech.

Milton's most famous tract, *Areopagitica* (November 1644) uses this speech. In the context of a larger debate about religious toleration, this work argues passionately against the limiting or suppression of publications. It advocates the use of rhetorical invention to sort truth from error and virtue from vice. Milton argues that confronting error is a better way to refute it than suppressing it, and suggests that conflict stimulates discovery. Even if myriad falsehoods were to be let loose by freedom of publication, Milton maintains, the public contest between truth and falsehood would allow falsehood to be refuted (*CPW* II, p. 561).

Miltonic invention requires combat over truth even among those who feel good will toward each other, because in the face of censorship, truth turns herself into "all shapes, except her own" (*CPW* II, p. 563). But vehement speech casts off the splinters and errors that result from conflict. Discovering truth is a process of birth, of bringing to light, but also of struggle, competition, and victory.

To those who might argue that the wrathful style of such pamphlets as *Animadversions upon the Remonstrants Defence against Smectymnuus* (1641) and *An Apology against a Pamphlet* (1642) is excessive, Milton insists that accommodating oneself to the opinions of others can be dangerous and false. His choice of confrontational public speech is illuminated by Cicero's strictures against flattery. The latter's dialogue *De amicitia* ("Of friendship") identifies truth-telling with friendship and flattery with tyranny. The capacity of a friend to speak frankly and, if necessary, sharply to a friend distinguishes "true and false friends and flattery and good counsel" (*Sovereign Amity*, p. 49). Flattery, on the other hand, is incompatible with freedom, and hypocrisy "pollutes truth and takes away the power to discern it" (*De amicitia* 96, p. 201). Cicero claims that if one is careful, one can distinguish hypocrites and truth-tellers even in the public assembly. One can "usually see the difference between a demagogue – that is, is a smooth-tongued, shallow citizen – and one who has stability, sincerity, and weight" (*De amicitia* 95). One who always assents and agrees cannot tell the truth. Milton's early prose speaks vehemently against such assent.

Although some writers distrust emotion because it can destabilize judgment (Aristotle, *Rhetoric* 1. 1, 1354a), Milton links bold virtuous speech to strong emotions of love and anger, and makes pathos an important source of credibility when he argues that bold speech springs from ardent love. He asserts the moral power of indignation, drawing on Antonius' defense of strong emotion in Cicero's *De oratore*. Antonius insists that he does not act or dissimulate in court. Instead,

> I was myself overcome by compassion before I tried to excite it in others . . . not by way of technique . . . but under the stress of deep emotion and indignation – I mean my tearing open his tunic and exposing his scars . . . [My invocation] was accompanied by tears and vast indignation on my own part; had my personal indignation been missing from all the talking I did on that occasion, my address, so far from inspiring compassion, would positively have deserved ridicule. (2. 195, vol. I, pp. 339–41, my brackets)

Antonius emphasizes the strength and appropriateness of emotion, the reality that occasions his indignation and pity. He argues that in order for speech to be persuasive, and legitimately so, the speaker must really experience the emotions expressed through his language and tells how his indignation arose when he saw Manius Aquilius (whom Cicero actually defended), a former commander-in-chief, cast down, crippled, and oppressed by the charges. Antonius' indignation and pity arose at an unjust action being perpetrated by the prosecutors, and he opened the emotional and factual truth to the light when he tore open the man's tunic and exposed his wounds. So *Animadversions* defends the role of indignation: Milton's love of the souls of men cannot countenance their oppression by seducers and liars. Reworking this idea, *Paradise Lost* represents Satan as simulating "indignation" to Eve's "wrong" (*PL* IX. 666).

But *An Apology against a Pamphlet* does not limit itself to a single highly emotional, vehement style. Although it shows that combative, emotional rhetoric may be needed to expose error, it argues that mild conversation may also help to discover truth. Styles and arguments need to be attuned to the different characters and emotional types found among humankind. Milton's insistence on the need for a variety of styles accompanies an argument for rational and ethical standards in choosing among them. He includes a broad range of human types and problems in conversation, drawing on Cicero and Augustine's defenses of variety, but going further than they do in the range of styles he recommends.

Cicero divides style into three kinds, following Hellenistic precedent: "the grand or vehement style, which stirs the emotions; the middle, which persuades, through pleasure; and the plain which proves points" (*Orator* 69, p. 257; *De oratore* 2. 128–9; see above Chapter 2, p. 26). But, as we saw in Chapter 2, B. A. Krostenko shows that for Cicero style is appropriate to topics, not "*per se,*" but "*in view of some objective.*" If one wishes to pursue a property claim, the plain style works best, but if one wants to celebrate the greatness of the republic to arouse anger against her betrayer, vehement language works better ("Text and context," p. 39).

As I argued in Chapter 3, Augustine modifies this distinction between styles in a manner that influences Milton. He distinguishes the styles on the basis of their function in relation to an audience rather than on the basis of topic and purpose (*Sacred Rhetoric*, p. 44). If hearers are to be taught, the speaker should address them in the plain style. If hearers have trouble attending, the speaker should use a pleasant style, and if they understand and attend, but do not wish to act, he should use the grand (vehement) style. Three different styles could presumably be used with reference to the same subject (*CD* 4. 6–7, pp. 120–1; 7–8, pp. 121–2; 27–8, pp. 136–7; 39, pp. 146–7; see above Chapter 3, p. 42). *An Apology* retains Augustine's emphasis on audience, but extends the multiplicity and irreducible difference of human types. Many styles are needed to reach these types. Each person needs to be drawn to belief in his or her own distinct way. None should be forced to give up the defining characteristic of his or her nature, whether that be a "predominance of... anger," a dejectedness "of spirit," or a nature "over-confident and jocund" (*CPW* I, p. 900).

Milton notes that the "rules of the best rhetoricians," and the most famous examples of the Greek and Roman orations support vehement rhetoric (*CPW* I, p. 899). But because objections to his fierce style are made on religious grounds, he turns to the Bible for illustrations of decorum (see above Chapter 2, p. 26). Jesus was capable not only of the mild and the bitter, but of all the powers later divided among the disciples and teachers in the church (*CPW* I, p. 900). Like Milton he often speaks plainly even with those who thought he should have held them "in more respect" (p. 899). At other times, when he could not teach, he used "bitter angry rebukes" to deprive his opponents of any excuse (pp. 899, 900).

Jesus allotted distinct styles to different types of teachers. The "severe" and sadly grave were given the ability to win the sad and "check" those "of nature over-confident and jocund." The "cheerfull," and "free" drew others who are cheerful "to salvation" and strengthened the "too scrupulous, and dejected of spirit." Drawing on humanist discourse, Milton creates a rich human world in which every type of rhetorician finds an audience that needs what he or she is best suited to give it. All of these persuasions encourage, but do not compel, belief. Milton indirectly defends his own vigorous polemical spirit when he writes that no one is forced to "dissolve that groundwork of nature which God created in him." Even the angry person does not need to drive out all his anger as long as he does not sin. Instead each humor and passion may be "corrected" and "made the proper mould and foundation" of each person's gifts (*CPW* I, p. 900). In all these varieties, Milton defends the distinctness of the human person and his or her particular gift against a unitary model of rhetoric.

Milton urges brotherly understanding for the perturbed, but rage against the deceptive, and argues that the need for a multiplicity of approaches springs from human imperfection. Imperfection makes us differ from one another, and yet Milton makes it a means for persons to connect with one another. The "cheerfull and free" strengthen the "dejected of spirit," and the derisive and scornful bruise the "perverse and fraudulent" (*CPW* I, p. 663; see also pp. 664, 903–4).

With all his references to the choleric, the severe, and the jocund, Milton does not exclude moderation from his list, a quality often associated with his opponents, the defenders of the state Church. "Soundnesse of argument" does "teach" the rational and "sober-minded." But, he argues, in extraordinary times of reformation, "of opposition . . . against new heresies arising, or old corruptions to be reformed," even a wise mildness is not enough. He calls on prophetic voices to express power and "indignation" against deceptive seducers. He appeals to these prophets to authorize "a sanctifi'd bitternesse against the enemies of truth" (*CPW* I, p. 900).

Milton's defense of verbal anger can be understood in light of Aristotle's *Rhetoric*. Philip Fisher's *The Vehement Passions* helps to clarify why. Fisher argues that Aristotle treats anger as restoring worth to one whose honor has been slighted. Whereas our "therapeutic" culture treats anger as something to be controlled or understood, the classical model presents anger as a positive moral state (p. 172). Fisher notes that when Aristotle defines anger as a "desire" for a "conspicuous" revenge because of a slight, he emphasizes that the slight is "without justification" (*Rhetoric* 2. 2, 1378a; *Vehement Passions*, p. 178). A person's anger at unjust insult asserts her self-worth and restores justice. Fisher goes on to explain that because the slight is directed "against oneself or those near to one," the angry response to it must be distinguished from mere immediate and selfish reaction. Anger restores justice to important others in one's world (*Vehement Passions*, p. 173). Linking anger to concern for others, Milton's *Animadversions* asserts that Joseph Hall's insidious argument so misleads the innocent that they transport those "who love the soules of men" into "a well heated fervencie." The love of souls is the "dearest love, and stirs up the noblest jealousie" (*CPW* I, p. 663).

Milton draws on Aristotle's rhetoric of emotion to shame the leaders of the English Church for misleading the people. He expresses powerful indignation at the projects and strategies of his antagonists. *An Apology* denigrates the pamphlet writer who attacked Milton for being less than pure when young (*CPW* I, p. 895), and recommends using anger to teach ordinary people, "for when [fools] are punisht *the simple are thereby made wise*" (Proverbs 21: 11). Even when the proud cannot be taught, scorn teaches the simple that the arguments of the proud are empty. The text justifies invective against oppressors by the authority of the martyrs, who in the midst of their sufferings, "were not sparing to deride and scoffe their superstitious persecutors" (*CPW* I, p. 903).

But vehement speech is not always appropriate. Milton's approach to invention and persuasion requires that language be accommodated to the audience. Each kind of audience and each style possess distinct opportunities for rhetorical invention. Mildness can be efficacious with those who err unknowingly. And because truth may appear in unfamiliar shapes and people may mistake her, we need gentle discussion with them. *Areopagitica* makes discussion a moral duty:

> And if the men be erroneous what withholds us but our sloth, our self-will, and distrust in the right cause, that we doe not give them gentle meetings...that we debate not and examin the matter throughly with liberall and frequent audience; if not for their sakes, yet for our own? seeing that no man who hath tasted learning, but will confesse the many waies of profiting by those who not contented with stale receits are able to manage, and set forth new positions to the world. (*CPW* II, p. 567)

This passage makes clear that ethical shortcomings inhibit proper rhetoric. Sloth should not prevent the more well informed from conversing with the less so because the former can benefit from considering new positions. Debate and the examination of truth inform everyone because they lead to freshness of ideas. The reference to "stale receits" suggests that even what is true (in some sense) loses its grounds when it becomes a tired, received doctrine.

Paradise Lost exhibits both strong and mild speech. Abdiel uses angry confrontational speech, and Adam and Eve use mild speech. Both vehement and gentle speeches play a role in bringing to light Satan's sophisms and hypocrisy. The poem explores the tensions between the vehement and mild styles by representing confrontations between Satan and Abdiel. It discriminates between Satan, whose malice and intentional errors require strong refutation, and Adam and Eve, whose afflictions call for gentle speech. At the same time, it deepens our understanding of the psychology of deception and flattery by exploring the dissolution of Satan's self as he takes on the roles of demagogue, flatterer, and seducer.

Milton's early pamphlets argue that only vehement language can cut through deceptive, malicious rhetoric. The next section shows why Satan's seductive rhetoric requires Abdiel's strong speech. It moves from Satan as a parody of the Ciceronian orator, to his distorted rhetoric, to Milton's defense of biting rhetoric in his early prose, and finally to Abdiel's use of a similar rhetoric to defeat Satan in *Paradise Lost*. Abdiel's strong speech is then contrasted with Adam and Eve's mild speech. When both these types of speech are properly used, new and better arguments are discovered.

Satan as Flatterer and Adam and Eve as Counselors

Paradise Lost's Satan is a demagogic orator, a deceiver, a consummate actor, and seducer, the antithesis of the plain-spoken Abdiel. He manipulates the emotions of others by merging with their desires, disguising himself, and becoming polymorphous. He breaks down the boundaries between self and other, and, finally, between God, human, and beast. Satan is like a "Proteus who converts himself into everything he desires and takes everything as his material" (*Emperor of Men's Minds*, p. 111). Satan in *Paradise Lost* and error in Milton's prose are "slie" and "shifting" (*CPW* VII, p. 261). *Areopagitica* implies that error needs "policies . . . stratagems . . . shifts, and defences," that are unnecessary to truth, which is "strong" (II, pp. 563, 562). *Paradise Lost*'s Satan employs these shifts and stratagems.

Rather than stating his beliefs openly to Eve, Satan insinuates himself into her psyche. He relies on *actio*, persuading through the visual and auditory images he creates by means of his body. Just as he penetrates the snake, and his words and his own image make their way "into the heart of Eve" (*PL* IX. 550, 732). He lurks about like a tiger in order to overhear Adam and Eve's conversation and find information that he may use to deceive them. Similarly, Antonius in Cicero's *De oratore* claims that in order to explore the "mind of the judge" carefully, he would "scent out with all possible keenness their thoughts, judgements, anticipations and wishes," discerning the direction in which they may be led by the oration (*De oratore* 2. 6). Again, like a great Ciceronian orator, Satan

> with show of zeal and love
> To man, and indignation at his wrong,
> New part puts on, and as to passion mov'd,
> Fluctuates disturb'd . . .
>
> (*PL* IX. 665–8)

Satan identifies himself with the injustices he alleges were suffered by Adam and Eve under what he represents as their contemptuous treatment by God ("Satan as Orator," p. 141). However, the text unmasks Satan's sincerity when it refers to the "new part" he "puts on," for though the Ciceronian orator is a great performer, he must feel the emotions he expresses (see *De oratore* 2. 195). As an orator, lover, serpent, and friend to Eve, Satan's self becomes a mirror image of what he discerns her to be.

Such deceptive strategies prevent debate; through them *Paradise Lost* interprets the "policies" and "stratagems" that make error vicious (*CPW* II, p. 563). The text makes insinuation, accommodation, and flattery signs of error. These strategies entail not only faulty logic but also a psychological indirectness that discloses

Satan's fluctuating, incomplete self. Satan attempts to work his way into Eve's good graces when he calls her "fairest resemblance of thy Maker fair," implying that she is more like God than Adam is (PL IX. 538). He accommodates himself to her by appealing to her consciousness of others' praise: "thee all things living gaze on . . . and thy celestial beauty adore" (PL IX. 438–9). He takes the role of flatterer, and flatterers mold themselves to others. Plutarch argues that

> since the flatterer has no single foundation for his attitudes as a source of stability . . . and since he moulds and adjusts himself by reference to someone else, then he is not straightforward or single, but complex and multifaceted; he is always streaming from one place to another like water in the process of being poured. ("Flatterer'" 52A)

Satan ingratiates himself with Eve and rolls from one place to another as he leads her to the fruit (PL IX. 631).

Satan, though a snake, copies human speech and moves with Eve as she walks. But he also leads her into the trap of viewing the fruit. He is busy, always involved in other people's affairs like the envious man described by Francis Bacon, "a man that is busy and inquisitive is commonly envious . . . Neither can he that mindeth but his own business find much matter for envy. For envy is a gadding passion, and walketh the streets, and doth not keep home" (Essays, pp. 354–5). Satan rushes from hell to chaos to earth; he meddles in the lives and marriage of Adam and Eve.

Satan passes on to Eve the very rhetorical topoi that inflate his longing, envy, and sense of injury. As Nancy Hagglund Wood argues astutely, he uses Aristotle's topics of anger to make Eve feel slighted ("Satan as Orator," pp. 141–6). By showing that he, a mere serpent, has been elevated while Eve has been neglected, Satan implies that God has contempt for her. Satan also asserts that God instituted the prohibition to keep Eve low, and to elevate himself, "an insult Aristotle calls hubris" (The "Art" of Rhetoric 2. 2, 1378b, pp. 175, 174; "Satan as Orator," p. 142). Satan's words infuse a sense into Eve that her merit has been injured, that her desire for godhead has been blocked by God's contempt for and rivalry with her.

Vehement Rhetoric

Milton's early prose argues that such indirect and deceptive rhetoric can only be confronted by angry vehemence. It uses anger to uncover and attack pernicious assumptions in the arguments of opponents. Mild speech does not penetrate to the error and bad faith that underlie slippery persuasions, but vehemence shocks in two senses; it uncovers fissures in deceptive approaches and it brings to light the moral ugliness hidden under euphemistic language. This approach to vehemence, articulated in Animadversions and An Apology, and exemplified in later prose such as

The Readie and Easie Way to Establish a Free Commonwealth (1660), provides a model in terms of which we can understand Abdiel's spirited attack on Satan.

Animadversions defends truth by dissecting what it claims are the sleights and wily stratagems of its opponent, Joseph Hall, teaching readers to recognize the argumentative measures by means of which this opponent befuddles them and distracts them from important issues. Milton wrathfully uncovers the deceptiveness of his opponents' stratagems by opening their methods to plain view. Epistemological and rhetorical concerns lie at the center of his anger. He accuses Hall of enclosing the reader "insensibly within" the ambush "of worst errors." The metaphor of the ambush suggests that Hall's arguments leave no way out to the reader. Milton also claims that Hall confuses his readers, "with a slye shuffle of counterfeit principles chopping and changing till hee have glean'd all the good ones out of their minds." Clever logical moves and appeals to principle shift and cut short better arguments until the readers have forgotten the issues they cared about. Focusing their attentions, for example, on the need for hierarchy in running a church, Hall, Milton claims, distracts his readers from their need to attend to what is right in conscience. "Counterfeit principles" come to the fore. His opponent "leaves [his readers] at last" in "a desperate stupidity," befuddled by these principles (*CPW* I, p. 663).

Milton turns invective against misleading arguments and toward the defense of his central values. He also attacks what he views as the disingenuousness of Hall's arguments. He opposes himself to deceit, not just to falsehood. But the deceit may or may not be consciously intended, and for this reason Milton's strictures have appeared unfair to many. But he believes he is justified in turning his ire against the deception latent in certain *ways* of thinking. For example, when his opponent defends his preface on the grounds that it was a fair complaint against the number of libels that he believes he found in the previous pamphlet (*CPW* I, p. 667), Milton sees an allusion to censorship and quickly exposes the "inside nakedness" of his opponent, whom he accuses of advocating censorship to suppress opinions that disagree with his own.

Paradise Lost represents Abdiel as adopting a similar approach, using conflict to test truth. Abdiel brings out Satan's misleading assumptions and challenges his ideas. For example, in answer to Satan's charge that it is "unjust to bind with laws the free," Abdiel asks, "Shalt thou give the law to God ... who made/Thee what thou art?" (*PL* V. 819, 823–4). He changes the grounds of the dispute and recontextualizes Satan's accusation. He also reverses the relation Satan asserts between the power of the questioner (Satan) and of the questioned (God), asserting God's supremacy as creator. Even more interestingly, he rejects the implications of the argument that in elevating the Son, God demoted the other angels and made them pay "knee-tribute" (*PL* V. 782).

Abdiel expresses his outrage against the idea that God would offend angelic dignity. Instead, Abdiel insists "of our dignity/How provident he is" (*PL* V. 827–8).

Far from wanting to make the angels less, God wants to "to exalt our happy state" (V. 829–30). Abdiel maintains that God originally created the angels and "crown'd them with glory" (V. 839), and when the Son is "reduc't" to the status of angel, the whole angelic host becomes elevated and glorified (V. 843–5). In short, the angelic host is honored when the Son becomes one of them. Satan has egregiously insulted God and the Son; he has interpreted them to be so tyrannical and hungry for power that he should, Abdiel tells him, hasten to appease their just anger (PL V. 846–7). In the Miltonic and Aristotelian rhetorical framework, the failure of God and the Son to feel anger in this context would be for each to care little about his own self-esteem or for the worth of the other.

Abdiel does not have the last word, however. Interestingly, Satan becomes the vehement respondent as he struggles against the bold statements of Abdiel. He brings into the open assumptions he regards as invidious in Abdiel's speech. To the point that God created them, Satan derisively argues that there is no evidence that they were created. Instead they are "self-begot," a momentous statement whose implications go beyond what I can analyze here (PL V. 860). Satan asserts the angels' power to test their strength, using the concept of heroic combat: "Our puissance is our own, our own right hand / Shall teach us highest deeds, by proof to try / Who is our equal" (PL V. 864–6). Attempting to retain the stature appropriate to Homeric heroes who define status through acts of prowess, Satan rejects the entire framework of honor proposed by Abdiel. Abdiel registers this rejection when he calls Satan "alienate from God," a "Spirit accurst," and "Forsak'n of all good," and leaves him to the thunder of God (V. 877–8).

Paradise Lost links Abdiel's anger to constancy and honest speech, distinguishing them from the tyrant's deception and the sycophant's flattery. Anger is an emotion of the resistant intellect and heart. Abdiel "unmov'd,/Unshak'n, unseduc'd, unter-rifi'd" by the scorn of Satan and his followers, exhibits "retorted scorn" as he turns his back "on those proud tow'rs to swift destruction doom'd" (PL V. 898–9, 904–7). The adjective "unshak'n" and the heroic simile underscore the strength and durability of emotions that defend honor by energizing struggle.

Milton's The Doctrine & Discipline of Divorce (1644) similarly celebrates steadfast independence, drawing attention to the author's own courage in being "the sole advocate of a discount'nanc't truth; a high enterprise Lords and Commons, a high enterprise and a hard" (CPW II, p. 224). God's praise of Abdiel resonates with this characterization:

> Servant of God, well done, well hast thou fought
> The better fight, who single hast maintain'd
> Against revolted multitudes the cause
> Of truth, in word mightier than they in arms.
>
> (PL VI. 29–32)

The individual's defense of truth against the multitudes shows the greatest heroic constancy and force. Similarly, *Areopagitica* famously interconnects the virtues of discernment and abstention:

> He that can apprehend and consider vice with all her baits and seeming pleasures, and yet abstain, and yet distinguish, and yet prefer that which is truly better, he is the true warfaring Christian ... Assuredly we bring not innocence into the world, we bring impurity much rather: that which purifies us is triall, and triall is by what is contrary. (*CPW* II, p. 515)

Apprehending and considering, abstaining and distinguishing are activities that create a pause in the action sufficient to allow discovery of "that which is truly better."

Abdiel's stand against sophistry and his strong speech cut through Satan's deceptiveness, but not all error can best be met with vehement speech. Mild speech is more efficacious when a person errs innocently. For example, when a distraught Eve confesses a disturbing dream to Adam in which Satan tempts her to eat of the fruit, Adam responds with in the gentle mode of counsel. He does not inveigh against her with harsh language, but bids her to be of good cheer, leaving nothing unsaid which might mitigate her pain (*PL* V. 95–106). Adam "cheer'd" his spouse, and uses his reason to explain how fancy operates in dreams in ways that leave the dreamer guiltless. Instead of attacking Eve, Adam finds commonality between them, saying that the trouble reflected in her thoughts "affects me equally" (*PL* V. 97). He comforts her and tells her to "be not sad." Evil may come and go ... and "leave no spot or blame behind" (V. 116–18). Using mild speech he recalls her thoughts from trouble to more "cheerful and serene" looks and employments (V. 123–4).

Reciprocally, when Adam is caught in an endless series of despairing, self-destructive emotions, Eve intervenes gently to bring him back to himself. Reinterpreting the injunction to "Delightfully, increase and multiply," as now implying death, Adam asks what can he multiply but "curses on my head" (X. 729–31). He tosses and turns various ideas of death, each more horrible than the last. His dilemma, and the remedy for it, can be understood in light of Francis Bacon's essay "Of friendship" (see above Chapter 5, pp. 79–82). Whereas classical and Renaissance models of ideal friendship praise the friend who responds to a partner's lack of virtue with sharp, frank speech, Bacon, while recognizing the need for honest counsel, ranks sympathetic listening as the first fruit of friendship. He praises the "true friend" as one "to whom you may impart griefs, joys, fears ... and whatsoever lieth upon the heart." And he asserts, "it is a mere and miserable solitude to want true friends; without which the world is a wilderness ("Of friendship," *Essays*, p. 391). Adam falls into this solitary wilderness after eating the apple and, in his new state, his circling anger and despair turn back on themselves. He finds no ease to his relentless thoughts until Eve approaches. She offers "soft words to his fierce passion," but he is unable to accept them. Instead he berates her with bitter misogynist terms. Undeterred, she supplicates him, asking forgiveness and seeking once again to benefit from his "gentle looks" (X. 918). Her humility and request for aid and counsel lead to his change of heart as he commiserates with her.

Adam's acceptance and forgiveness of Eve's imperfection provides the occasion for mild conversation between them. During this conversation, Eve discloses that she, like Adam, experiences the despair of the fallen state. She believes that it may be better not to procreate and to commit suicide. She benefits from Adam's counsel once he regains his self-respect, and he, once his relation to her is re-established, becomes capable of new interpretations of events and, hence, of very different emotions from those he experienced in the intense solitude of his lamentations. The shift in his attitude toward the ideas of cursed procreation and suicide dramatizes what it means to be restored to Eve's society. Earlier, Adam's wish for death leads only to the despair that he cannot die, whereas when Eve voices the intention to die, his "more attentive mind" raises better hopes. Instead of an imagination that proliferates ever more terrible visions of deathless misery, he counsels a "safer resolution . . . calling to mind with heed / Part of our sentence" (X. 1029–30), that Eve's seed shall bruise Satan's head. Memory of specific promises replaces the global terror under a divine voice that earlier Adam imagines "would thunder in my ears." Milton represents him as using language similar to Aristotle's in the *Rhetoric* and reiterated by Juan Luis Vives, and Thomas Hobbes, who wrote about rhetoric in the sixteenth and seventeenth centuries. These writers comment that images of imminent destruction create much fear, whereas images of far distant or mild threats create little fear. Instead of the frightening images of divine anger he imagined in his solitary state, Adam now remembers specifically "with what mild and gracious temper he [God] both heard and judg'd / Without wrath or reviling" (X. 1046–8). Adam's judgments become more empirical, more sane, and more hopeful, as he remembers how God providently supplied clothes for their nakedness. Adam infers from this action that God will also teach them how to shun the inclement seasons, to use fire, and to remedy the evils that beset them.

By meeting together in mild discourse, Adam and Eve become more resourceful at thinking of better possibilities for the future. Having joined together against a common foe instead of attacking one another, they discover a new basis for marriage. This new community provides the grounds for more inventive delibera-tive activity. Although the fall has limited their range of action, their inventiveness in considering their new circumstances allows them to find new ways to act. Whereas the polemical rhetoric of Abdiel, God, and the Son seeks to overcome the confusion and willfulness of an audience, Adam and Eve's mild rhetorical capacities help them see their situations and difficulties from new points of view.

Though they are exiled from Eden at the end, *Paradise Lost* insists that "The world was all before them, where to choose/Their place of rest," lines that make the end of the poem a new beginning (XII. 646–7). Mutual company, providence, and a capacity for a deliberation informed by rhetoric offer grounds for the choices that *Paradise Lost* envisions as at the center of human, cosmic, and religious transformations.

Chapter 7

Prudence and Eloquence in Jane Austen's *Persuasion*

Anne Elliot and Captain Wentworth, characters in Jane Austen's *Persuasion*, use rhetoric to found marriage as a discursive community in which ends are shared and actions deliberated. But they achieve this community only after Anne becomes able to use eloquence and Wentworth is able to listen to it. Their communication cannot be taken for granted. Unlike the works analyzed previously in this volume, Jane Austen's *Persuasion* (1818) explores multiple social groups with different, often conflicting, beliefs and ends. Most of the characters are trapped in their discursive worlds, at the beginning, Anne is not heard at all, and Wentworth cannot hear. The novel explores the obstacles and opportunities that difference creates for the characters. The aristocrats of Kellynch Hall, the heroine's home, value rank and personal attractiveness above everything else; at Uppercross the focus is on the happiness of the family; and in the navy effectiveness and honor are paramount. The different ends of these "commonwealths," as Austen calls them, are accompanied by differences in the topics that animate conversations and in what counts as persuasive. The novel challenges its characters to negotiate these differences.

If marriage and friendship serve as sites of counsel in *Paradise Lost*, the "social commonwealth" provides the context for communication in *Persuasion*. For, as the heroine Anne Elliot reflects, "every little social commonwealth...dictates[s] its own matter of discourse." Only within such a community can a person's words be heard and understood. The novel educates Anne and its readers in the "art of knowing our own nothingness beyond our own circle" (ch. 6, p. 41). Within her family at Kellynch Hall, Anne's "word had no weight; her convenience was always to give way; – she was only Anne" (ch. 1, p. 7). But by the end of the novel, her speech pierces Wentworth's soul (ch. 23, p. 222; *Some Words*, p. 246). This change has required Anne's discovery of a new social and discursive context and her rhetorical skill in defining a new community with an equal. Anne changes from being a "nobody" with her family, who always gives way, to an eloquent, passionate orator on the subject of her feelings and beliefs (*Rethinking*, p. 151) and an assertive, intelligent, and vigorous leader. She is most able to deliberate, to judge, and to find means of persuasion in a contingent, changing world. But at the beginning she is rarely consulted and her family does not attend to her words.

Persuasion is one of five novels by Austen that criticize "female confinement" and that influenced modern feminist novelistic protests against the domestic confinement of women ("Virago," pp. 140–65). At the beginning, the novel represents the wasting of a woman who is imprisoned within a trivial and unsympathetic family and who, though mature, is unable to achieve fully adult autonomous action. She makes thankless efforts to be useful to relatives among whom she is "nobody" (*Persuasion*, ch. 1, p. 7). Although her "elegance of mind and sweetness of character... must have placed her high with any people of real understanding," she is useless and uninteresting to those around her (ibid.).

But Anne breaks out of the defining social milieu of her family by recognizing the differences within the rhetorical communities in which she lives. As James L. Kastely argues in an excellent chapter on rhetoric in *Persuasion*, "Anne, who has been forced to look at communal life from both the margin and the outside, can appreciate the truth that a self is relative to membership in a discursive community" (*Rethinking*, p. 154). My chapter analyzes the rhetorical ends that shape each community and Anne's rhetorical inventiveness in finding agency within the limits of each. As she discovers a more capacious commonwealth, she finds opportunities to act and be heard. Her rhetorical skills and character strengthen, become more intelligent, and finally blossom. Austen draws on her contemporary Hugh Blair (influenced by Cicero and Quinitilian) and on Shaftesbury (influenced by Aristotle) to represent this process. By the end, Anne forges her own rhetorical community with a man who is her equal (Captain Wentworth) (*Rethinking*, p. 154).

Austen differs from her predecessors in this volume by construing rhetorical communities as plural. Whereas Aristotle, Cicero, and the others base rhetorical arguments on the beliefs of a single polis, republic, or political commonwealth, Austen traces the different ends and discourses that shape a diversity of social milieux in early nineteenth-century England. Anne Elliot distinguishes herself from other characters in the novel by recognizing this plurality. She acknowledges it "to be very fitting, that every little social commonwealth should dictate it own matters of discourse; and hoped, ere long, to become a not unworthy member of the one she was now transplanted into" (i.e., the families at Uppercross) (*Persuasion*, ch. 6, p. 41). Anne's practical wisdom and ability to use language to enlarge her possibilities for action makes her a discerning member of her communities. But her eloquence only gradually brings her into the full independence and agency she deserves and desires.

Eloquence in the novel must be understood in the fullest Ciceronian sense. Eloquence, as Blair's *Lectures on Rhetoric and Belles Lettres* (1819) phrases it, is not "a certain trick of speech; the art of varnishing weak arguments plausibly; or of speaking, so as to please and tickle the ear." Instead, in his words, "to be truly eloquent, is to speak to the purpose . . . to influence conduct, and persuade to action" (p. 234). Anne always speaks to the purpose, even when no one listens to her. Her few words at her home, Kellynch Hall, define the recognition that the English ought to give to the navy: "The navy . . . who have done so much for us, have at least an equal claim with any other set of men, for all the comforts and all the privileges which any home can give" (*Persuasion*, ch. 3, p. 20). She characterizes exactly the office and experiences of Admiral Croft, the prospective tenant of Kellynch: "He is rear admiral of the white. He was in the Trafalgar action, and has been in the East Indies since" (p. 22). But eloquence requires more than purposeful, accurate speech. Blair continues, "the power of eloquence chiefly appears when it is employed to influence conduct, and persuade to action" (*Lectures on Rhetoric*, p. 234). It is Anne's fate not to be heeded. To Anne's praise of the navy, her father raises "two strong ground of objection . . . First, as being the means of bringing of persons of obscure birth into undue distinction" and secondly, because "a sailor grows old sooner than any other man" (*Persuasion*, ch. 3, p. 20). A member of the hereditary aristocracy, Sir Walter cannot bear the idea of social mobility and any claim on his gratitude for the services of those who have risen by their own achievements must fall on deaf ears.

Anne cannot be heard because the social and rhetorical world of her father and sister is organized around ends and values that she does not embrace. Austen's skill in defining these ends and values can be understood in terms of the classical (Aristotelian and Ciceronian) emphasis on common beliefs as the premises for rhetorical arguments. Aristotle comments that rhetoric examines "what seems true to people of a certain sort" (*On Rhetoric* 1. 2, 1356b, p. 41), and he comments that dialectic depends on "generally accepted opinions" (*Topics* 1. 1, 100a18). Austen complicates this view when she represents the ends and *topoi* that define a rhetorical community as varying from one discursive commonwealth to another.

Sir Walter Elliot, Anne's father, and Elizabeth, her sister, are guided by the ends of the older order of landed property owners. Sir Walter is a baronet, the lowest rank of the aristocracy, but one on which he prides himself. He, as the first line of the novel describes him, "was a man who, for his own amusement, never took up any book but the Baronetage . . . he could read his own history with an interest which never failed," and his favorite book was always opened to: "Elliot of Kellynch-Hall" (*Persuasion*, ch. 1, p. 5).

Aside from reading in his favorite book, he enjoys perusing his own reflection in his numerous mirrors. For "he considered the blessing of beauty as inferior only to the blessing of a baronetcy; and the Sir Walter Elliot, who united these gifts, was the constant object of his warmest respect and devotion" (p. 6). Because his rhetorical world is defined by the values of good looks and rank, he cannot accept Anne's praise of the navy. He is indignant that a man "whose father we all know to have been a country curate, without bread to eat" once took precedence over him. The man's appearance makes the insult worse, his face being "the colour of mahogany... all lines and wrinkles" (ch. 3, p. 20). Austen reserves her most caustic satire for Sir Walter, Elizabeth, and their aristocratic relatives.

Because she cannot subscribe to the ideas of good that her family embraces, Anne, though prudent, remains unheard and little valued. Whereas Mrs Clay, an ambitious flatterer, is deemed to be invaluable by Sir Walter and Elizabeth, Anne is perceived as of being of no use. Elizabeth comments that Anne had better stay at Uppercross with her other sister Mary "for nobody will want her in Bath." Anne is "rejected as no good at all," and she is "no good" in light of the beliefs and values of her family (ch. 55, pp. 32–3). Not embracing their vanity and snobbery, she cannot influence their conduct. Though they desperately need her prudent advice, because Sir Walter faces a serious financial crisis, they cannot be persuaded by her but only manipulated rhetorically by their lawyer Mr Shepherd.

Anne's rhetoric fails for a second reason that can be illuminated by looking at Blair's book on rhetoric. Having outlined two functions of eloquence, namely to speak to the purpose while influencing conduct and persuading to action and to inform, to instruct, to convince (something Anne can do with a rational person such as her friend Lady Russell), Blair emphasizes a "third, and still higher degree of eloquence," It is one "wherein... we are not only convinced, but are interested, agitated and carried along with the speaker... We enter into all his emotions; we love, we detest, we resent, according as he inspires us; and are prompted to resolve, or to act, with vigour and warmth" (*Lectures on Rhetoric*, p. 236). This highest kind of Ciceronian eloquence requires passion and is nourished by a liberty that, according to Longinus but in Blair's words, "animates the spirit, and invigorates the hopes of men." Blair psychologizes Ciceronian rhetoric (as represented also in Quintilian), painting a picture of faculties that are invigorated and warmed by imagination. But the animation and genius that Blair envisions as the fount of eloquence eludes Anne through much of the novel. For "her bloom had vanished early" and "she was faded and thin" (*Persuasion*, ch. 1, p. 7). Anne lost her bloom after a failed courtship with Captain Wentworth, who, when he sees her seven years later, is reported to have found her "so altered that he should not have known her again." For, Anne believes, "the years... had destroyed her youth and bloom" (ch. 7, p. 57). She is "silent," and "pensive," belonging to an elegiac landscape (ch. 13, p. 115). But her eloquence has not utterly died for, although she was persuaded seven years ago by the prudent advice of her friend, Lady Russell, to give up Captain Wentworth (who had no fortune), now "how eloquent could Anne Elliot have been, – how eloquent, at least were her wishes on the side of early warm attachment, and a cheerful confidence in futurity" (ch. 4, p. 29). How eloquent she *might* have been, but *is not* because Captain Wentworth does not wish to hear her and because her own vitality has faded, depriving her of the life and energy that inspires ardent speech.

Anne's case is not hopeless, however, because she is granted the opportunity to move beyond the confines of those for whom she is nobody and not worth consulting. Her entrance into a second rhetorical commonwealth gives her perspective and awareness that reconfigure her relation to discourse. The opportunity to live in two communities introduces her to the phenomenon of rhetorical plurality, and she learns a critical edge and sees an opportunity for change that provides a way out of her isolation.

In order to grasp the importance of her new insight, we need to recognize that her blight and loss of hope at her abandonment of her engagement with the only person with whom she could speak fully and freely took place because she confused two modes of discourse about what it means to be practically wise. She had confused practical wisdom with a prudence founded upon an interest in rank and property, even though she herself did not value the latter. She had loved a man who was without wealth or place but "full of life and ardour," warm-hearted, active, and effective (ch. 4, p. 27). But her old friend, Lady Russell, abhorred boldness and feared for Anne's welfare. Anne, respecting her as a guardian, was persuaded by her advice. Hence, the novel's interest in the question of when and under what circumstances one ought to be persuaded.

But behind Lady Russell's advice lies the difference between her discursive commonwealths and Anne's. In the social and rhetorical worlds of inherited property, a man lacking rank with chancy prospects for achieving wealth was not esteemed to be a good candidate for marriage. But the novel also focuses on a new economic order that depends on the individual action and risk-taking that produce social mobility (*Rethinking*, pp. 146–7; Tanner, *Jane Austen*, p. 228). As Kastely puts it, "what made one a man was the ability to rise to and master the fluctuations of fortune (*Rethinking*, pp. 146–7). Captain Wentworth obtains a ship and "excels in his profession" of pursuing French ships and confiscating the goods of pirates (*Persuasion*, "Introduction," p. 26). He wins a fortune and has returned to England ready to marry.

Excellence in this sphere depends on people's ability to accept the reality of their circumstances and shape them into the best outcomes possible. So Mrs Croft, Captain Wentworth's sister, scolds him for not wanting a woman on board his ship: "women may be as comfortable on board, as in the best house in England" (*Persuasion*, ch. 8, p. 64). She rejects the idea that women should be treated as fine ladies: "But I hate to hear you talking so, like a fine gentleman, and as if women were all fine ladies, instead of rational creatures. We none of us expect to be in smooth water all our days" (p. 65). The new order calls for action that is rational and effective. For example, Captain Harville, although he is lame, is amply endowed with the practical abilities that define those who live by their own efforts. His house shows the "the ingenious contrivances and nice arrangements . . . to turn the actual space to the best possible account" (ch. 11, p. 92; *Some Words*, p. 284). Practical inventiveness, the ability to turn limited circumstances into good arrangements, characterize self-made men and women in the professional class.

Whereas the rhetoric of the landed aristocracy is based on the perceived goods of title, reputation, and personal beauty, the rhetoric of those who achieve excellence in a profession by their own efforts is based on a belief in the importance of rationality, inventiveness, and realism. As a young woman Anne grew up with the former but was drawn to the latter. But she was not very clear in her own mind about the differences and, as a result, she allowed herself to be persuaded by Lady Russell that her engagement with Captain Wentworth was imprudent and wrong. The novel tells the story of her education into different social and rhetorical worlds.

In order to understand Anne's choice to renounce her engagement even though she did not agree with her father about the importance of wealth and rank, we need to understand that the subculture of the aristocracy is represented in the novel as having two modes of discourse, one based on precedence alone and the other founded on an ethics of nobility. Anne and Lady Russell share an ethical language that requires more from people than mere adherence to the proprieties of status. When Lady Russell, unlike the Elliots, consults Anne about the need for the family to reduce their expenses, Anne's every emendation of her friend's suggestion "had been on the side of honesty against importance." Lady Russell is a good, right-thinking woman who aligns the "true dignity of Sir Walter Elliot" with his being "a man of principle," who must support the "character of an honest man" (ch. 2, p. 13). "Honesty" and "dignity" refer, according to the OED, to "honourable position or estate; high rank; respectability" and "the quality of being worthy or honourable." The words go back to the humanists and to the Ciceronian praise of *honestas* (virtue or the honorable) and *dignitas* (worth, self-respect, honor). Anne and Lady Russell speak in terms that define nobility not just by rank, but also by what is ethically good. Sir Walter and Elizabeth, by contrast, have reduced the full range of aristocratic discourse to the concern for precedence and reputation.

Agreeing with Lady Russell as she does about duty, Anne is persuaded by her that her engagement to Captain Wentworth is "wrong," "improper," and "not deserving success." Wanting to be "prudent" she gives up the engagement for Captain Wentworth's sake. But she does not notice that, in being prudent, Lady Russell believes that there is "a great deal . . . due to the feelings of the gentleman," meaning by "gentleman" a man of property and "the head of a house" (ch. 2, p. 13). She is "as solicitous for the credit of the family, as aristocratic in her ideas of what was due them, as any body of sense and honesty could well be." Lady Russell "had prejudices on the side of ancestry" and "a value for rank and consequence" (p. 12). In other words, she values rank in a way Anne does not. When Captain Wentworth appeared, without wealth or title and yet confident that "he should soon have a ship, and soon be on a station that would lead to every thing he wanted" (ch. 4, p. 27), Lady Russell was horrified. She had no taste for boldness, confidence, and action, and expects Anne to marry a man of property. Anne does not think it is right to reject the advice of the woman who has befriended her after the death of her own mother, but she does not understand fully the implications of her choice. Her interactions with Lady Dalrymple and Mr Elliot bring home to her the degree to which she does not value rank or landed property. The novel tells the story of how Anne clarifies for herself the kind of community she wishes to join and to create.

In order to choose a community, Anne needs to become more self-consciously aware of the differences between groups. Her trip from Kellynch to Uppercross, the home of her other sister Mary, affords her this opportunity. It brings home to her that "a removal from one set of people to another, though at a distance of only three miles, will often include a total change of conversation, opinion, and idea" (ch. 6, p. 40). Again, if Aristotle and Cicero emphasize that rhetoric depends on common opinions, Anne witnesses the variety of opinions that differentiate social groups.

Each commonwealth absorbs the attention of its inhabitants in its concerns and subjects. Before Anne arrived at Uppercross, her heart had been "full of the subject" which had been "completely occupying" Lady Russell, herself, her father, and Elizabeth, namely how her family could move to Bath with something like honor and dignity (however differently defined by the two groups) (ch. 6, p. 40). But she finds that the inhabitants of Uppercross have little interest in the subject. Anne does not mourn their lack of interest; indeed, she "acknowledged it to be very fitting that every little social commonwealth should dictate its own matters of discourse; and hoped, ere long, to become a not unworthy member of the one which she was now translated into." She chooses "to clothe her imagination, her memory, and all her ideas in as much of Uppercross as possible" (ch. 6, p. 41). This mental clothing proves to be worthwhile because Uppercross offers her more opportunity for action and persuasion than Kellynch did. People listen to her and seek her aid. She can adopt the goals and ideals of Uppercross as her own, whereas she could not respect or embrace the egoism and snobbery of her family. Indeed, because the commonwealth of Uppercross revolves around the welfare of the family members and especially of the children, Anne finds employment and interest there.

The inhabitants of Uppercross aim at the ends of mutual affection, happiness, and, for the young girls, dancing and young men. Anne shares these aims, in a sense, but the fact that she is not the daughter of the Musgroves and that she can openly love no young man (for she must love Captain Wentworth in silence) deprives her of the opportunities for mutual affection. Yet she aims to be as happy as possible in the situation. The fact that she cannot be fully happy illuminates the full relationship with another that a speaker and member of a discursive community needs to have in order to achieve eloquence. What Anne lacks can be understood if we examine Austen's deployments of the *topoi* "happiness," and "use" or "usefulness." Anne achieves moderate happiness by being useful, but her happiness is blunted when others use her without esteeming her. She serves their ends but is not valued for her own ends or for herself. She lacks friendship understood as a relationship of reciprocity and mutuality.

Anne is eloquent at Uppercross insofar as she can persuade others to do what is practically wise. Austen uses the strategy exemplified in Aristotelian topics that link opposite terms into a mean, probably influenced by Shaftesbury, whose 1711 work recast "the copious and elastic discriminations of which Aristotle had been the discoverer" into an English mold ("Jane Austen," pp. 182–3; *Characteristicks*, pp. 232–7, 252–74). Gilbert Ryle argues for Aristotle's doctrine of the mean from the *Nicomachean Ethics* as the precursor to Austen's use of opposite terms to describe and judge characters, virtues, and faults ("Jane Austen," pp. 183–4). But Aristotle and Cicero's emphasis (in *On Duties*) on using opposite topics had also been reiterated, extended, and given a rhetorical interpretation by the humanists. Drawing on these influences, Austen represents her characters as too persuadable or not persuadable enough, and Captain Wentworth discovers that Anne's "character" maintains "the loveliest medium of fortitude and gentleness" (ch. 23, p. 226). He learns to "distinguish between the steadiness of principle and the obstinacy of self-will, between the daring of heedlessness and the resolution of a collected mind," by seeing the near-fatal consequences of Louisa's obstinacy and the restorative power of Anne's resolution (p. 227).

Austen's skills in using opposed topics are dramatized by showing how she makes the terms meaningful in relation to particular circumstances rather than falling into skepticism. More than a century and a half before *Persuasion* was published in 1817, Thomas Hobbes introduces a skeptical note into his analysis of the evaluation of praiseworthy and blameworthy qualities through the use of opposite terms. He uses the term "glory" to show how subjective judgments of virtue and vice can be. Hobbes qualifies glory by writing that "this passion, of them whom it displeaseth, is called *pride*; but them whom it *pleaseth*, it is termed a just valuation of himself" ("Human nature," pp. 40–1). Drawing on analysis of style from Aristotle's *Rhetoric* (3. 2, 1405b), Hobbes dramatizes how the choice of words colors judgment about a thing and argues that names depend arbitrarily on what pleases or displeases the person using them. This skepticism undermines social agreement about what factors appropriately discriminate glory from vainglory.

Austen's narrator and characters clarify terms that might otherwise seem arbitrary by using them to judge particular situations. Austen's goal is not to teach that readers should aim, for example, at the mean between the extremes of stubbornness and weak-mindedness, but to discern when and how to exhibit the virtues of constancy and flexibility. Captain Wentworth errs with regard to Anne when he regards her as weak-minded and with regard to Louisa when he admires her for her apparent firmness. After Lousia's accident, which occurs because of her unwillingness to listen to Captain Wentworth, Anne muses that universal judgments about the desirability of certain qualities are probably mistaken. She "wondered whether it ever occurred to him now, to question the justness of his own previous opinion as to the universal felicity and advantages of firmness of character; and whether it might not strike him, that, like all other qualities of the mind, it should have its proportions and limits. She thought it could scarcely escape him to feel, that a persuadable temper might sometimes be as much in favour of happiness, as a very resolute character" (*Persuasion*, ch. 12, p. 108). Anne does not deal in universals independent of fact, but like other rhetoricians before her, uses ambiguous words to sort through probable truths. She uses terms to explore particular cases and to articulate judgments about them.

However, Austen complicates the challenges of skepticism by examining the ambiguity that arises from the way different social groups use the same word. Whereas Hobbes finds the usage of terms like "pride" and "just valuation of oneself" to be arbitrary because it depends on what pleases or displeases an individual, Austen tests the social bases of such pleasure and displeasure. Her novel inquires into words such as "gentleman" by testing socially defined differences in their meanings in relation to different kinds of behavior. Clashes in the meanings of the word "gentleman," for example, become apparent in an interchange between Anne, the lawyer Mr Shepherd, and her father. Mr Shepherd describes a gentleman whose name he cannot remember, and Sir Walter cannot recall any such person. Finally, Anne responds in her brief, accurate fashion: "You mean Mr Wentworth, I suppose." Her father replies "Wentworth? Oh! Ay, – Mr. Wentworth, the curate of Monkford. You misled me by the term *gentleman*. I thought you were speaking of some man of property: Mr. Wentworth was nobody" (ch. 3, p. 24). According to Sir Walter, only those who appear in his favorite book or possess landed property can be "gentlemen" or "somebodies." Anne, on the other hand, judges that Captain Harville, a lame man but an excellent officer who lives rather poorly at Lyme, "was a perfect gentleman, unaffected, warm and obliging." His being "kindly hospitable" to the friends of his friend, Captain Wentworth, shows him in Anne's eyes to be a gentleman *par excellence*, far superior to the Mr Elliot who appears later, a person whose manners are superb but whose heart is hollow (ch. 11, p. 91).

Analogously, the episode at Uppercross makes use of ambiguities in the ideas of "usefulness" and "happiness" that show Uppercross must be for Anne a transitional discursive world that leads her closer to eloquence without allowing her to speak fully in her own voice. Anne goes there because Mary is feeling unwell. Mary thinks "a great deal of her own complaints" (being a self-centered Elliot), and very little of Anne's preferences (ch. 5, p. 32). Anne is there to help Mary fulfill her desires.

At Uppercross, Anne's rhetorical skills are turned to the purposes of others. She is "too much in the secret of the complaints" of each person so that Charles, her brother-in-law, wishes she would tell Mary not to fancy herself ill whereas Mary complains that if she were dying, Charles would think nothing was the matter with her (ch. 6, p. 42). From their points of view, Anne's job is to persuade each to follow the wishes of the others. Anne finds only a small space for agency. She cannot "set all these matters to rights," so she "listen[s] patiently, soften[s] every grievance, and excuse[s] each to the other" (p. 44).

Even in her musical performances at Uppercross, Anne finds herself to be useful to the purposes of others but not valued for her own taste. She plays well, better than either of the Musgrove girls (the sisters of Mary's husband, Charles), but "having...no fond parents to sit by and fancy themselves delighted, her performance was little thought of, only out of civility, or to refresh the others...She had never...since the loss of her dear mother, known the happiness of being listened to, or encouraged by any just appreciation or real taste" (p. 44). Anne is not heard fully at Uppercross any more than she is at Kellynch. But Anne takes pleasure in the Musgroves' "fond partiality for their own daughters' performance" (p. 44), and, because the girls "were wild for dancing...Anne...played country dances to them by the hour together" (p. 45). She does so with good humor, until the girls dance with Captain Wentworth and she finds the tears filling her eyes, for, of course, she would rather be dancing with him herself.

If Anne creates a place for herself at Uppercross by being useful, Charles and Mary pride themselves on being useless and the interchange between them explores the difficulties and opportunities presented by the rhetorical topics "useful" and "useless." Certainly, Anne's usefulness does not seem very desirable, even though it is better than nothing. But uselessness involves problems as well. For example, when Charles and Mary's child becomes ill, someone must stay home from a party at the Musgroves to take care of him. As the narrator renders Charles's thoughts in free indirect discourse, it is a "female case" and "it would be highly absurd in him, who could be of no use at home, to shut himself up. His father very much wished him to meet Captain Wentworth" (ch. 7, p. 52). Mary complains that "because I am the poor mother, I am not to be allowed to stir," and, defending her right to go to the party, asserts, "I am more unfit than any body else to be about the child...I have not nerves for the sort of thing" (p. 53). Pleasure and the fulfillment of desires precede the value of usefulness. Anne expresses her willingness to help. And then "They were gone, she hoped, to be happy, however oddly constructed such happiness might seem" (pp. 54–5). Anne's use of the word "happy" and her implied criticism suggests a connection between usefulness and happiness, but she also notes the strengths and weaknesses in her own ability to unite the two: "She knew herself to be of the first utility to the child; and what was it to her, if Frederick Wentworth were only a half a mile distant, making himself agreeable to others!" (p. 55). Even if she feels satisfaction from being useful, as long as her more ardent wish cannot be satisfied, her happiness is limited. The novel makes a more subtle point too. As long as the others in her circle do not share her desires and pleasures, she will be only a partial member of the community. For she subordinates her energies and persuasive abilities to helping others pursue their ends without being fully animated by those ends herself, except in her genuine concern for the child and for the welfare of others.

A romantic conclusion to the novel that gives Anne Captain Wentworth could not by itself have solved the problem that Austen poses. If Anne had married Wentworth without solving the problem of the disjunction between her aims and those of others, she still would have been useful without being fully happy. Yet happiness requires appropriate usefulness. Anne experiences this conjunction when she goes to Lyme and enters into a new relationship with Captain Wentworth. Lyme represents a transition between rhetoric as an instrument of usefulness to others and rhetoric as full eloquence. Three things happen at Lyme to facilitate Anne's eloquence in Blair's second sense, namely "when the speaker aims not merely to please, but also to inform, to instruct, to convince" (Lectures on Rhetoric, p. 236). First, Anne increases her acquaintance with members of the navy and enjoys a sense of kinship with those who are able to use practical wisdom to turn their immediate circumstances to the best account. This gift has been Anne Elliot's from the beginning and has enabled her to survive her imprisonment within narrow unsympathetic social commonwealths. Second, she and Captain Wentworth become friends who deliberate and use their rhetorical skills for the welfare of others. In two new ways, Anne finds that she shares the common ends that unite usefulness, concern for others, and respect for effectiveness into socially valued qualities. Third, an accident occurs because of the folly of Captain Wentworth and Louisa that calls forth Anne's persuasive wisdom. When all is chaos Anne says " 'A surgeon!' . . . He [Captain Wentworth] caught the word; it seemed to rouse him at once" (Persuasion, ch. 12, p. 102). The man who had closed himself off from her is not just taught but "roused" by her word.

Let us examine Anne's new discursive commonwealth more closely. First with regard to the navy, let us recall that men use their own resourcefulness to encounter fortune and advance by means of their achievements (Rethinking, p. 149). Agency does not disappear when circumstances rob Captain Harville of the normal use of his leg and of a good income. Even under these circumstances, Anne recognizes the power of his agency. Initially surprised that he and his wife could invite so many to dine in such small rooms, her astonishment was soon lost in the pleasanter feelings which sprang from the sight of all the ingenious contrivances and nice arrangements of Captain Harville, to turn the actual space to the best possible account...Some few articles of a rare species of wood, excellently worked up, and with something curious and valuable from all the distant countries Captain Harville had visited, were more than amusing to Anne: connected as it all was with his profusion, the fruit of its labours, the effects of its influence on his habits, the picture of repose and domestic happiness it presented, made it to her a something more, or less, than gratification...His lameness prevented him from taking much exercise; but a mind of usefulness and ingenuity seemed to furnish him with constant employment within. (ch. 11, p. 92)

Captain Harville possesses the vision to find opportunities for "usefulness and ingenuity" that create a space fit for the domestic happiness he enjoys with his family. His inventions are kindred to the rhetorical inventiveness that finds possibilities for action in recalcitrant circumstances and articulates them in speech. "Use" and "happiness" are brought together in his world, and Anne Elliot, who has sought without being able to achieve that union sees and admires his work. For Captain Harville's contrivances make life better for himself, his wife, his friends, and the friends of his friends. He demonstrates his "attachment to Captain Wentworth," a "degree of hospitality so uncommon, so unlike the usual style of give-and-take invitations, and dinners of formality and display, that Anne felt her spirits not likely to be benefited by an increasing acquaintance among his brother officers. 'These would have been my friends'," was her thought (ch. 11, pp. 91–2). Anne is beginning to discern the kind of commonwealth to which she would like to belong, one aimed at mutual affection, ingenuity, accomplishment, and generosity.

Anne begins to find her rhetorical role when she responds to the emergency of Louisa's fall. Captain Wentworth is uncharacteristically at a loss in this situation. Whereas he had been the successful man in a new merchant and military economy, when Louisa falls he feels despair and his strength leaves him: "Is there no one to help me?" he asks (ch. 12, p. 102). Anne cries out in full concern for Louisa and Captain Wentworth: " 'go to him, go to him' cried Anne, 'for heaven's sake go to him. I can support [Mary] myself.' " Her goals become the same as his, and as I noted, Captain Wentworth is shocked into listening to her. When he begins to fetch the surgeon, Anne cries out " 'Captain Benwick, would not it be better for Captain Benwick? He knows where a surgeon is to be found.' Everyone capable of thinking felt the advantage of the idea" (pp. 102–3). Anne demonstrates her superiority as a deliberative thinker. The group forms a little social commonwealth around the accident with Anne as the leader and orator. Captain Wentworth no long blocks her out, refusing to hear her, but he attends to her and respects her opinion and her capability.

The episode at Lyme does not resolve the problems faced by Anne and Captain Wentworth because they lack a full understanding of one another's values and beliefs. When Captain Wentworth urges warmly that Anne should stay with Louisa because there is "no one so proper, so capable as Anne!" Anne must pause "a moment to recover from the emotion of hearing herself so spoken of" (p. 106). But very shortly, when it turns out that Mary insists that she must stay and Anne returns to Captain Wentworth in the carriage, "his evident surprise and vexation, at the substitution of one sister for the other... made but a mortifying reception of Anne; or must at least convince her that she was valued only as she could be useful to Louisa" (p. 107). In making this inference, Anne falls back into the assumptions that governed her at Uppercross, that she was valuable to others only insofar as she was useful to their goals. But such misunderstandings cannot be prevented until she and Captain Wentworth create their own discursive community (*Rethinking*, p. 151). That creative act requires Anne's eloquence.

In order for this community to come into being, Anne and Captain Wentworth must converse, but the presence of other characters makes conversation difficult (*Rethinking*, p. 163). The propitious accident must befall them, and Anne shows her ability to work rhetorically in a world of chance when she takes advantage of Captain Harville's invitation to debate with him about Captain Benwick's constancy. A kind man who grieves for his dead sister, Captain Harville possesses the passion necessary to eloquence, and he expresses his distress that Captain Benwick, recently a widower because of her death, is now engaged to Louisa. He exclaims "Poor Fanny! She would not have forgotten him so soon!" Anne replies "It would not be the nature of any woman who truly loved," initiating a debate on man's and woman's constancy (ch. 23, p. 218).

The debate elicits the full force of Anne's eloquence and an expression of her strong beliefs and fervent desires. As Blair puts it, an effective speech is one "wherein we are not only convinced, but are interested, agitated and moved with the speaker; our passions are made to rise together with his; we enter into all his emotions" (*Lectures on Rhetoric*, p. 236). Anne's eloquence is of this order. To be eloquent, speakers must be impassioned and carry others along with their emotions. Healed from the confinement that robbed her of her bloom, given a sympathetic listener who shares her ideas of life, Anne carries Harville and Wentworth (who overhears her) into her impassioned defense of the constancy of woman's feelings. As Kastely puts it, "passion begets eloquence, which, in turn, calls forth more passion and more eloquence" (*Rethinking*, p. 165). Recognizing the value of the active life that forces men into "exertion" and into "continual occupation" that soon weaken[s] impressions," she, nevertheless, articulates a defense of woman's virtue relative to their tender feelings. Whereas men can exert themselves in the professions, "we live at home, quiet, confined, and our feelings prey upon us." Finally, Anne brings her past experience into a community that listens to her. In response to Harville's assertion that men's feelings are strongest, she defends woman's constancy, "'Man is more robust than woman, but he is not longer-lived; which exactly explains my view of the nature of their attachments'" (ch. 23, p. 219). When Harville cites the historians on his side of the issue, Anne rejects them because they are men and education has been "in their hands" (p. 220). Stimulated by the vigorous arguments on both sides of the question, Anne clarifies and articulates the ethos of each gender: " 'I believe you equal to every important exertion, and to every domestic forbearance, so long as . . . you have an object. I mean, while the woman you love lives, and lives for you. All the privilege I claim for my own sex . . . is that of loving longest, when existence or when hope is gone' " (p. 221). Anne defines the ends of her strongest commitment and the basis of a commonwealth in which she is a most fit citizen. She articulates her own identity, the heroism of her sex, and she "pierces" the soul of Captain Wentworth, who hears her even when her voice falls: " 'You sink your voice, but I can distinguish the tones of that voice, when they would be lost on others' " (pp. 222–3). His penetrating hearing (unlike his former deafness to her) makes him a worthy partner.

At the conclusion, Austen sharply realigns the commonwealths explored earlier. The older order of hereditary nobility and property is cleanly rejected in favor of the newer world of enterprise and achievement. Captain Wentworth, worth twenty-five thousand pounds and "as high in his profession as merit and activity could place him, was no longer nobody" (ch. 24, p. 232). Sir Walter, who had been somebody, in his own view at least, appears as a "foolish, spendthrift baronet" able to give only a small part of Anne's dowry to her. The Crofts and Harvilles are welcome members of the new circle but Lady Russell must abandon her admiration for rank and landed property to be admitted. She had been completely wrong about Mr Elliot, whose lack of openness and passion, one might say his lack of eloquence, had made Anne suspicious of his real motives. Lady Russell had misjudged Captain Wentworth, who lacked fortune and rank but whose confidence was rewarded with achievement. She abandons the commonplaces that had formed the basis of her life. "There was nothing less for Lady Russell to do, but to admit that she had been pretty completely wrong, and to take up a new set of opinions and of hopes" that make her a valued member of Anne and Captain Wentworth's discursive community. Captain Wentworth finds himself able to be useful to Mrs Smith, a valued friend whose "cheerfulness and mental alacrity did not fail her" (p. 235) "Anne was tenderness itself, and she had the full worth of it in Captain Wentworth's affection," as they flourish in their new commonwealth (p. 236).

Part III

Rhetoric and Contemporary Disciplines

Introduction

Part III argues that contemporary thinkers in literary studies, politics, and law draw on the classical ideas of ethos, logos, and pathos, along with rhetorical arguments, to redefine the boundaries and relevant materials of their disciplines. Each chapter shows how they adapt *topoi* and arguments to the problems and opportunities of their inquiries. Recent decades have brought rhetoric to the forefront in many fields of study, and this section introduces readers to the diversity and power of scholarly and critical rhetorical inventions.

If Milton's works and Austen's *Persuasion* disclose the challenges to rhetorical sharing posed by sectarian conflict, civil war, and sociocultural diversity, the writings examined in the next three chapters show twentieth- and twenty-first-century writers innovating rhetorical means to facilitate communication in a pluralistic, often divided and fragmented world. Rhetoric can heal misunderstanding and even abuse, making it possible to respect others as distanced and distinct from our selves. Modern and postmodern thinkers use language with an awareness of how it alters with time and shifts in community values. Diversity, pluralism, and change are central foci in literary studies, politics, and law.

Chapter 8, "Literary criticism and rhetorical invention," analyses how Wayne C. Booth and Stephen Greenblatt use terms rhetorically to open up new areas of inquiry. Booth's *The Rhetoric of Fiction* (1961) redefined literary studies for decades by using distinctions of ethos, logos, and pathos, writer, work, and audience to explore hitherto unknown facts and arguments about how novels can be read more inventively and with more fidelity to their communicative possibilities. Confronting dogmatic universals that had led critics to reject many novels and novelistic techniques, the work tests maxims against empirical evidence, fashioning new distinctions that facilitate the communion between an implied author and an implied reader. Recognizing that the task of finding common ground with an author may not be easy, it opened the way for readers' greater sensitivity to the values of a work and educated their judgments about them. Booth's *topoi* are inventive because he brings out unrecognized features of the narrator and of narrative technique. *The Rhetoric of Fiction* teaches a practice of reading that goes far beyond what the work itself has space to articulate or evaluate. Many other critics took up his terms and continued the inquiry (e.g., *Companion to Rhetoric*, pp. 325–54).

Stephen Greenblatt's *Marvelous Possessions* is similarly ingenious in using topical distinctions to explore materials in new ways, even though the author begins with assumptions and goals nearly the opposite of Booth's. Booth celebrates the communion of implied author and implied reader and the ability of great works to lead readers to more adequate values and judgments. Stephen Greenblatt, on the other hand, turns away from the veneration of Shakespeare that he was taught as a student of New Criticism to examine "a stubborn unassimilable otherness, a sense of distance and difference" between modern readers and Renaissance texts ("Resonance," p. 275). Nevertheless, he shares with Booth a rhetorical inventiveness that allows him to look at literary interpretation from fresh angles that bear rich fruit. Using argument by example in novel ways, *Marvelous Possessions* and "Resonance and wonder" focus on "engaged representations" that are "local, and historically contingent" (*Marvelous Possessions*, p. 12). They look at texts in light of an abundant variety of textual contexts. Unlike Booth, who tends to focus on the interaction between the implied author's ethos and the implied reader's values, Greenblatt emphasizes the instrumentalities of communication, the material or textual artifacts that have meaning in relation to a "zone of social practice." But both critics use *topoi* to illuminate new, broad-ranging rhetorical and literary practices. Chapter 8 explores *Marvelous Possession*'s deployment of *topoi* of admiration, possession and dispossession, agency, constraint, and authority to illuminate the uses of wonder in Renaissance European colonialist and anti-colonialist texts.

Chapter 9, "Faction, politics, and rhetorical invention," investigates two reinventions of practical rhetoric that heal seemingly irresolvable divisions in splintered, oppressive societies. In the aftermath of colonialism, which produced distrust in citizens in the United States and in South Africa, political leaders needed to foster what Danielle S. Allen and Eugene Garver identify as the trust-building powers of rhetoric to create a more equitable discourse between persons with different interests. Drawing on Ralph Ellison's concept of sacrifice to recognize the distinctively political character of Elizabeth Eckford's courageous walk to Central High School in Little Rock, Arkansas, Allen formulates an idea of political friendship that acknowledges the self-sacrifice of others. Offering an original, illuminating reading of Aristotle's *Rhetoric* in *Talking to Strangers*, she shows how speakers as friends use rhetoric to demonstrate that they care for the interests of others, that they have good practical sense, and that they are virtuous. They use rhetoric to create equitable relationships. She also shows how speakers use rhetoric to stabilize the uncertainties of political life and heal emotions arising from the audience's or listener's pain of not having their interests addressed.

Eugene Garver thoughtfully reinvents Aristotelian rhetoric to analyze the way in which South Africans used epideictic rhetoric after the civil upheavals to fashion a new, more democratic ethos for their country. When trauma has occurred because of the oppression of one group by another, distrust makes communication impossible. Words were regarded suspiciously so that communication and deliberation became difficult or impossible. Garver argues that the Truth and Reconciliation Committee built trust by pursuing the truth of what had happened. Seeking agreement was not enough. Speakers and hearers discerned many kinds of truth: factual, perspectival, and narrative truths. Speakers also needed to discover a way for everyone's interests to be addressed. Then common interests and new truths established new grounds for a community-building ethos. Garver illuminates the rhetorical means for facilitating discovery of truth and for creating political friendship.

If Danielle Allen and Eugene Garver find ways for speakers to establish more ethical, equitable relationships with their audiences and to debate the values that define communities, Edward H. Levi's *An Introduction to Legal Reasoning* (1949) argues that the law serves as a forum in which communities debate the common ideas and values of their societies. This process serves as a focus for Chapter 10, "Legal reasoning, historical contingency, and change." Levi shows how legal rules or words provide an ambiguous space where discussion can take place and change can be made more rational. Ambiguous words (topics) allow conflicting ideas to be expressed and adjudicated. Levi's analysis of the history and practices of exemplary cases in nineteenth- and twentieth-century English and North American law shows how topics guide lawyers and judges' deliberations and judgments. His work investigates legal reasoning by analogy or by example, one of the two main kinds of rhetorical argument. Legal theorists such as Cass R. Sunstein and Richard Posner refer to his book as the classic treatment of reasoning by analogy; it has implications for current debates on the kinds of agreement and argument necessary for cogent legal reasoning. By examining this book, I show how practical reasoning addresses things and values that change through time. I also compare Levi's analysis to other legal theorists' treatments of rhetorical invention and legal argument. Levi's thinking is exemplary for the present volume in its alertness to the interaction between evolving categories and historical change. It discerns the (sometimes fragile) cogency of reasoning about recalcitrant particulars and historically shifting values.

Chapter 8

Literary Criticism and Rhetorical Invention: Wayne C. Booth's *The Rhetoric of Fiction* and Stephen Greenblatt's *Marvelous Possessions*

Ethos, Logos, and Pathos in the Rhetoric of Wayne C. Booth

Whereas ancient rhetoricians seemed confident that they shared common ground with their audiences, modern rhetorical writers must often *discover* common ground. Wayne C. Booth, for example, in his essay, "My life with rhetoric," recalls that his years as a Mormon missionary gave him in "an education in rhetorology," the art of "probing beneath rival arguments to find common ground (*topoi*, places) on which the rivals can stand in agreement as they pursue truth together" (p. 498). In looking back at the writing of *The Rhetoric of Fiction* (1961), and *A Rhetoric of Irony* (1974), Booth recalls that the former argues that the most important task for a writer of fiction is to create "a communion between an implied author and an implied reader," and that the latter stresses "rhetorical bonding" between author and reader as the primary achievement of irony ("My life with rhetoric," p. 500). In our pluralistic world where we often do not share values, readers and authors work to find the common ground that allows them to communicate and interpret judgments, evaluations, and emotions.

Booth's literary critical works take up the rhetorical distinctions of author, work, reader, of ethos, logos, and pathos, of topic, argument, deliberation, and judgment to discover previously unnoticed facts and arguments about how English and American novels can be read judiciously. Although Booth did not originally intend to write a rhetorical analysis of fiction, setting out instead to fashion a poetics in the manner of the neo-Aristotelians at the University of Chicago, his approach became deeply rhetorical. Booth read Aristotle's *Rhetoric* intensely as a young man. He remarks, "For some miraculous reason that I can't recover, I found myself assigned to the daunting task of reading Aristotle's *Art of Rhetoric*, preparing for an examination with no classroom instruction. After several rereadings, the book became for me a fantastic revelation, and its influence has continued until today" ("My life with rhetoric," p. 499). Like Aristotle, Booth rejects universal necessary truths as the ground for rhetorical arguments about particulars. *The Rhetoric of Fiction* questions the universals that had guided literary criticism previously and tests them against particular novelistic techniques to examine their adequacy. It emphasizes that judgments of means need to be evaluated according to how well they fulfill the ends of a particular novel.

The Rhetoric of Fiction subjects universal statements about the ideal author and novel to a vigorous refutation. Indeed, the project of the book arose from Booth's objections to these universal rules. He recalls that the project "began as an attack on those 'New Critics' who argued that only with Flaubert's rejection of telling in favor of 'showing' did fiction begin to achieve the status of 'poetry'," and have "genuine aesthetic value" ("My life with rhetoric," p. 499). Flaubert had recommended that novelists treat "the human soul with the impartiality which physical scientists show in studying matter" (quoted in *Rhetoric of Fiction*, p. 68). From this and similar formulations, Booth distills three rules that novelists and readers were supposed to follow, and he refutes supposed universal truths about the author, the work, and the reader. According to one rule, authors were supposed to be "objective," "detached," "dispassionate," and "ironic," and, according to another, readers similarly aspired to being "objective," "ironic," or "detached" (*Rhetoric of Fiction*, p. 38). Some critics argued, following a third set of rules, that the novel must be "natural, realistic, or intensely alive," while others "would cleanse it of impurities, of the inartistic, of the all-too-human" (p. 37).

Booth refutes these universal requirements by looking at individual novels to see whether, in fact, detached authors, realist novels, and objective readers are always superior. His use of commonsense beliefs to discover evidence in particular cases marks his work as rhetorically inventive. Similarly, his willingness to overturn previous critical commonplaces in favor of more adequate guides to interpretation displays invention; *The Rhetoric of Fiction* realigned and invigorated criticism of the novel for decades.

For example, in questioning the belief that naturalness of technique is always desirable, the text points out that although some believe "that a story should be told as it might be told in real life," in fact "Conrad's Marlow, in *Lord Jim* could not possibly have told all that he does tell in the allotted time" (p. 57). Booth believes that in seeking realism as a good end for all novels, critics confused means and ends. For, he affirms, "no quality, however desirable, is likely to be suitable in the same degree in all parts of a work" (p. 60).

Analogously, the author's neutrality may be a desirable quality, and Booth maintains that what he calls "unacknowledged narrators" or "reflectors" in the words of Henry James can achieve important effects such as allowing "characters to work out their own destinies or tell their own stories" unmediated by a dramatized or fully present authorial voice (p. 273). But no novel can dispense entirely with authorial commentary, an argument Booth again supports with many examples. Symbols and patterns of imagery serve as a sort of commentary even when the author's voice is silent. More important, the neutral or objective author is only one kind among many, effective for some ends but not for others (p. 153). And all reflectors are not the same; they differ "markedly according to the degree and kind of distance that separates them from the author, the reader, and the other characters of the story" (p. 155).

Booth says that no fiction ever evades the presence of some impression of the author, an impression which he calls the "implied author." "However impersonal he [or she] may try to be, [the] reader will inevitably construct a picture of the official scribe who writes in this manner" (p. 71). Likewise, although many believed that "true art ignores the audience," for Booth, "every stroke" an author uses to imply a "second self will help to mold the reader into the kind of person suited to appreciate such a character and the book he [or she] is writing" (p. 89). Acknowledging that few people would agree with the beliefs about human beings of writers such as Baron Corvo or Ezra Pound and that the disagreement need not affect our engagement in their art, he takes issue with a position expressed by I. A. Richards among others that " 'we need no beliefs, and indeed we must have none, if we are to read *King Lear*'." Instead, says Booth, "the implied author of each novel is someone with whose beliefs on all subjects I must largely agree if I am to enjoy his work" (p. 137). Indeed, as we read (when we are reading well), our beliefs become more and more aligned with those of the implied author, so that we may understand and enjoy the work. Booth draws on the rhetorical category of the audience as shaped by the speech (or work), but even more importantly, on the shared beliefs in which fictional and other rhetorical works are grounded. Far from disregarding Shakespeare's beliefs, he argues, "Shakespeare requires us to believe that it is right to honor our fathers, and that it is wrong to kill off old men like Lear or grind out the eyes of old men like Gloucester" (p. 141). Shared beliefs or rhetorical common topics may be difficult to discover at times, but Booth argues vigorously for their presence and importance.

The amplitude and flexibility of Booth's distinctions (*topoi*) lay out a field of rhetorical discovery for the book and for subsequent critics. He "expands the variables we use to describe narrators going beyond grammatical person and degrees of knowledge" to fashion terms for dramatized and undramatized narrators, self-conscious and unaware narrators, privileged or omniscient implied authors and those limited to a single point of view, implied authors and narrators, as well as reliable and unreliable narrators ("Wayne C. Booth," p. 55). The point of these distinctions and many others is not to find boxes for classifying things but to promote thinking about how particular kinds of narrators serve as a means to certain ends but work less well for others. These *topoi* are inventive because they bring to light features of the narrator that had not been noticed previously and because, by using them, his readers may explore specific narrative techniques that Booth himself does not analyze. The distinctions are adaptable and open-ended, sensitive to differences among particulars rather than rejecting those that do not fit a universal rule.

The work's use of examples is also inventive and persuasive. For instance, having distinguished undramatized narrators (which occur in novels and short stories that do not refer directly to an implied author, such as Hemingway's "The killers,") from dramatized narrators, whose novels make them into characters, he analyzes the function of *Tristram Shandy*'s narrator, Tristram, who is "in some way the central subject holding together materials which, were it not for this scatterbrained presence, would never have seemed to be separated in the first place" (*Rhetoric of Fiction*, p. 222). Although the novel had seemed extremely disjointed and ill-fashioned to some previous critics, Booth argues that Sterne's treatment of the dramatized narrator achieves wonderful comic effects once one grasps the role of the narrator: the novel is the "mad kind of book it seems" because of the qualities of the teller upon whom it focuses (p. 229). By comparing the narrator of *Tristram Shandy* to the narrator of Swift's *Tale of a Tub* and the implied author of Montaigne's *Essays*, Booth makes his readers more sensitive to the distinct effects achievable by treatments of dramatized authors.

Instead of setting up dogmatic criteria for judging techniques of narrative (like the claim that all commentary is bad), Booth offers a variety of flexible distinctions between kinds and degrees of distance. Narrators may be *more or less distant* from the implied author, the narrator may be *more or less distant* from the characters and so forth. The variety of degrees and kinds allows Booth to clarify the intricacies of the implied author's distance from other characters. "Jane Austen, for example, presents a broad range of moral judgment (from the almost complete approval of Jane Fairfax in *Emma* to the contempt of Wickham in *Pride and Prejudice*), of wisdom (from Knightley to Miss Bates or Mrs Bennet), of taste, of tact, of sensibility" (*Rhetoric of Fiction*, p. 158).

The most famous distinction between reliable and unreliable narrators organizes the argument of the book and enables Booth to explore and admire the distinct effects produced by a broad range of narrators. Reliable narrators express attitudes and norms that agree with those of the implied author, whereas unreliable narrators depart from the attitudes and norms of the implied authors. To those who objected to reliable commentary in novels, the book points out that without such commentary, authors would be unable to heighten readers' anticipations by, for example, writing as Henry James does in *The Ambassadors* " 'this was the very beginning with him of a condition as to which, later on, as will be seen, he found cause to pull himself up' " (quoted in *Rhetoric of Fiction*, p. 173). Nor would novels be able to create dramatic irony, an effect that requires the author and audience to share information withheld from characters (p. 175). By dramatizing the degrees and kinds of variations of distance, Booth lays the groundwork for the analysis of complex literary effects. In his analysis of *Emma*, the heroine serves as a model, not to be slavishly imitated by readers, but to be thought through in order that they may perceive new effects and learn to use distinctions clearly and tactfully. Austen's skills in using degrees and kinds of sympathy and distance to create a heroine who has serious but comic and remediable flaws makes *Emma* a thought-provoking object for thoughtful critical activity. Austen maintains the reader's sympathy for Emma by telling the story through her eyes. She provides a corrective to any blindness this technique might produce by making the character Mr Knightley the reliable commentator on Emma's shortcomings. This combination of sympathy and judgment teaches the reader, but Austen goes beyond teaching to using a reliable narrator whose judgment provides clues to the reader of how exactly Emma goes astray. The tensions between this narrator's judgments and those of Emma produce comic irony and intellectual delight.

The last sections of *The Rhetoric of Fiction* focus on impersonal narration – the technique that provides the least amount of commentary. By telling the story through the characters, authors create sympathy for them and allow readers to imagine vividly their situations and experiences. But, Booth fears, because readers tend to sympathize with a character whose point of view they share, the absence of a judging narrator can lead to their accepting morally flawed narrators such as Humbert Humbert in Nabokov's *Lolita*. Booth prizes the meeting of minds and values that can occur in reading and defends communion against what he perceives as its misuses.

New Historicism: The Rhetoric of Stephen Greenblatt

Although many classic rhetoricians focus their inquiries on shared beliefs, post-modern critics tend to stress the differences that separate us from other cultures and times. For example, Stephen Greenblatt, resisting accounts that display an "air of veneration" toward Shakespeare and Elizabethan culture as precursors to our own worldviews, defines New Historicist critics as "more interested in unresolved conflict and contradiction than in integration" ("Resonance," p. 168). They seek "a stubborn unassimilable otherness, a sense of distance and difference" between culture and critics (p. 169). In this respect, they share goals with cultural anthropologists.

Greenblatt draws on the work of cultural anthropologist Clifford Geertz, who writes that anthropologists focus on the "said" of social discourse in order "to construct a system of analysis" ("Impact," p. 27). Their analyses interpret meaning in relation to symbolic cultural patterns. By acting in terms of these symbolic forms, human beings organize their common life. Culture is understood as "a set of control mechanisms – plans, recipes, rules, instructions (what computer engineers call 'programs') – for the governing of behavior" (p. 44). Only by understanding these recipes, rules, and instructions can one hope to interpret the actions and words of other cultures.

Like Geertz, Greenblatt rejects knowledge of universal "man" in favor of empirical knowledge of "selves fashioned and acting according to the generative rules and conflicts of a given culture." These selves are "conditioned by the expectations of their class, gender, religion, race and national identity." Although New Historicism "does not posit historical processes as unalterable and inexorable," "it does tend to discover limits or constraints upon individual intervention" ("Resonance," p. 164).

Nevertheless, in spite of his emphasis on constraint, Greenblatt's writings on wonder discover multiple uses of wonder in the acts of possessing and renouncing the possession of lands in the New World. "Resonance and wonder" and *Marvelous Possessions* exemplify this inventiveness. Greenblatt focuses more specifically than Geertz on studying "particular, contingent cases" ("Resonance," p. 164). Rather than providing a general analysis of a culture's symbolic patterns, he chooses anecdotes that have a recalcitrant particularity. Greenblatt's fascinating, highly charged grappling with cryptic meanings share with other rhetorically inventive works the attempt to discover terms and examples that probe the probable and contingent without making the particular an instance of a general rule, pattern, or idea of "man." That is not to say, however, that Greenblatt focuses on anecdotes only in their singularity. Instead, he seeks *"representative anecdotes."* These anecdotes cannot be subsumed by larger patterns, but they can "gesture" toward a "larger strategy." For this reason, the anecdotes do not lose the "provisionality" that "marks them as contingent" (*Marvelous Possessions*, p. 3).

The idea of the representative anecdote has puzzled some analysts of New Historicism. Jean Howard, for example, asks how "representative" is "the illustrative example," and notes that "there is often no observation or consideration of a culture's whole system of signifying practices which would allow one to assess, relationally, the importance and function of the particular event described" ("New Historicism," pp. 38, 39). But instead of providing such an analysis, which would, after all, be anthropological, Greenblatt focuses on seeking "a vehement and cryptic particularity that would make one pause or even stumble on the threshold of history." New Historicists looked for certain sorts of anecdotes: "outlandish and irregular ones held out the best hope for preserving the radical strangeness of the past by gathering heterogeneous elements." These anecdotes would not exemplify "epochal truths" but instead would "undermine them" (*Practicing New Historicism*, p. 51).

As Joel Fineman argues in an essay published more than ten years before *Practicing New Historicism*, anecdotes are aporetic. Fineman insightfully ties the anecdote to the Baconian aphorism ("History of the anecdote," p. 63). Neither the anecdote nor the aphorism provides complete, rounded-off knowledge; both introduce disjunction into previous interpretations, so that inquiry strikes out in new directions. But unlike Bacon, Greenblatt does not use anecdotes to discover more adequate universals. Rather, he uses rhetorical *topoi* to explore the particular workings of salient anecdotes in Renaissance writing across a broad range of rhetorical practices and situations.

I focus on one set of anecdotes, those associated with wonder and with the symbolic means that early European writers used in responding to the New World. These writers did not supply what Greenblatt calls "detached scientific assessments," rather they provided "engaged representations, representations that are . . . local, and historically contingent" (*Marvelous Possessions*, p. 12). The interest expressed in them focuses not on "knowledge of the other but practice upon the other," so their effect can be described more accurately as rhetorical (inventive and effective) rather than as analytic (pp. 12–13).

An anecdote representative of one element of the argument in *Marvelous Possessions* ties the European fantasies of possession of the New World to the experience of wonder. Columbus writes:

> I have taken possession for their highnesses, by proclamation made and with the royal standard unfurled, and no opposition was offered to me. To the first island which I found, I gave the name *San Salvador*, in remembrance of the Divine Majesty, Who has marvelously bestowed all this." (quoted in *Marvelous Possessions*, p. 52)

Greenblatt argues that Columbus uses the wonder associated with the gift of possession to complete his formal legitimating gestures and words. Wonder's uses in rituals and processes of possession and dispossession serve as organizing *topoi* for Greenblatt's broader argument. For example, wonder and seizing (but also giving) function as "characteristic rhetorical features[s]" of Columbus's "Christian imperialism" (*Marvelous Possessions*, p. 70). But Greenblatt also explores Mandeville's refusal to take possession, and a use of wonder as providing a path away from ownership (p. 27) and toward "many divers folk and divers kinds of beasts, and many other marvelous things" (*Mandeville's Travels*, i. 102, quoted on p. 29). The argument moves from a sphere of intention where the writer makes a choice to renounce his own possessions, to a dispersal of signs that take on a life of their own as they proliferate.

This focus on instrumentality (rather than, say, on the author's intention alone) occurs frequently in Greenblatt's writing. "Resonance and wonder," for example, begins with a "round broad-brimmed Cardinal's hat" in a glass case at Oxford that turns out to be a "material referent" and an "element in a complex symbolic construction" as it travels from Cardinal Wolsey's head possibly to become a costume in a theater company and then, definitely, to the library at Oxford (pp. 161–2). Greenblatt traces the material sign "from one zone of social practice to another" to explore the signifying possibilities within Renaissance culture ("Resonance," p. 163).

However, Greenblatt does not reduce his analysis to signs as instrumentalities of cultural meaning. The *topoi* of wonder, possession, and dispossession help to display the many cultural and individual uses to which wonder is put. The fact that Greenblatt's account is not exhaustive does not diminish its value, because he seeks to explore a spectrum of distinctive uses. Mandeville the author disappears from the work called *Mandeville's Travels*, and the work becomes a stitching together of significant, unfolding bits and pieces of the wonderful, but wonder for Columbus becomes "a calculated rhetorical strategy" serving a formal process designed to legitimate the Spanish possession of the New World (*Marvelous Possessions*, p. 73). The book moves from renunciation of possession to the assertive, even possessive use of rhetoric. Far from ignoring human agency in the production of meaning, Greenblatt uses the *topoi* of agency and constraint to examine the intricacies of writers' relationships to the signifying processes that do cultural work in Renaissance Europe. "Resonance and wonder" sees selves as "fashioned and acting according to the generative rules and conflicts of a given culture," and Greenblatt shows great skill in probing the interconnectness of the *topoi* of "fashioned and acting." The complexity of agency emerges in his characterization of human "behavior":

> Every form of behavior, in this view, is a strategy: taking up arms or taking flight is a significant social action, but so is staying put, minding one's business, turning one's fact to the wall. Agency is virtually inescapable. (*Marvelous Possessions*, p. 164)

Inescapable but not simple: New Historicism does not posit historical processes as unalterable and inexorable, but it does discover limits and constraints upon individual intervention. Actions that appear to be single are disclosed as multiple; the apparently isolated power of the individual genius turns out to be bound up with collective, social energy; a gesture of dissent may be an element in a larger legitimation process, while an attempt to stabilize the order of things may turn out to subvert it ("Resonance," pp. 164–5). Greenblatt calls agency "inescapable," but warns that individual purpose and action do not produce intended social and political effects. The meaning and force of the words of geniuses may express collective energies beyond their own ken. For these reasons, Greenblatt focuses on the tension between the constraints of cultural systems and the individual's use of those systems in communicative acts.

The argument locates separate authorial intention and action within the web of signifying practices of which they are parts. *Mandeville's Travels*, for example, actively turns away from possession but as the quotations within it proliferate, the author disappears in a chain of signifiers. "Mandeville," who initially expresses a "dream of recovery [of the Holy Land], return, reoccupation, and hence repossession," makes, at the "mid-point in his text... his decisive, peculiar, and unexplained move, turning abruptly from the Holy Land to the rest of the world," a "turning... toward diversity, difference, the bewildering variety of 'marvellous things'" (*Marvelous Possessions*, pp. 28, 29). Once he makes this turn, a rich set of accounts of the wonders of his travels unfolds, accounts of experiences that in fact Mandeville never had but which were recorded by others and found their place in *Mandeville's Travels*, a text that leaves its author behind, becoming "a fictive body made up of the fragment of other bodies" (p. 35). So, like Cardinal Wolsey's hat, the experiences of wonder recorded in *Mandeville's Travels* take on a life of their own as they circulate within the signifying system.

Columbus imagines that he takes possession of the land by means of a set of linguistic acts that include an appeal to wonder. Fulfilling a list of formal conditions meant to effect ownership, he takes "possession for their highnesses." These examples provide evidence for the thesis that animates Greenblatt's book, namely that "the marvelous" is "the object of a range of sharply differing uses" (p. 24). The book offers a rich variety of these uses, along with a study in the tensions between human activity and undergoing. Greenblatt investigates "different and conflicting ways of seeing and describing the world," although "the variety is not infinite" (p. 23). Noting that in "Descartes or Spinoza wonder precedes recognitions of good and evil," and that "in Aristotle or Albertus Magnus... it precedes knowledge," he argues that this status "conferred upon the marvelous a striking indeterminacy." These indeterminate resources for rhetorical use can be drawn on in many ways.

The yield of Greenblatt's approach is rich and full of surprises. For example, he notes that from antiquity the marvelous had produced not only "fascination" but also "authentication" (p. 30). Sources of authority become a focus for his study. The appearance of wonders cited in earlier works that are quoted in *Mandeville's Travels* seems to have made Mandeville esteemed as an authority. The text accentuates this effect by elaborating the role of the eyewitness to each marvel. The surprise unfolds when Greenblatt argues that the "details" given by the eyewitness in each case turn out to be a "fabrication," and, in fact, the text itself, as Jonathan Haynes has shown, was believed because it "seconded the wildest rumors of Pliny or Vincent of Beauvais" (pp. 32, 35; *Humanist as Traveler*, p. 31). The papacy ratifies the text, Greenblatt notes, by saying " 'all was sooth that was therein'," because everything had already been 'written down in another book'," a book that "Mandeville" validates by saying he saw it (*Mandeville's Travels* 1, p. 207, quoted in *Marvelous Possessions*, p. 35). The analysis illuminates a culturally and historically distinct understanding of authority. There is no Mandeville as authoritative author but a movement of the text. Like the locus of authority, the range of beliefs pertinent to the account is opened up. The text moves from "a possessive insistence on the core orthodox Christian belief to an open acceptance of many coexisting beliefs." For "Mandeville" writes, " 'I trow that God evermore loves well all those that love him in soothfastness and serve him meekly and truly... Men [should] despise no men for the diversity of their laws. For we wot not whom God loves ne whom he hates' " (quoted on p. 35).

Columbus, on the other hand, constructs a very different kind of authority and ethos; he is confident that he can *take* possession of the New World. He identifies himself as a representative of the king and queen; he speaks before competent witnesses; and seals official papers to be taken back to Spain. Of course, the people who should ratify the performative act of possessing by not opposing it do not understand his language and could not oppose it. Even though Columbus is "not concerned with a particular subjective consciousness responding to the proclamation and hence with consent as an inner act of volition but with the formal absence of an objection to his words" (p. 59), the lack of informed consent threatens the validity of the act of possession.

Here wonder comes into play as "a sense of the marvelous that in effect fills up the emptiness at the center of the maimed rite of possession" (p. 80). Wonder accompanies Columbus's intuition that the "Divine Majesty... has marvelously bestowed all this" (*Select Documents* 1. 2, quoted on p. 52), filling in any ambiguity left by the non-response of the inhabitants. The language of gift invokes a rhetoric of "Christian imperialism" that yokes the discourse of the circulation of commodities with the discourse of the transformation of souls. Columbus uses the paradoxical (Pauline) language of opposites to denote the marvel of spiritual/financial transmutations: he "takes absolute possession on behalf of the Spanish crown in order to make an absolute gift; the wicked natives... will be enslaved in order to be freed from their own bestiality... the conversion of commodities into gold slides liquidly into the conversion and hence salvation of souls" (pp. 70, 71). Later, in the third voyage, when the gold promised to the sovereigns who finance his journey has not materialized, Columbus uses the "marvelous" to stand for "the missing caravels laden with gold; it is – like the ritual of possession itself – a word pregnant with what is imagined, desired, promised" (p. 73). Greenblatt's brilliant association of wonder with the deferred but hoped for object of desire informs a broad range of his interpretations. Wonder magically gives that which is beyond imagination: new worlds, wealth, salvation of souls. It serves as a sign of the danger it poses to whomever Columbus visits. The perfection of wonder and its madness merge when Columbus imagines himself as king of the promised land: "He gave thee for thine owne . . . Of the barriers of the Ocean sea, which were closed with such mighty chains. He gave thee the keys; and thou wast obeyed in many lands and among Christians thou hast gained an honourable fame" (2. 90–2, quoted on p. 85).

Lest the explorers' uses of the marvelous to possess and enslave seem to exhaust its meaning, Greenblatt turns to Montaigne to show that wonder is available (serves as a rhetorical resource) for "decency as well as domination" (p. 25). Greenblatt does not try to balance or make up for the cruelty of the explorers by analyzing Montaigne's essay "On cannibals," but suggests another use for wonder. He finds in Montaigne the "critical and humanizing power of the marvelous" (p. 25). Montaigne does not offer himself as a trustworthy witness. Rather, Greenblatt argues, he uses distinctions between the elaborately rhetorical and the plain style, the peasant and the nobleman, the living and the dead, distinctions taken from his own culture, to find distance and difference in the New World and then to use what he discovers to criticize war-torn France. Eschewing a rhetorically shaped, ornate language that masks its subject, he seeks the plain, humble style of a servant. Greenblatt shows that this imaginary witness, a servant, allows Montaigne to insist on the lack of class distinctions and servitude in the New World so that he can criticize its presence in the old. He shows how Montaigne discovers *topoi* in that class structure, quoting his statement: "Between my way of dressing and that of a peasant of my region . . . I find far more distance than there is between his way and that of a man dressed only in his skin" ("Of the custom," p. 167, quoted on p. 149). Whereas Columbus dreamed of possessing the New World, wonder in Montaigne turns "toward shame." The *topoi* of cannibalism (whether of eating a man alive or dead) capture the horror of the civil war in France:

> I think there is more barbarity in eating a man alive than in eating him dead; and in tearing by tortures and the rack a body still full of feeling, in roasting a man bit by bit . . . than in roasting and eating him after he is dead. ("Of cannibals," p. 155, quoted on p. 150)

Greenblatt closes by insisting that Montaigne refused to "possess the souls of others." He truly articulates, whereas *Mandeville's Travels* could only intimate covertly, that "we are incomplete and unsteady, we are go-betweens, we do not know whom God loves and whom He hates." Greenblatt allows himself one final moment of identification in a work that eschews communion in favor of strangeness and difference, finding a solitary point of connection between "us" and "them" in the go-between that is neither fully a part of the old world nor part of the new one.

Chapter 9

Faction, Politics, and Rhetorical Invention: Eugene Garver's *For the Sake of Argument* and Danielle S. Allen's *Talking to Strangers*

Modern liberal democracies confront citizens with divisions that threaten the trust and mutual deliberation upon which community depends. The roots of these conflicts can be found in the Reformation. Medieval Christianity has been thought to provide an authoritative set of beliefs, but when competing authoritative systems emerged within the same society during the Reformation, sectarian warfare proved irresolvable. As a result, citizens agreed to end religious warfare without reconciling their differences (*Political Liberalism*, p. xxiv). In order to avoid destructive conflict, pluralists accepted the fact of religious and philosophical differences and found grounds for agreement in the political process ("Incompletely theorized agreements," pp. 1733, 1735, 1736 n. 8).[1]

But this deliberative process depends on trust, and the aftermath of colonialism has produced distrust. Too often, as Danielle S. Allen shows, "frustration – with unemployment, crime, and public education – is understood" in racial or factional terms (*Talking to Strangers*, p. xiii). "Black" and "white," "right" and "left," "evangelical" and "secular," are labels that make differences rigid, threatening the common ground that supports democratic deliberation. In the absence of common ground, we might despair of the possibility that the art of deliberative rhetoric could enable wise, effective, practical thinking.

Despair would be premature. The framers of our constitution drew their ideas of democracy from classical republicanism, which valued homogeneity. However, as Cass R. Sunstein argues, they did not believe that "heterogeneity and difference were destructive to the deliberative process" (*Partial Constitution*, pp. 23–4, quoted in *For the Sake of Argument*, p. 212 n. 36). In fact, they believed that difference is advantageous because, after all, deliberation presupposes at least two perspectives from which to examine an issue. And we can look to what Allen calls the trust-building power of rhetoric to heal divisions and create political partnerships.

However, we should not underestimate the difficulties. Liberal democracies are plagued with inequities that interfere with mutually respectful deliberation. When one group's interests are systematically sacrificed to those of another group, when truth becomes the property of a dominant faction so that one must acquiesce to the statements of another because of the latter's class or position, then the respectful deliberative mode of thinking becomes impossible. Citizens can no longer use rhetoric to form a community.

Two books examine the breakdown in the polity that takes place when one group pursues its interests at the expense of another. Both reinvent the trust-building power of Aristotle's *Rhetoric* to address modern factional strife. Eugene Garver's *For the Sake of Argument: Practical Reasoning, Character, and the Ethics of Belief* (2004) argues that the rhetorical search for truth was indispensable to reconciliation after the civil upheaval in South Africa. He demonstrates that rhetoric's power to discover factual and perspectival truth in particular helped to heal trauma and to discover a new, shared ethos that would guide deliberation in South Africa. And Allen's *Talking to Strangers: Anxieties of Citizenship since Brown v. Board of Education* (2004) demonstrates that rhetoric, properly used in liberal democracies, can foster equity between speakers and hearers and heal the pain caused by inequitable decisions.

Political Friendship and Rhetoric

Talking to Strangers discloses the injuries that occurred when American citizens failed to recognize the self-sacrifice of Elizabeth Eckford in the face of verbal assaults and physical threats from Hazel Bryan and other white persons in front of Central High School, Little Rock, Arkansas, September 4, 1957 (*Talking to Strangers*, pp. 3–24), during an action supporting the abolition of segregation in schools. This event becomes a representative anecdote for the betrayals of trust that undermine liberal democracy. By not recognizing the sacrifice of people such as Eckford, citizens lost the opportunity to create more equal relationships and to establish a community that was whole and healthy, and that served the interests of all its citizens.

Allen shows the consequences of a polity's repeated failure to serve the interests of their citizens. When citizens lose faith that a political organization will attend to interests, they flee, withdraw, or look for new political allegiances. Hardened distrust leads emigrants, for example, to leave their homes for countries that they believe will leave protect their interests. And, Allen argues, during the civil rights movement in the United States, African American citizens shifted their loyalties from their state government to the federal government (*Talking to Strangers*, p. xvii). Distrust can be remedied only when groups of citizens whose interests differ can work together for their mutual benefit (p. xix).

But even joint deliberation does not always produce a perfect political solution; some groups will have to sacrifice without having their interests met in return, perhaps for a long time. Allen draws on Ralph Ellison's concept of sacrifice from *The Invisible Man* to recognize the African American invention of a new kind of citizenship and a new political heroism. When Elizabeth walked alone to Little Rock High School, suffering the jeers and taunts of people who called for her lynching, she acted politically to set in motion the workings of the federal legal system that had forbidden segregation in the schools to be sanctioned by state law (*Talking to Strangers*, p. 30). Allen maintains that her heroic self-sacrifice was intended "to generate enough political friendship to secure a democratic legal system" (p. 31).

Yet this voluntary ordeal was not seen by some as a heroic act. Allen demonstrates that Hannah Arendt's hard distinction between "private, social, and political spheres" (p. 26) prevented her from recognizing the heroism of African American children and parents. Arendt's *The Human Condition* strongly differentiates the intimacies of personal life from the activities that achieve economic security as well as from political action and speech among free, equal persons (*Human Condition*, pp. 22–49). Intimacy presupposes privacy and individualism, whereas the behavior of members of society is conformist and directed toward satisfying the necessities of life. Political action, on the other hand, exemplified in archaic and classical Greek writings, is "permeated by a fiercely agonal spirit, where everybody had constantly to distinguish himself from all others, to show through unique deeds or achievements that he was the best of all (*aien aristeuein*)" (p. 41; *Iliad* vi. 208). When labor movements appeared in the political realm, "men acted and spoke *qua* men – and not *qua* members of society." The improvement of economic status was "incidental" to political action (p. 219). In an article published in *Dissent*, Arendt criticized the parents of Little Rock, whom she thought exploited their children for mere economic gain. But Allen demonstrates how she misread their actions.

Allen makes the distinction between social behavior and political action flexible and rhetorically inventive, drawing on Ralph Ellison's concept of self-sacrifice to redefine African American actions in Little Rock as heroic and political. Ellison shows that Arendt had failed to understand "the *ideal* of sacrifice" among "Southern Negroes." He argues that a parent in Little Rock expected a child to face fear "because he is a Negro American" and willing to make "one more sacrifice" (*Who Speaks for the Negro*, pp. 343–4, quoted in *Talking to Strangers*, p. 27).

Allen shows that self-sacrifice needs to be understood in terms of Ellison's concept of democratic consent. In liberal democracies, decisions are supposed to involve the citizens' consent but "never really do" (*Talking to Strangers*, p. 27). Joint decisions necessarily benefit some people at the expense of others (p. 28). She argues, "Recognition of the necessary fact of loss and disappointment in democratic politics vitiates any effort, such as Arendt's, to hold the social firmly separate from the political" (p. 29). Instead citizens need to strive for political friendship and equality and use rhetoric to heal the social, economic, and political injuries that inevitably occur as a result of political decisions. *The Invisible Man* calls on citizens "to invent new forms of citizenship."

Rejecting utopian philosophical attempts by Hobbes, Kant, and Habermas to arrive at unanimity, Allen argues that we need to address the irreducible differences in the interests of citizens. Differences of opinion do not cause trouble; conflicts of interest do. But these conflicts cannot be eradicated, nor should they be. Instead, Allen draws on Aristotle's concept of "utility friendship" as a model for cultivating habits of citizenship that heal "rivalrous self-interest" and "*pleonexia*, the problem of 'wanting more than' " (p. 126). Friendships based on usefulness are imperfect, but by "bringing the techniques of friendship to bear on rivalrous self-interest," citizens move toward trust and equity (p. 127).

Trust arises, Allen argues, when those who sacrifice are confident that in the long run their interests will be addressed. Because no political decision can serve everyone's interests, the losing group needs to be shown that their turn will come. Allen asserts, "How sacrifices are handled affects the ability of a democracy to maintain institutional allegiance and trust among citizens" (pp. 111). She shows how Aristotle's idea of political friendship provides the "core practices" necessary for productive citizenship (p. 120). Utility (as distinct from Aristotle's pleasurable or virtuous) friendships establish working relationships and reduce rivalry. Utility friends learn to share power. They have conflicting desires, but they seek reciprocity (pp. 130–1). Allen argues that the practices of friendships based on usefulness can be adapted to relationships with strangers (pp. 135–9). Avoiding the extremes of domination and submission, political friends seek the mean; Allen formulates her own maxim: "Equity is friendship's core" (p. 129).

Allen devises a practice for increasing equity. If a friendship is to survive, friends must be convinced that the sacrifices and benefits of friendship are roughly equal, that each person recognizes and respects the other, and that both have "equal agency within the relationship" (p. 129). But because not all interests can be addressed by any political decision, one person will have to sacrifice without having his interests met, perhaps for a long time. Aristotle writes that the equitable person "is content to receive a smaller share although he has the law on his side" (*Nicomachean Ethics* 5. 10; *Talking to Strangers*, p. 132). Allen demonstrates that friendship (not law alone) needs to sustain cooperation. Friends do not make all issues matters of litigation. Rhetoric provides tools for generating trust and preserving reciprocity when outcomes are unfair. But first, citizens with equitable self-interest treat the interests of others as their own. They recognize that a social bond is in everyone's interest and that there are many kinds of interest that need not always be in competition with one another.

Rhetoric fosters trust and equity. Persuasion does not manipulate audiences into heedless action. Instead the speaker makes the best possible argument and leaves the decision up to the audience (p. 141), preserving independence and autonomy. The people's free obedience, based on persuasion, generates legitimate consent. Allen relates political persuasion to friendship, arguing that in Aristotle "persuasion is treated solely as the speech of a friend" and not as an interchange in a "hierarchical model" (p. 142). The speaker, to be persuasive, must address the audience as equals, however diverse they may be in other respects. She draws on Aristotle's argument that speakers create trust and equity by displaying their "good sense, virtue, and good will" (*The "Art" of Rhetoric* 2. 1, 1378a). They demonstrate that their facts and factual analyses are sound and will resolve the particular problems under discussion, and they "dispel . . . interpersonal distrust" (p. 146). Allen focuses her analysis on the challenge of dealing with interpersonal distrust.

Talking to Strangers draws on Aristotle's treatment of the maxim to show how argument establishes ethical trust. Aristotle praises maxims because they make "speeches ethical" (*The "Art" of Rhetoric* 2. 21, 1395b). And speeches are ethical "in which the moral purpose is clear" (ibid.). These effects are important because "moral character is the most effective proof" (1. 2, 1356a).

Allen uses Aristotle's maxim that "the true friend should love as if he were going to be a friend forever" (*Rhetoric* 2. 21, quoted on p. 146) to establish a rhetorical practice that promotes political friendship. She argues that speakers need to use "universal principles" and "fashion rules in the present" that they will abide by in the indefinite future (p. 147). By stating such principles, they manifest their commitments over the long run and stabilize uncertainty. They show that they themselves will be subject to the same rules that they propose for others.

Trustworthy leaders also debate ethical and political doctrines in addition to analyzing facts. Sometimes facts are not available. Before the Iraq war, for example, citizens were unable to discover factually whether there were weapons of mass destruction in Iraq and whether Iraq was working with the Al-Qaeda terrorists. But they could have debated the ethical and political question of whether "the doctrine of pre-emptive strike is compatible with democracy" (p. 147). Public discussion of doctrine in light of the basic standards of the community could have strengthened adherence to the rule of law.

But arguments that manifest ethical commitments (ethos) cannot generate trust by themselves. Even when an audience is convinced by a speaker's analyses of facts and her equitable, rule-abiding character, painful emotions like anger, fear, indignation, and envy may persist. These emotions need to be addressed. For example, Allen observes, in the Iraq war, the British were partly successful at promoting a "rule-of-law" ethos by wearing soft berets and dispensing with body armor, making themselves as vulnerable to attack as the people were. But they could not completely overcome the fear and anger of the Iraqi people.

Allen draws on Aristotle's analysis of political emotion (pathos) to show how speakers can change negative emotions such as anger and fear into positive ones like mildness and confidence. By moving the listener out of pain, the speaker "deals with the impact of feelings of loss on politics." She uses the examples of anger and indignation to show how people feel at first when they do not receive the honor that they believe is due to them. Since anger depends on their belief that they have been slighted, it can be changed through persuasion. "One can counteract the anger, for instance, by proving that no slight occurred, or that it was unintentional" (p. 150).

Thus speakers can overcome the pain of sacrifice by being sensitive to particular emotions and learning how the rhetorical art can deal with them. They need to be attuned to "how proposals look" from the different points of views of various citizens. Allen asserts "no decent judge, [Aristotle] argues, would consent to an argument in which a speaker does not establish a rule-of-law ethos, display equity, and cultivate good will in addition to making logical arguments" (p. 155). Equity comes into being in the relationship between speaker and hearer. The genius of Allen's account is to show how rhetoric, properly used, creates this relationship. For the imperfect outcomes of the political process repeatedly erode trust; but "political friendship" and trust-building rhetoric "achieve community where trust is a renewable resource" (p. 156).

Political Friendship, Practical Truth, and Reconciliation

The first chapter of Eugene Garver's *For the Sake of Argument* draws on Aristotle's ideas of political friendship and rhetoric to explore the problems that arise when "trust breaks down," as it did before, during, and after the South African revolution. The South Africans faced the problem of finding a shared memory and a "common ethos" for their new country (p. 22) when one group had traumatized another group. Jonathan Shay formulates the difficulties of enacting a democratic process when trauma has occurred. Democratic governance requires deliberation, persuasion, and compromise, but "these all presuppose *the trustworthiness of words.*" Trauma produces severe distrust. Tortured persons reinterpret the meanings of words; "fair offers from opponents are scrutinized for traps, every smile conceals a dagger" (*Achilles in Vietnam*, pp. 180–1, quoted in *For the Sake of Argument*, p. 28; see also *When Words Lose their Meaning*, pp. 5, 14, 59–92, on Thucydides). Distrust destroys the social and deliberative capacities that allow people to shape their future.

Garver demonstrates that the Truth and Reconciliation Committee (TRC) in South Africa moved toward trust by pursuing truth. But truth does not imply agreement. Like Allen, he argues that overcoming differences of opinion by finding agreement is not at issue in trust-building. We do not trust others simply because they share our philosophical or religious opinions. Rather, we trust them because of their integrity, reliability, and good will along with their ability to discern factual and perspectival truths. Garver writes, "Truth is less a correspondence between statement and reality than a relation between speaker and hearer. This is the connection between truth and trust that will be a theme throughout this book" (p. 18).

Like Allen, Garver examines political friendship and trust-building rhetoric as the keys to living together when citizens' beliefs and interests sharply diverge. Both look to Aristotelian same-mindedness or concord for a commonality that is practicable in pluralistic democracies. Far from advocating a complete joining of selves, likemindedness is "limited to the objects of deliberation" (*For the Sake of Argument*, p. 22). Aristotle focuses agreement on the practical:

> Concord is not merely agreement of opinion, for this might exist even between strangers. Nor yet is it agreement in reasoned judgments about any subject whatever, for instance, astronomy, termed concord ... Concord is said to prevail in a city when the citizens agree concerning their interests ... choose the same things ... and act on their common resolves ... Concord then refers to practical ends, and practical ends of importance, and able to be realized by all or both parties. (*Nicomachean Ethics* 9. 6; see *Talking to Strangers*, p. 124; *For the Sake of Argument*, p. 22)

Whether or not citizens share universal religious or philosophical beliefs, they can come to agreement about what is advantageous to them. But, Garver shows, South Africa was so painfully divided that the TRC needed to discover "a common history and a common *ethos* for the new South Africa" (p. 22). He describes how its inventive use of epideictic rhetoric, and its insistence on discovery of factual and personal or narrative truth, produced that history and ethos.

Garver argues that political friendship lives within the rhetorical situation itself, when speakers present arguments that articulate their beliefs and "charitably interpret the arguments for others' beliefs" (*For the Sake of Argument*, pp. 33–4). Even when traumas had destroyed trust and friendship seemed impossible, political friendship permitted the South Africans to achieve reconciliation. Rhetorical discovery of truths known only to a few disclosed new grounds for community-building ethos. *For the Sake of Argument* explores the kinds of fact-finding and discoveries of truth that make reconciliation possible.

Garver acknowledges that South Africa's Truth and Reconciliation Committee took a bold risk in deciding to explore victims' stories. He points out that Eastern

Europe, contrarily, let go of truth about the past in order to move on, fearing that disclosure could only deepen wounds. The work of the TRC might have made people angrier and exacerbated racial conflict, as Archbishop Tutu emphasizes: "It would be naïve in the extreme to imagine that people would not be appalled by the ghastly revelations that the Commission had brought about" (*Truth and Reconciliation Commission Report* 1, p. 6, quoted in *For the Sake of Argument*, p. 16). Garver demonstrates the need for the (rhetorical) discovery of what really happened in achieving true reconciliation. As Archbishop Tutu argues,

> There are erroneous notions of what reconciliation is all about. Reconciliation is not about being cozy; it is not about pretending that things were other than they were. Reconciliation based on falsehood, on not facing up to reality, is not reconciliation at all. (*Truth and Reconciliation Commission Report* 1, p. 6)

But what kind of truth did the Commission need to find? Would all stories be admissible as representing someone's point of view? Would victims' statements always be accepted as legally binding? What would the Commission do with conflicting accounts?

Garver, along with Anthea Jeffrey, argues that the TRC could not rest with the assumption that there are two kinds of truth: "objective information or subjective opinions" (*Truth about the Truth Commission*, p. 10, quoted in *For the Sake of Argument*, p. 17). Rhetorical truth bridges this gap. The Commission "named four kinds of truth: factual, objective information, 'personal or narrative truth, social or dialogue truth, and healing or restorative truth' " (*For the Sake of Argument*, p. 18). This multiplicity of truths enlarges our understanding of what rhetorical argument includes and what it can do. Truth is not relativistic; believing that someone's stories were only "true for them" would have meant not taking the stories seriously. Truth was not a matter of opinion; facts and experiences that came to light had an evidential quality, though they were not always appropriate to be used in a trial. Yet the truths had consequences. They limited the lies that could be told about what had happened; they initiated contests over what was true ("Articles of faith," p. 113). They also created a new place, a new common arena for a sharply divided people to find an ethos and a community. For truth-telling relates to ethos and pathos. Mondli, a colleague of Anthea Jeffrey, uses the metaphor of the table to express this idea:

> "For me, justice lies in the fact that everything is being laid out on the same table...The truth that rules our fears, our deeds, and our dreams is coming to light. From now on you don't only see a smiling black man in front of you, but you also know what I carry inside of me. I've always known it – now you also know."
> "And reconciliation?"

"Reconciliation will only be possible when the dignity of black people has been restored and when whites become compassionate. Reconciliation and amnesty I don't find important. That people are able to tell their stories – that's the important thing." (quoted in *Country of my Skull*, p. 15; quoted again in *For the Sake of Argument*, p. 18)

Shared knowledge of people's stories becomes the basis for community. This is what Garver means when he writes, "truth is less a correspondence between statement and reality than a relation between speaker and hearer."

But Garver warns that interpreting victims' stories as having "expressive value and not truth" would not have given the victims "moral standing" (*For the Sake of Argument*, p. 17). Nor did the TRC limit itself to common knowledge about what had happened. This knowledge is important when it is attainable, because crimes against humanity must be punished. And, in Chile, Argentina, and Brazil, Michael Ignatieff argues, the "relatives of victims preferred the facts to the false consolations of ignorance" and many of them "preferred the truth to vengeance or even justice" ("Articles of faith," p. 111). But in these countries discovery of factual truth alone did not change the locus of power or produce reconciliation: "a truth commission cannot overcome a society's divisions. It can only winnow out the solid core of facts upon which society's arguments with itself should be conducted. But it cannot bring these arguments to a conclusion." Truth commissions work best in societies that "have already created a powerful political consensus behind reconciliation, such as in South Africa" (p. 113).

Truth commissions need to find not just factual truth (though that is crucial) but also moral truth. But Ignatieff insists the moral truth may be elusive. Many people define themselves in terms of who they are not. "To be a Serb is first and foremost not to be a Croat or a Muslim. If a Serb is someone who believes Croats have a historical tendency towards fascism and a Croat is someone who believes Serbs have a penchant for genocide, then to discard these myths is to give up a defining element of their own identities" ("Articles of faith," p. 114). Truth commissions have difficulty overcoming these differences in moral evaluations. "The truth that matters to people is not factual or narrative truth but moral or interpretive truth. And this will always be an object of dispute in the Balkans" (p. 114).

Garver argues that rhetoric is useful in such ongoing disputes. Granted, rhetoric cannot create progress in all of them. There needs to be a willingness to listen. "The *Rhetoric* shows me how to have ethical relations with people with whom I can talk and to whom I can listen" (*For the Sake of Argument*, p. 35). To the challenge that groups filled with enmity toward each other do not listen, his argument replies that discussion requires that "we share interests." That is Aristotle's great insight. In South Africa whites listened only when they "had no choice but to listen to blacks. This necessity was . . . a product . . . of interest" (p. 36). Rhetorical invention helps people identify their interests.

Finding a common interest does not mean everyone will agree on a truth about the past. Bishop Tutu affirms, "instead of a single set of true beliefs, we have a 'new shared, and ceaselessly debated memory'." The memory South Africa seeks is not a "stifling homogenous nationhood," nor is it "every individual's mental ability to retain facts and arguments," although "collective memory is helpful." Instead, "shared memory, in the intended sense, is a process of historical accountability" (*Reconciliation through Truth*, pp. 9–10, quoted in *For the Sake of Argument*, p. 25). By telling and listening the people recognized, adjudicated, and shared truth. Garver argues that epideictic rhetoric changed knowledge from something individual victims knew to something all the people knew and could use as the basis for deliberation (p. 39).

Rhetoric promotes healthy change by making knowledge explicit. Lawrence Weschler's account shows why explicitness matters:

> Fragile, tentative democracies time and again hurl themselves toward an abyss, struggling over this issue of truth. It's a mysteriously powerful, almost magical notion, because often everyone already knows the truth – everyone knows who the torturers were and what they did, the torturers know that everyone knows, and everyone knows that they know. Why then, the need to risk everything to render that knowledge explicit? (*A Miracle*, p. 2, quoted in *For the Sake of Argument*, p. 213 n. 45)

Professor of law and philosophy Thomas Nagel came upon the answer in a conversation at a conference at the Aspen Institute: "It's the difference . . . between knowledge and acknowledgement. It's what happens and can only happen to knowledge when it becomes officially sanctioned, when it is made part of the public cognitive scene" (*For the Sake of Argument*, pp. 213–14 n. 45). Garver argues that making knowledge truly common through epideictic rhetoric creates "collective responsibility as opposed to individual guilt" (p. 39).

Even if common knowledge does not solve the political divisions and heal prejudice, it creates a beginning; Garver's concept of rhetoric is intensely dynamic. Practical reason not only establishes a common ethos; it can develop that ethos. In order to trace this dynamism, Garver contrasts the way Lincoln and Douglas conceptualized the beliefs of the people. Douglas believed that the nation should "privatize" disagreement and allow different people to believe different things about slavery. Lincoln *developed* the ethos of the Nation by arguing that the Nation should "commit itself to the truth of the proposition that all men are created equal" (p. 36). Like Allen's treatment of the maxim, Garver's analysis of this proposition stresses that commitment to a principle is an action that creates political stability (p. 36). Second, Lincoln used rhetoric dynamically to extend the proposition into action. His ethos and commitment to argument transformed "shared dedication to equality into a new commitment to abolish slavery" (p. 38).

Garver sees a connection between this dedication and TRC's commitment to developing South Africa's new ethos. The witnesses, judges, and people exercised practical rationality in offering and hearing testimony, in person and on the radio. They engaged in a vast discussion, deciding when to accept multiple but conflicting truths, when to insist on a single factual truth, and when to agree to disagree. Those rhetorical activities produced democratic friendship. Friendship lay within the activities of telling, listening, disputing, and deciding. By doing these things, South Africa "persuaded itself that it was a democratic nation, and so became one" (p. 42).

Note

1   I am grateful to Nicholas Olmsted for this reference.

Chapter 10

Legal Reasoning, Historical Contingency, and Change: Edward H. Levi's *An Introduction to Legal Reasoning*

Historically rhetoric was intimately connected to the law courts. In classical Greece, rhetoric was taught to citizens so that they could defend themselves in the court and deliberate in the assembly.[1] In Rome, advocates used oratory to plead on behalf of their clients. Indeed, law as a subject taught in its own right did not emerge until the twelfth century ("Lawyers and rhetoric," pp. 274–91). Law students continued to be educated in rhetoric well into the Early Modern period, and today knowledge of rhetoric illuminates decision-making activities of lawyers, judges, and law students ("A night in the topics," pp. 212, 273 nn. 2 and 3, and p. 224).

Legal cases show how rhetorical topics and community values shift through time. Rhetoric reflects social mores, but it also changes people's ideas about their interests. It allows those trapped by oppression or conflict to debate values within the legal forum. Chapter 9 showed how Danielle S. Allen and Eugene Garver articulate ways that rhetoric helps to establish equitable relationships between deeply opposed speakers and listeners. There we found that rhetoric heals emotions associated with loss by changing people's interpretations of events and by discovering new factual and narrative truths. This chapter argues that legal reasoning takes thinking beyond its current position to discover new interests and values that will alter people's relationships to one another.

Legal rules, the recurring forms of argument in legal briefs and judgments, *"are topics in the classical sense"*, and topics offer a "path to pursue" in finding facts and arguments; they are "a place from which to begin one's investigations" ("A night in the topics," pp. 218, 214). Topics are flexible words, strategies of argument, and commonplace propositions that can be adapted to new circumstances. Edward H. Levi's classic treatment of reasoning by example or by analogy argues that rules (topics) change "from case to case and are remade with each case" (*Legal Reasoning*, p. 2; see also "On analogical reasoning," p. 741 n. 3, p. 747 n. 25, and p. 758 n. 65). He traces the history of this process through nineteenth- and early twentieth-century English and North American law. His book considers legal deliberation under conditions of uncertainty as it responds to and influences community values. The legal process does not necessarily resolve conflict, even though judges determine judgment in particular cases. But the process makes change more rational and democratic:

> The examples or analogies urged by the parties bring into the law the common ideas of the society. The ideas have their day in court, and they will have their day again. This is what makes the hearing impartial, rather than any idea that the judge is completely impartial. (*Legal Reasoning*, p. 5)

Although reasoning by analogy is the most common form of legal reasoning, not all legal theorists embrace it. Richard A. Posner distinguishes between "top-down" and "bottom-up" theories of reasoning:

> In reasoning from the top down, the judge or other legal analyst invents or adopts a theory about an area of law... and uses it to organize, criticize, accept or reject, explain or explain away, distinguish or amplify the decided cases to make them conform to the theory and generate an outcome in each new case as it arises that will be consistent with the theory and with the cases accepted as authoritative within the theory. (*Overcoming Law*, p. 172)

Posner identifies himself with the top-down theory that understands the common law on the assumption, for example, that "judges try to maximize the wealth of society" (pp. 172–3). His approach is enthymematic; it adjusts particular cases to general rules, seeking an idealized correspondence. Levi, on the other hand, illuminates the extent to which reasoning by example actually shapes legal terms and arguments in the history of legal reasoning.

Accepting a degree of indeterminacy in legal reasoning, Levi's analysis shows that ambiguity is indispensable because it creates a space where discussion can take place and change can happen. The ambiguity of topics like "inherently dangerous" and "prostitution, debauchery, and any other immoral purpose" focuses debates about cases while leaving room for the discovery of pertinent facts and issues. Although most of Levi's examples are cases that have "reached the appellate stage," the process he describes involves "fact determination" as much as it does "rule making" (*Legal Reasoning*, p. vi). And, as Cass R. Sunstein argues, the "concreteness of analogical reasoning is a large advantage." "People can often think far better about particular problems than about large-scale approaches to the world" ("On analogical reasoning," p. 772). In order to dramatize how Levi embeds his analysis in the facts and circumstances of cases, I will address ways other legal thinkers have argued that rhetoric informs legal reasoning.

Legal thinkers have linked rhetorical invention to legal reasoning by showing the relevance of rhetorical topics to legal arguments ("A night in the topics," *Legal Discourse, Legal System, Reading the Law, Word of the Law*). It will be recalled that for classical rhetoricians, topics indicate things to talk about and strategies of argument for investigating a subject. They can also be understood as propositions that serve as premises for arguments. Although topics "do not predetermine the result of the investigation, they shape the nature of the inquiry" ("A night in the topics," p. 214). To illuminate topics, J. M. Balkin focuses on the topic "from part and whole" as a means of recognizing problems and solving them. This topic allows one to investigate the parts of an elephant in relation to the whole organism, or the elephant as a part of a larger genus, or a single elephant in relation to a herd (p. 213). These arguments may seem simple until we consider that the *Federalist Papers* use relations of whole to part to discover the safest and most beneficial whole of which states may be parts. Paper 5, for example, argues that without the union as whole, the "disunity among states might invite dangers from other sovereign powers." Papers 6 through 8 consider the *states* as wholes, and Paper 9 considers the disturbances among states considered, again, as wholes ("Cultivating deliberating," p. 198). Most famously, faction is a whole that endangers all the other parts of society. Thus, in richly interconnected ways, arguments from parts and wholes investigate possible consequences of forming a union or of failing to do so.

Balkin finds topics operating in similar ways in the law. He argues that lawyers use "recurring forms of arguments" to "justify legal doctrines" ("A night in the topics," p. 216). For example, in tort law, Balkin says, the defense might argue that there is "No liability without fault," to which the plaintiff responds, "As between two innocents, let the person who caused the damage pay" (quoted on pp. 216–17). Whereas the defense emphasizes fault, the plaintiff stresses causal responsibility. "But the plaintiff can also argue that the defendant was at fault ('One who is at fault should be liable'), and the defendant can also deny causal responsibility ('No liability without causation')" (p. 216). Both sides can draw on the topics of "fault" and "cause." For example, in *Vosburg* v. *Putney* a young boy kicked his comrade in the leg, and the comrade's leg became diseased. The defendant could have argued that the kick was harmless, and that he should not be held liable because he was not at fault. He could also have argued that he had not caused the disease. But the plaintiff could answer that the boy kicked him "wrongfully" and that he himself was innocent. "The plaintiff was no less injured because the defendant meant no harm" (p. 217). Both sides use arguments drawn from the topics of fault and cause.

One could survey tort law to discover the range of topics that lawyers and judges use, thus broadening awareness of the available means of persuasion ("A night in the topics," p. 274 n. 18). By becoming conversant with a range of topics and their interconnections, lawyers and judges increase their ability to invent arguments. Topics are heuristics, not formulas or proofs in themselves (p. 219). They provide ways of formulating and discussing problems; solutions need to be defended by argument.

An Introduction to Legal Reasoning considers legal rules or topics in the context of their use in particular cases. Levi emphasizes the *interaction* between rule and case and between rule and fact. Recalcitrant circumstances are important to the book's argument understood in its own terms and because Levi wrote the book in response to legal realism. Legal realists argued that the legal process is uncertain and arbitrary. Levi's book acknowledges uncertainty and arbitrariness but shows how judges use ambiguous words to grapple with uncertainty. In tracing the ways in which ambiguous topics served as places for discussion and adjudication and by showing changes in their uses and meanings, he discerns patterns, possibly making the law seem more coherent than it is. But the vicissitudes of change also receive their due as the lawyers and judges make rational judgments about them. In addition, by showing historical change through the nineteenth and twentieth centuries, Levi dramatizes the degree to which community values are debated when judgments are made. The specificity of social values and historical circumstance stands out when we try to understand the past.

The changes in topics and historical circumstances emerge clearly in Levi's analysis of the history of the "inherently dangerous" rule. We may wonder why courts refused to declare liability for the manufacture of a defective carriage and an exploding lamp that injured someone but awarded it for an exploding gun and defective hair wash that did the same thing (*Winterbottom v. Wright* (1842) and *Longmeid v. Holliday* (1851)). In order to understand why, we need to know that manufacturing was in its infancy and judges were unwilling to hold manufacturers liable for injuries to third parties. They were less convinced than they are now that manufacturers are responsible for injuries caused by their products, partly because manufacturers had less control over the safety of their products. But the *change* in the judgments needs also to be understood in terms of words and interpretations of words.

The discovery of the topic "inherently dangerous" emerged from the consideration of specific cases and things. The court in *Winterbottom v. Wright* refused to consider whether the defective carriage was dangerous. In *Longmeid v. Holliday* the court judged that it would be going too far to argue that if "a machine not in its nature dangerous" (such as a carriage) "but with a latent defect" should be lent to someone who was injured by it then the lender or manufacturer should be liable for the injury (155 Eng. Rep. 752 (1851), quoted in *Legal Reasoning*, p. 13). The court accepted the category of "in its nature dangerous" only when a judge compared the lamp to the carriage and the gun and not before (*Longmeid* v. *Holliday*).

The *topoi* distinguishing "inherently dangerous things" and "things not of themselves dangerous" changed their meanings and their relation to one another as they were used to classify new things. Once the distinction became clear, it was used to classify objects; "loaded guns, defective guns, poison, and hair wash were considered to be things in their nature dangerous, whereas a defective lamp was a thing which became dangerous by an unknown latent defect" ("Uses of rhetoric," p. 239; see also *Legal Reasoning*, pp. 13–27).

> As new situations and problems arose, ideas about the meaning and importance of "inherently dangerous" things shifted. Later the rule was that "if the nature of a thing is such that it is reasonably certain to place life and limb in peril, when negligently made, it is then a thing of danger." (Levi quoting Judge Cardozo in *Legal Reasoning*, p. 32; see also "Uses of rhetoric," p. 239)

Levi argues, "what was only latently dangerous in *Thomas* v. *Winchester* [namely a carriage] now became imminently dangerous or inherently dangerous, or, if verbal niceties are to be disregarded, just plain or probably dangerous" in an automobile (*Legal Reasoning*, p. 23). Levi traces the evolution of legal topics to show how meanings evolve as terms are brought to bear on new situations such as automobiles rather than carriages. Legal rules need this ambiguity and flexibility because things that change raise new problems for judgment ("Uses of rhetoric," p. 239).

The topic "inherently dangerous" was ambiguous when the court used it in *Longmeid* v. *Holliday,* but its meaning became more determinate as courts classified objects inside and outside the category. Of course, not all legal topics are equally ambiguous. Case law is flexible because "what a court says is *dictum*" but "what a legislature says is a statute" (*Legal Reasoning*, p. 6). *Dictum* can be disregarded by future courts, but the words of statutes and their meanings are supposed to remain the same. Thus the indeterminacy characteristic of all rhetorical discourse varies in degree from one discursive context to another. Whereas the court's judgment may or may not be followed later in case law, the judgment of a statutory case sets the direction for interpreting its words in future cases. Levi argues that the Constitution offers more flexibility than statutory law because it "sets up the conflicting ideals of the community in certain ambiguous categories" (p. 7). Lawyers and courts develop satellite concepts (sub-topics) that give initial definition to reasoning by example. We shall see how powerful these satellite concepts can be in focusing judgments.

Although legal scholars have been disturbed that legal canons and rules are indeterminate and can be used effectively both for and against issues, Levi defends the ambiguity of legal rules: "In an important sense legal rules are never clear, and if a rule had to be clear before it could be imposed, society would be impossible." Legal reasoning requires "differences of view and ambiguities of words" (*Legal Reasoning*, p. 1). The community participates in "resolving the ambiguity" by discussing policy within ambiguous legal topics.

Levi shows how this process works when he traces reasoning by example. Similarity between cases is discerned and then "the rule of law inherent in the first case is announced" and applied to the second case. Levi calls reasoning by example "necessary for the law," although its characteristics "might be considered imperfections" (*Legal Reasoning*, p. 2). The fact that "rules change from case to case and are remade with each case" makes law dynamic. It also roots legal reasoning in facts. The meaning of a rule "depends on a determination of what facts will be considered similar to those present when the rule was first announced" (p. 2). Each judge in case law determines similarity and difference. Since the things compared change through time just as the social values in terms of which judges decide also change, the topics and their meanings evolve. For example, the words "inherently dangerous" are abandoned when their meaning can no longer be differentiated from "latently dangerous" in thinking about a defective automobile.

If rules and categories were determinate, there would be no room for the introduction of new ideas. Even the words of the Constitution come "to have new meanings," so that it can express the current values of a community (p. 4). Of course, Levi insists, some ideas will be erroneous, but reasoning by example corrects and changes ideas once they have been accepted.

The degree of flexibility of rules and examples also varies with the stage of legal reasoning. But Levi argues that the legal concept never enables a purely deductive inference. Rules are not imposed on cases or facts. Rather, Levi shows that some movement that is required because "as Judge Cardozo suggested in speaking of metaphors, the word starts out to free thought and ends by enslaving it." This maxim is true of topics more broadly. First, they suggest a direction for investigation, but eventually they become blinkers that limit discovery. Levi discerns a "circular motion" in case law (p. 8). In the first stage, lawyers and judges create topics that accumulate as they compare cases. In the second stage, topics or concepts become more fixed and reasoning by example classifies things inside and outside of the topics. In the third stage, the concept breaks down. In rhetorical terms, we would say that the topic has become too determinate and suggests meanings that are no longer functional (pp. 8–9).

In the first stage of case law, courts may fumble for a word that expresses what is at stake when, for example, guns go off, carriages break, and lamps explode, injuring those who use them (p. 8). Levi comments, "similarity is seen in terms of a word, and inability to find a ready word to express similarity or difference may prevent change in the law" (p. 8; see "Uses of rhetoric," p. 244). The discovery of a legal topic such as "inherently dangerous" occurs as lawyers and judges compare cases to determine who is responsible. This is a heuristic activity, and legal reasoning cannot get going until a word is found to define what is wrong from a particular point of view ("Uses of rhetoric," p. 243). Words such as "fraud," "negligence," "direct dealing," and "inherently dangerous," are raised, used, accepted, or rejected. Concepts like "dangerous in themselves" are urged but lose favor before the courts adopt them.

In the second more stable stage things are classified inside and outside of the categories. For example, a "loaded gun...a defective gun, mislabeled poison, defective hair wash, scaffolds, a defective coffee urn, and a defective aerated bottle" have been classified as inherently dangerous. "A defective carriage, a bursting lamp, a defective balance wheel for a circular saw, and a defective boiler" were judged as "only latently dangerous" (p. 18). This stage of reasoning is the most conservative and the most extended in time.

In the third stage of the "inherently dangerous" rule, the concept breaks down. In *MacPherson* v. *Buick* (1916), Judge Cardozo radically enlarged and changed the concept of dangerous objects, realigning cases. He collapsed the distinction between "inherently dangerous things" like guns and "latently dangerous" or "not-dangerous things" like "a defective carriage, a bursting lamp, a defective balance wheel for a circular saw" (*Legal Reasoning*, p. 18). His intervention may seem arbitrary at first glance, but Levi shows how new things change judges' and lawyers' understandings of words. Whereas it seemed inconceivable in 1842 that a coachman should recover from the maker of a defective carriage that injured him, the counsel for the plaintiff in *MacPherson* v. *Buick* (1916) urged that an automobile resembled a locomotive more than it did a wagon. New things made lawyers and judges rethink the meaning of "inherently dangerous."

Change can seem arbitrary and, no doubt sometimes is. When Cardozo complains about "verbal niceties" employed in the defendant's distinctions "between things inherently dangerous and things imminently dangerous," or dangerous through want of care, he refers to the inherently dangerous rule that had been used to classify cases since *Longmeid* v. *Holliday* (1851) (quoted in *Legal Reasoning*, pp. 22–3). That distinction no longer carries the same weight with him: "If the danger was to be expected as reasonably certain, there was a duty of vigilance, and this whether you call the danger inherent or imminent" (quoted in *Legal Reasoning*, p. 23). Cardozo defends this change in the rule by arguing, "precedents drawn from the days of travel by stagecoach do not fit the conditions of travel today," and "the principle that the danger must be imminent does not change, but the things subject to the principle do change" (quoted on p. 21). Changing facts require new meanings and uses of language. But these uses can be reasonable. Cardozo finds a principle (that there is a duty of vigilance when a thing is dangerous) behind the principle that there is a duty of care for inherently dangerous things. He also discerns an extension in the range of objects included under the "inherently dangerous" rule after *Winterbottom* v. *Wright*). The court in that case had deemed that belladonna mislabeled as extract of dandelion had put Mrs Thomas's life in danger (p. 14). When later courts added hair wash, a large coffee urn, and scaffolding to the list, Cardozo wrote that the urn and scaffolding may "have extended the rule of *Thomas* v. *Winchester*," but "if so, this court is committed to the extension'" (quoted on p. 22). The rule no longer has the narrow meaning it once had. The new dangers posed by previously unconsidered things like scaffolding, and later, locomotives and automobiles, required a reassessment of the topics that guided legal judgment.

The flexibility of case law means that topics are corrected over time in light of new things and new values. But statutory law does not have the flexibility of case law. Once the legislature establishes the words of the statute, they ought not to change. Whereas relative indeterminacy holds sway in case law, statutory law aims for greater determinacy. The words express the will of the legislature. If courts find the words ambiguous at first they can look to the intention of the legislature.

Levi's analysis of statutory law shows several important features of topics. Even statutes contain ambiguous language, and although courts look to the intent of the legislature, that intent is itself ambiguous. Ambiguous words allow community values and ideas to be expressed and reasoned about in the legislature and the courts. More surprisingly, perhaps, the growing determinacy of words in a statute may actually become a problem for judges. Levi's analysis demonstrates that determinate language is not necessarily a desirable feature of legal reasoning, as I shall argue in a moment.

In order to resolve the initial ambiguity of statutory words, lawyers and judges follow rules for operating "a given classification system. The problem is to place the species inside the genus and the particular cases inside the species." For example, lawyers and judges who made arguments about the Mann Act had to relate "debauchery" and "any other immoral purpose" to "prostitution" by aligning the words with each other and with the case at hand. The ambiguous words of the statute are made more determinate by interpreting them "in light of the meaning given to other words in the same or related statute" (p. 28). But even when interpreted in this way, words remain ambiguous and courts look to legislative intent to determine meaning.

However, legislative intent itself can be ambiguous. Thus the faith expressed in a book such as E. D. Hirsch's *Validity in Interpretation,* that valid meanings of texts are determined by considering authorial intention, must be qualified in the case of legislatures. Levi believes that members of a legislature do not need to agree on "the precise effect of the bill" (*Legal Reasoning,* p. 30). Nor do they need to look at cases or facts to determine the meaning of a bill. They may debate different things and will use committee reports and speeches to introduce their particular beliefs about what the bill should mean and do. On the other hand, their opinions may result from ignorance. The members of the legislature that enacted the Mann Act, for example, were often confused about what evil it was intended to fight. Was it sexual immorality or enslavement of underage women for the purposes of sexual exploitation? Because of such confusion and conflict, the court's task of interpreting legislative intent is not easy. Levi's analysis of legislative discussion of the Mann Act dramatizes how sharply the members of the legislature differed in their knowledge of the facts and in their values. But the legislature provides the initial forum for deliberating about moral and legal issues like prostitution of minors and organized crime. And the court's search for intent "results in an initial filling-up of the gap" of ambiguity and that gives "broad direction to the statute" (pp. 31, 32).

Levi's analysis of the history of the Mann Act shows the extent to which legislatures and courts are influenced by community values and how they in turn influence those values. Congress formulated the Mann Act at a time when prostitution occurred in defined areas of cities and people believed that men captured innocent girls, transported them across state lines, and confined them to houses of prostitution (*Legal Reasoning*, p. 34). Members of Congress debated conflicting and fundamental values: the importance of home rule (in policing immoral acts) and the power of the federal government, the importance of ending the use of interstate transportation for immoral purposes, on the one hand, and the goal of stamping out prostitution, on the other hand, as well as the desirability or undesirability of insisting that only moral people use tickets on railroads that crossed state lines (pp. 37–9). Congress passed the bill without agreeing on these issues. Levi writes:

> There was no common understanding of the facts, and whatever understanding seems to have been achieved concerning the white-slave trade in retrospect seems incorrectly based. The words used were broad and ambiguous. There were three key phrases: "prostitution," "debauchery," and "for any other immoral purpose." (p. 40)[2]

Once a statute has been passed, reasoning by example aligns a case under the major topics of the statute. The problem for the Mann Act is determining how "any other immoral purpose" serves as a genus for debauchery and debauchery for prostitution. Does "any other immoral purpose" suggest criminal sexual behavior analogous to prostitution or does it refer to all sexual behavior deemed immoral in a broad sense? Lawyers and judges argue about facts and values within such ambiguous topics. Initially Justice McKenna in *Hoke and Economides* v. *United States* (1913) interpreted the words in the narrower sense. He saw analogies between the use of interstate transportation for "the demoralization of lotteries, the debasement of obscene literature, the contagion of diseased cattle or persons, the impurity of food and drugs" on the one hand and for "the systematic enticement to and the enslavement in prostitution and debauchery of women, and more insistently of girls," on the other (quoted in *Legal Reasoning*, p. 40). Levi comments that his judgment emphasized organized crime, the unwillingness of the girls, and "the belief that many... were minors" (p. 40). But the limitation did not hold up; in another case in the same year, *Athanasaw v. United States* (1913), McKenna held that debauchery could include sexual advances as well as "sexual intercourse" (p. 41).

Later courts extended the Act to cases where the women were willing and could even be punished for transporting themselves (pp. 41–2). Finally, the court in *Caminetti v. United States* (1917) established that the women did not have to be involved in organized crime in order to be at fault. In that case, two women had been transported across state lines to become a mistress and a concubine. Considered in modern terms, this behavior was a purely private matter. The counsel for the defendants drew on the legislative history and the "House Committee Report" to show that "commercial traffic alone was in view" (*Caminetti v. United States* 242 U.S. 474, quoted in *Legal Reasoning*, p. 42), but the court ruled on the "plain meaning" of "for any other immoral purpose." But the meaning was not plain to everyone; the debate in the *Caminetti* case centered on the issue of whether this topic included only sexual acts in the context of organized vice or whether it extended to all immoral sexual acts. Canons of interpretation were debated. Does one include the title, the committee reports, and the debate in Congress in defining the terms? What constitutes plain meaning of the words? What seemed plain about the meaning of "immoral act" to this court in 1917 looked very different to other and later eyes. But *Caminetti* set the direction for the Act. One might argue that the topics "prostitution, debauchery, and any other immoral purpose" became too determinate. "Immoral purpose" came to include Mormon polygamy. But once the direction had been set, it was followed. "The restriction thus placed upon the freedom of the Court to realign cases sets legislative interpretation apart from the development of case law. The dissenting judges have complained about the loss of freedom" (*Legal Reasoning*, p. 54). In these circumstances, the Constitution becomes a resource.

Whereas interpretation of statutes can become too fixed, constitutional legal reasoning involves very ambiguous terms. If in case law, one case is set next to another and similarities and differences are sought, and in statutory law words and a case are placed in the relation of genus and species, according to Justice Roberts, in constitutional law the Constitution is placed next to the statute and the court judges whether there is a connection (*Legal Reasoning*, p. 58).

Levi argues that legal reasoning in constitutional law uses the most ambiguous language of the three kinds because the court need not follow earlier cases. The Constitution, not interpretations of the Constitution, informs judgment. "The Constitution in its general provisions embodies the conflicting ideals of the community" (p. 58). It provides the places, the topics, in which discussion takes place.

Interpretations are not as consistent as they are in case and statutory law. There is development and pattern, but there are also "abrupt changes in direction" (pp. 59–60). The next few pages will introduce the topic of the commerce clause, trace vacillations of interpretation that ended by declaring the Mann Act constitutional, and show the dramatic changes in topics that were used to examine shifts in community values and historical changes in the character of transportation and commerce. (The commerce clause decrees: "The congress shall have the power to regulate commerce with foreign nations, and among the several States, and with the Indian tribes" (*Legal Reasoning*, p. 63).)

The words of the Constitution differ from those used in case law and statutory law because the major topics in the Constitution express "conflicting ideals." The commerce clause offers an opportunity to celebrate the power of the state *and* the power of a nation. Moreover, judges develop satellite concepts or sub-topics that interpret the broader word in the Constitution. The variety of satellite concepts and the conflict between them mean that no one concept can determine judgment. In addition, Levi argues, because the problem of judging is one of seeing a "connection between what is sought to be done and the ideals of the community, connection and consequence must be argued." Hypothetical cases are proposed to clarify consequences, thus giving the process even more freedom (p. 60).

Levi's emphasis on the importance of changes in community values and historical circumstances to decision-making, and his focus on ambiguous topics, shows keen awareness of the rhetorical character of legal reasoning. His analysis of the commerce clause is a beautiful model of sensitivity to topics and their interrelations. The "language" of the clause "is simple and ambiguous: 'The Congress shall have the power to regulate commerce, with foreign nations, and among the several States, and with the Indian tribes.'" He argues that even if one tried to follow the literal meaning, one would struggle with the implications of "among" and "commerce" as judges indeed did. "Among" might mean "between" or "intermingled with" ("That commerce which concerns more states than one," quoted in *Legal Reasoning*, p. 63). "Commerce" might refer to the whole "moneyed economy" including manufacturing, or be limited to the "exchange of goods" already made (p. 63). Other questions might arise. Does the commerce clause bestow a negative power that removes obstacles that states might create to commerce among the states? Or is there a positive power as well? (p. 64).

Levi traces the history of the development and modification of topics in light of cases. *Gibbons v. Ogden* (1824) raised the issue of whether New York might "grant a monopoly of the right to use steam navigation within its territorial waters" (p. 65). Does commerce include navigation or should it be limited to "buying and selling" as the "counsel for the appellee" argued? Is commerce not only "traffic," but "intercourse"? (Marshall in *Gibbons v. Ogden*, quoted in *Legal Reasoning*, p. 66).

The question of whether persons could be considered "articles of commerce" stimulated much thinking. The court in *The Mayor* v. *Miln* (1837) said they were not. But when it came to "vagabonds and paupers," Justice Barbour thought that the states had a right to regulate (p. 68). The topic of "moral pestilence" came into being. It could confer power on the states or the federal government (p. 69). This topic became extremely important for the Mann Act because it allowed items (or people) "to be excluded from the commerce power for one reason or another" but to be included under the commerce clause if they were morally pestilent. The development of this topic was part of a broader process in which "the satellite concepts" of "commercial intercourse, the exchange of commodities and navigation or transportation on one side, and inspection, health, and police regulations on the other side" slowly emerged (pp. 70–1).

In 1894 *Kidd* v. *Pearson* created a new distinction that would have consequences for a dramatic shift in interpretations of the commerce clause later on. The court referred to "commerce" as "interstate," and included navigation under commerce, suggesting that commerce is a flow (p. 71). Later, the question would arise whether this flow moved through manufacturing sites. Thus reasoning continued to use topics or places to articulate the clause in light of definite historical circumstances. *United States* v. *Knight* (1875) ruled that the commerce clause did not extend to controlling "the refining of sugar" because "commerce succeeds to manufacture and is not part of it" (*United States* v. *Knight*, quoted in *Legal Reasoning*, p. 72).

Courts used this intricate web of topics to shape decisions about the Mann Act; changing topics caused a dramatic shift in how later cases were decided. But in the meantime the category of "moral pestilence" helped judges struggle with the question of whether lottery tickets could be subjects of commerce. Were lottery tickets commercial articles? They are pieces of paper. Ultimately the category of moral pestilence and the idea that lotteries are hideous evils led the court to prohibit the tickets from interstate commerce (p. 75). Those decisions along with others about pure food and drugs made it easier to rule the Mann Act constitutional (see *Hoke* v. *Economides* (1913)).

The story up to this point has been one of gradual change, of adding satellite concepts and extending their meanings. But in 1917 a stage begins that leads to a startling change in the way cases are judged. Similar arguments used in the Child Labor case (*Hammer* v. *Dagenhart* (1918)) and the Fair Labor Standards Case (*United States* v. *Darby* (1941)) led to opposite judgments. Levi comments, "it was the community, not the briefs, which had changed" (p. 61). In 1917 the category of things being transported controlled decisions. Justice White ruled that intoxicating liquor could be regulated; the "exceptional nature of the subject here regulated is the basis upon which the exceptional power exerted must rest" (quoted in *Legal Reasoning*, p. 83). The complainant in the Child Labor case thought it would be bad to permit regulation of items made by children because then Congress could "prescribe a minimum wage scale" (quoted in *Legal Reasoning*, p. 86). By 1941 the Fair Labor Standards Act prohibited interstate transportation of things made by workers paid less than the minimum wage or working more than the maximum permitted number of hours. The objects were not pernicious, but the community had come to accept "government regulation by prohibition" (p. 101).

As historical circumstances and community attitudes changed, legal topics changed to come to grips with new situations. Topics advanced in the Child Labor Act of 1917 were rejected then, only to be accepted in 1941. The Act endeavored to prohibit things made by children from being transported across state lines. Child slavery was compared to white slavery and the products children made were compared to "lottery tickets, intoxicating liquor, adulterated articles, and goods misrepresented" (p. 84). The government argued that child labor was immoral and produced commodities that were in "unfair competition" with those produced elsewhere (pp. 84–5). But the complainant asserted that "the product of a factory is not unsanitary or adulterated or unwholesome because it has been touched during the process of manufacture, by a child's hand" ("Complainant's brief," *Hammer v. Dagenhart* (1918), p. 21, quoted in *Legal Reasoning*, p. 85). The court ruled that the Act was unconstitutional because the commerce clause "did not include such items as coal mining and manufacture. There was no authority to prohibit the movement of ordinary commodities." The court differentiated these commodities from "lottery tickets, adulterated articles, and women to be used for immoral purposes" because the latter three were covered by a "power to regulate." In these cases, interstate commerce was instrumental to the accomplishing of evil ends, whereas the goods covered under the Child Labor Act were "harmless" (p. 86). The court was concerned not to extend the government's power of regulating into places where ordinary objects were manufactured.

Chief Justice Hughes wrote an opinion on *Kentucky Whip & Collar* "about convict-made goods which almost pushed the *Child Labor* case out of the books." *Kentucky Whip & Collar* was a case about useful objects that "if permitted" in interstate commerce would "aid in the frustration of valid state laws." The judgment on this case converted the category (topic) of "illicit articles" into a category of "anticipated evil" that continued to be used along with the category of "local production" (Chief Justice Hughes, quoted in *Legal Reasoning*, p. 95). Although the majority of this court was "less amenable to a philosophy of increased government responsibility," certain phenomena like stolen automobiles and goods made by convicts led them to grant increased powers. Changed historical circumstances along with reasoning by example pushed the judges in a new direction (p. 96).

But on March 29, 1937, a shift occurred that strongly dramatizes the possibility of change in constitutional interpretations and judgments. Levi states that the "Court-packing plan made the shift more dramatic, but surely no more decisive than it would have been." The court upheld minimum wage legislation and the Railway Labor Act (p. 96). In support, Justice Stone argued that the inability to settle "grievances of railroad employees with respect to rates of pay, rules, or working conditions" was likely to " 'hinder interstate commerce' " (*Virginia R. Co. v. System* (1937), quoted in *Legal Reasoning*, p. 97). Conditions of manufacturing had changed so much that it was no longer possible to consider issues like wages, hours, and unionization as a local matter. A strike in one place could spread to others and cause cataclysmic interruptions of interstate commerce. Commerce extended through states and did not merely take place within them.

The shift continued. In 1941 the court in *United States* v. *Darby* rejected the judgments in the Child Labor cases. The government had argued that Congress had the power to regulate commerce, a category that applied "not only to the narrow concepts of sale or exchange, but to include the entire moneyed economy, embracing production and manufacture as well as exchange" ("Brief for United States," quoted in *Legal Reasoning*, p. 101). Community values had changed but so had the nature of the economy.

Whereas early interpretations of the Commerce Law were emphatic in excluding manufacturing from the concept of interstate commerce, now it was included. Levi writes that the "cases of illicit articles: intoxicating liquor, white slavery, lottery cases, adulterated articles, stolen articles, kidnapped persons, convict-made goods, and filled milk . . . had done their work," p. 102). But now the Chief Justice left them behind because, he argued, the distinction between pestilent or harmful things and ordinary commodities "was novel when made and unsupported by any provision of the Constitution" (quoted on p. 102). In fact, Levi notes, the distinction had been forgotten long ago.

The development and abandonment of the distinction in case law between things inherently dangerous and those only latently dangerous, along with the distinction in constitutional law between things evil or ordinary, dramatize how changes in society affected uses of topics, and how topics shifted to guide judgments about new situations. As manufacturing expanded and more things were invented, as the relationship between buyer and seller shifted from a local to a national level, the ways people viewed and categorized cars, locomotives, and guns changed. As manufacturing became less local and affected people throughout the nation, activities that were once deemed "remote and local" became "matters of national concern" (p. 103).

Levi emphasizes legal reasoning as a process that constantly assesses and reassesses such changing things and circumstances. Lawyers, the courts, and the community find new similarities and differences between cases. Levi calls it "the only kind of system which will work when people do not agree completely." The meanings of words and the words themselves change when the community understands them differently. In a sentence significant for modern controversies on pluralism and agreement, Levi writes, "the effort to find complete agreement before the institution goes to work is meaningless. It is to forget the very purpose for which the institution of legal reasoning has been fashioned" (p. 104). Like the rhetoric envisioned by Danielle S. Allen and Eugene Garver, legal rhetoric invites participants who have conflicting interests and interpretations to share loyalty to the institution and to use practical reasoning to articulate and judge conflicts and community values.

More than any of the other writers treated in this volume, Levi articulates the way topics guide and are reshaped through time as lawyers and judges use them to assess and reassess cases, things, and values. My volume aspires to achieve something of his sensitivity to conceptual shifts as particulars considered change through time. In economical language, Levi brings out strands of coherence in a constantly shifting, interactive process constrained by the recalcitrance of historical circumstance and community values.

Notes

1   I am grateful to Dennis Hutchinson of the University of Chicago for references and for stimulating conversation on change and legal reasoning. Of course, I take responsibility for my errors.
2   The Mann Act (June 25, 1910) that "shall be known and referred to as the 'White Slave Traffic Act'," states, in part: "Any person who shall knowingly transport or cause to be transported, or aid or assist in obtaining transportation for, or in transporting, in interstate or foreign commerce or in any territory or in the District of Columbia, any woman or girl for the purpose of prostitution or debauchery, or for any other immoral purpose, or with the intent and purpose to induce, entice or compel such woman or girl to become a prostitute or to give herself up to debauchery, or to engage in any other immortal practice ... shall be deemed guilty of a felony" (*Legal Reasoning*, pp. 33–4).

Index